"The stories and examples in this bool   )etter
business storyteller. You'll be inspired t   1at you
can in turn inspire your audience. Foll   boring
again."

JACK CANFIELD, Co-author
Chicken Soup for the Soul at Work

"Effective storytelling is critical to strategic business presentations and professional
selling. Doug Stevenson is a master storyteller. In his new book, Never Be Boring
Again, he shares insights and techniques for storytelling in ways that we all can use.
Read it!"

ED OAKLEY, CEO
Enlightened Leadership International

"Personal stories are the surest and most intimate way for a speaker to connect with
the heart, mind and spirit of their audience. This book provides a roadmap for you to
discover and develop your own personal stories."

MARIANNE WILLIAMSON, Author
A Return to Love and *Everyday Grace*

"Doug Stevenson taught my sales team how to tell better stories and close more deals.
I'm a results oriented guy and his method gets results. This book will teach your
salespeople how to get better results."

JOHN BUIE, Executive Vice President, Sales
Synygy

"As a professional speaker I have worked with Doug, but more importantly, I have
sent non-speaking professionals to his workshop. We need them to be comfortable
telling stories that help sell our services. Doug pushed them beyond their normal
comfort zones, and now they think telling stories to prospects is easy."

STEVE EPNER, President
BSW Consulting, Inc.

"I tell everyone who wants to become a better presenter that I have taken many
seminars and read many books on becoming a better speaker, but Doug's workshops,
tapes and now his book, are the ones I review all the time because they get to the heart
of what successful presentations are all about."

JEANNETTE HOLTHAM, Director, Organizational Leadership
Junior Achievement

"Doug Stevenson helped me to be a better speaker. He's one of only a handful of
coaches that I would recommend to work with top level executives. In this book he's
captured all the wit and wisdom of his live presentations and coaching. Read it today."

DAN MADDUX, Executive Director
American Payroll Association

"All great business presenters have learned to tell their 'compelling story.' Doug's book can help you learn to do that."

DR. SUZANNE SAVARY, Associate Professor
Marshall School of Business, University of Southern California

"Not only did I study The Story Theater Method with Doug, I hired him to keynote one of our leadership luncheon programs. The feedback was excellent; he even got a standing ovation. What else can I say? Doug is both a master storyteller and a master speaking coach. Read this book and you too will become a great storyteller."

DR. JEANETTE MITCHELL, Executive Director, Leadership Center
Cardinal Stritch University

"Through Doug's personal coaching, I have experienced the power of the techniques presented in this book. My storytelling skills have grown beyond my wildest dreams. By continuing to put into practice The Story Theater Method, I know I can become an awesome speaker! Thank you, Doug, for pulling together all the critical pieces."

LORI SILVERMAN, Co-author, *Stories Trainers Tell*
Owner, **Partners For Progress**

"This book reads like an intimate conversation that you'd have with your speaking coach. It's not a bunch of theory and sketchy ideas. This is down to earth stuff you can use immediately to become a better speaker. I highly recommend it."

HOWARD PUTNAM, Speaker, Author, Former CEO
Southwest Airlines and **Braniff Airlines**

"Having been in sales for 25 years and working for one of the best in the world of selling, Zig Ziglar—I have always felt that telling stories was Zig's secret to success. I believe Doug's new book will teach you how to do so as well. I truly believe that Doug Stevenson is the modern day Zig Ziglar in teaching how to tell stories."

DAVID CURRY, Sales Veteran
Crestcom International, Ltd.

"I never thought I was boring—but I also never realised that I had so much to learn about public speaking. Among my peers I'm regarded as a good speaker, but when you consider my before and after videotape at the Story Theater Retreat, it's staggering how much better I became. I have worked with Doug Stevenson as a teacher and coach and I'm convinced that if other executives spend some time with this book they will radically improve the communication skills that are critical to their success like I did."

RICHARD S. EYRE
Chairman of RDF Media and former Chief Executive of ITV

"Doug taught me how to tell my stories with my whole body and my whole heart in a dramatic yet genuine way. By unveiling my 'gifts', he freed me to be a more powerful and authentic speaker. If you want to be more powerful on the platform, this book will teach you how."

LEANN THIEMAN, Co-author
Chicken Soup for the Nurses Soul

NEVER
BE
BORING
AGAIN

MAKE YOUR
BUSINESS
PRESENTATIONS
Capture Attention,
Inspire Action, and
Produce Results

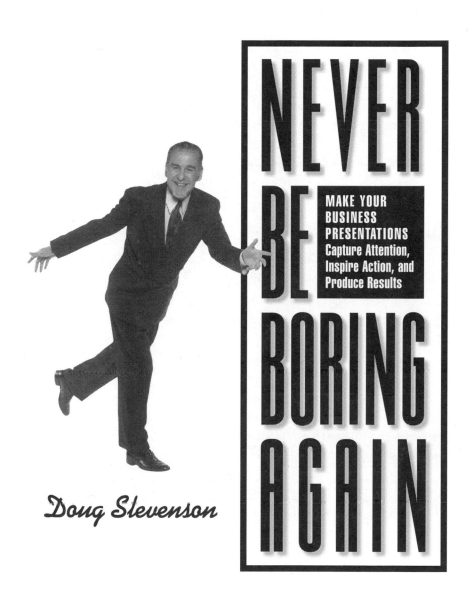

NEVER BE BORING AGAIN

MAKE YOUR BUSINESS PRESENTATIONS Capture Attention, Inspire Action, and Produce Results

Doug Stevenson

CORNELIA PRESS

COLORADO SPRINGS

CORNELIA PRESS
P.O. Box 9222
Colorado Springs, CO 80932-0222

1-800-573-6196 or 719-573-6195
www.storytheater.net

Cornelia Press books are available at special quantity discounts to use as premiums and sales promotions, or to use in corporate training programs. For more information contact the author at Deborah@DougStevenson.com or call 800-573-6196 or contact your local bookstore.

Library of Congress Catalog Number: 2003093671

ISBN: 0-9713440-9-4

For Deborah

You changed my world forever

For the better

And rewrote the story of my life

Contents

Make Your Business Presentations Capture Attention, Inspire Action, and Produce Results

Acknowledgements

Although my name is the only one that appears on the front cover of this book, it took a lot of people to make it happen. It took me a long time to learn this most important lesson: ask and you shall receive. I asked for help and the following people responded to my request with their time, talent, skill, feedback, advice, support and friendship.

My deepest thanks to my writing mentor, editor and constant cheerleader, Sam Horn. She is an author's dream co-creator. Her hands, heart and voice permeate and enliven this book.

My huge thanks to my father, Jerry Stevenson, for instilling in me a respect for language, and to my mother, Edith Stevenson, for being proud of me for every little thing. Thanks to my big sister, Ann McCormick, for loving me no matter what.

Thanks to Deborah Merriman for marrying me and giving me a ready-made family. Thanks to my stepson, Bennett Merriman, for building my wonderful websites and to my stepson, Mike Merriman, for hanging in there with me when the going got rough and for loving me forward. Thanks to both of you for teaching me how to be a dad. Because of the three of you, I know what it means to be a husband, father and friend. I am a better man because of you.

Thanks to my friend and fellow author, LeAnn Thieman, who has always believed in me and encouraged me to write this book. Thanks to Sam Silverstein, Carol Weisman, Ed Oakley, Mary LoVerde, LeAnn Thieman and Linda Evans Shepherd for reading early drafts.

Thanks to Pam Gordon for her love and support in the early days of Story Theater. To all of the hundreds of Story Theater Retreat graduates worldwide who have cheered me on and helped me to understand and refine my gift for coaching — I say thank you from the bottom of my heart. I have learned as much from you as you have learned from me.

Make Your Business Presentations Capture Attention, Inspire Action, and Produce Results

Thanks to Michael Morgan and Mark S.A. Smith for help in the early days.

Thanks to all the literary agents and publishers who helped in the molding of the final product. Thanks to the members of the National Speakers Association and the American Society for Training and Development who have embraced The Story Theater Method for storytelling in business. Thanks also to Paul Shadler who taught me how to see the big picture and to John Buie and Susan Kearney for friendship and partnership.

Thanks to Nancy Kelly and Carole Van Brocklin for helping me get started in the speaking business. Thanks to Marie Mosely for bringing me to England and Brendan Power for bringing me to Ireland.

Thanks to Lori Silverman and Mary Wacker for including me in their book, *Stories Trainers Tell.* Their contribution to spreading the word about Story Theater is immeasurable.

Thanks to Jim and Kelly Young and Jim and Joni Lyman for allowing me to camp out with my laptop at Rancho San Carlos in the beautiful Wet Mountains near Beulah, Colorado where I wrote much of this book. Thanks also to Mark Joyous and Lori Cohen for their hospitality.

Thanks to Barb McNichol for editing help along the way and to Shannon Parish for her wonderful illustrations. Thanks to Alan Bernhard of Argent Associates in Boulder, Colorado for his wonderful cover design and interior layout. Thanks to Dale Marich for spirited support.

Thanks to Dan Poynter for guiding me through the self-publishing maze and to Joe Sabah for his nurturing support and willing replies to emails and questions. Also to Rebecca Morgan and Ken Braly of SpeakerNet News for valuable insights and information on the speaking business.

Introduction

It was an odd reaction. I was in the middle of a customer service training session when my entire audience put down their pens almost at the same time, leaned back in their chairs and looked up at me with smiles and childlike innocence. It was as if a switch had been flipped in the room and all of a sudden the room was warmer. You know how you can hear the furnace turn on in the winter? It was like that, like the furnace turned on.

Up until that moment, the eighty people that were gathered in our chilly hotel room were listening to me, some more intently than others, while at the same time writing notes in their workbooks. They were listening, but they weren't really with me. I knew this because when I'd ask a question, it would take a minute for people to respond — like their brains were on screen saver and when I put them on the spot it made them realize they were daydreaming of a beach in Jamaica.

But when I said those magic words, "let me tell you a story about a customer that I had..." and I began telling a personal story, they all looked up and paid attention. They were right there with me hanging on every word. The only thing I can relate it to is a school of fish. You know how an entire school of fish turns left and then right and then left again at the same time as if they all have one brain? Like they are all one? Well the minute I started telling my story, it was as if we were all one. All of a sudden and without warning — we were connected.

At the end of that day, a number of people came up to me to thank me for the training. One lady commented on the story that I told and then launched into her own story about a customer she had. I

xiv NEVER BE BORING AGAIN

Make Your Business Presentations Capture Attention, Inspire Action, and Produce Results

didn't think much about it at the time — but it kept happening time and again at every program where I told that story. My story reminded her of her story, but now she understood her story better.

Have you ever channel surfed on the TV? You're sitting there on your comfy couch with a liquid beverage in one hand and your trusty remote in the other and you're just flipping channels. Nowadays you can really do some flipping, can't you? There are hundreds of channels to choose from and they're all sitting out there hoping you'll pick them. And you, you're looking for something that catches your attention.

Are you aware that your audience is doing something very similar while you're talking? They're sitting there a few feet away from you and they're listening to what you're saying but in their mind they're flipping channels, waiting for you to say something that catches their attention.

If you're doing a speech or a training session and what you're saying sounds anything like high school — lots of facts and figures and numbers that remind them of being bored to tears in chemistry class, they mentally flip the channel. They may be looking at you, but their heads are in Jamaica. That's right, they're watching the travel channel imagining themselves on a white sandy beach in Jamaica. Why?

Because they already did the school thing as kids and most of them didn't like it, so anything that sounds like school turns them off. All the while, you want and need their full attention. You have to be as interesting as Jamaica.

That's why you're not finished talking 'til you've told a story. When you start telling a story, and you really get into it by having fun and letting yourself go, then they listen with full attention. That's what it's all about — getting their full attention. In order to do that you've got to have something better for them to listen to, something more interesting than the noise going on inside their heads. You've got to catch their attention.

So what's your story? What are the stories from your life that are just like the stories from someone else's life that they will immediately relate to. Your first job as a speaker is to create a relationship, which means that you've got to find something to say that they relate to. Facts and figures and numbers don't do that.

Stories do — especially if they're personal stories, the ones that are part of everyday life. If you can find everyday stories, and then craft them to make a good solid point, you're a business storyteller. You're on the fast track to success because you understand something that most people around you don't — that stories are the best way to deliver content.

What was phenomenal about my customer service training experience was the sense of connection I had with that audience. At no other point during that entire day had I felt anything like it. One minute the room was chilly and the next minute it was warm. One minute the energy was scattered and the next it was focused. One minute I was trying to hold their attention and the next minute I had it.

I think you know what I mean. Every speaker who has ever stood in the front of a room to teach or speak or lead a meeting has experienced it. It's a palpable feeling. You either have it or you don't. It's a sense of connection that you have with your audience — a sense of oneness.

When it's not there, it's as if there is a gap between you and your audience. No matter how hard you try to connect, there is a hollow space that separates you. Speakers hate the gap. Audiences hate the gap. It serves neither speaker nor audience. What's needed is a bridge across the gap — something to connect speaker and audience.

Stories are that bridge. Here's what I've discovered over the years about storytelling in business:

- When training people, a story is the best way to help employees "grasp" an abstract concept. It helps them "buy into" a new idea or initiative. The story brings an intellectual idea into the "real world" so they "get" it. Listeners "see" what you're saying and visualize it — which means they internalize it instead of just hearing it.

- Using a well-crafted story is the key to winning over resistant audiences. If you have to give bad news, sharing a story often makes listeners understand a decision and accept it, even when they don't like it.

- Storytelling enhances your powers of persuasion. If you are proposing a product or service and your listeners aren't "buying it," telling them a story that paints a picture of how the product or service has been used successfully elsewhere "proves" its merit by allowing the listener to test drive the product or service.

- Storytelling has the power to connect with an audience as no other medium can. It bridges the gap and removes any sense of separation.

- Not all stories work. There are good stories and bad stories. The good ones create a bridge that connects the speaker and his or her audience. The bad stories fall flat or even worse — widen the gap.

- Storytelling is a skill that can be practiced, learned and perfected. It's like any other skill or discipline — the more you know, the better you become.

This book is about helping you connect with your audience by using stories — stories that are strategically chosen and crafted to make a business point. In these pages you'll discover a simple storytelling formula that will make you a better business speaker and storyteller.

Part One explains how you can use storytelling to move up the ladder of success and gain instant credibility as the speaker of choice in your organization.

Part Two explains how The Story Theater Method works. You'll learn how to connect with any audience and how to use the number one secret to being your best when you speak.

Part Three teaches you how to find stories and what to do with them once you find them.

Part Four shows you, in detail, how to write and develop your story for maximum impact using The Nine Steps of Story Structure.

Part Five explains how to take what you've written and put it on its feet using insider secrets from the worlds of acting and comedy.

Part Six prepares you to step in front of an audience and deliver your story with confidence and poise.

I've coached over 1000 business professionals using the exact steps described in this book. I've witnessed some amazing transformations and heard some wonderful success stories.

NOW, IT'S YOUR TURN!

This Book Is Right For You If...

- [ ] You don't think of yourself as a boring speaker but you want to be more dynamic.

- [ ] You're tired of being a boring speaker with good content but no pizzazz.

- [ ] You're interested in knowing how to capture and keep the attention of listeners, whether at a board meeting, conference, orientation, leadership retreat or trade-show.

- [ ] You're interested in being able to make your message memorable — so audiences remember what you said MONTHS later.

- [ ] You're interested in knowing how to make any speech or presentation come alive so audiences relate to what you're saying and want to hear more.

- [ ] You're interested in connecting with people so they care about you, your ideas, your products, your services, and your company.

- [ ] You are required by your job to be a speaker or trainer and you have to communicate important and sometimes dull information.

- [ ] You are climbing up the ladder of success and want to skip a few rungs.

- [ ] You're an entrepreneur who needs to speak in public to spread the word about your product or service.

- [ ] You're interested in using stories because you've seen how effective they can be.

Make Your Business Presentations Capture Attention, Inspire Action, and Produce Results

❏ You're a powerful leader but a weak speaker.

❏ You know you have what it takes to be a good speaker but you lack training and proper guidance.

❏ You want to add some humor and fun to your speeches.

❏ You've got some great stories but don't know what to do with them.

❏ You just got a promotion and will be doing more speeches and presentations and need to improve now.

❏ You just got passed over for a promotion by someone who is a better public speaker than you are and now you're angry enough to do something about it.

❏ You're a professional speaker or trainer who has great content but falls short in the storytelling area.

❏ There is a frustrated actor inside of you that wants to get out.

PART ONE

Understand that Storytelling is Your Passport to Professional Success

CHAPTER 1

Learn Why Storytelling is so Powerful

Think about all the people you interacted with at work today — on the phone, over the net, through correspondence, or in person.

Did any of those people tell you a story? Did they relate a conversation with a customer, explain how an employee gave them above-and-beyond service, or report in detail what happened at the annual trade show?

How about you? Did you tell a story today? Did you reassure a nervous new-hire by recalling your own first day on the job and by confessing how intimidated you felt? Did you pleasantly surprise staff members by starting the weekly meeting with a funny story about your shopping experience at a competitor's store? Did you convince a prospective client to sign on the dotted line by telling her a success story of another satisfied buyer?

John-Paul Sartre said, "We understand everything in human life through stories." It's true. We comprehend things better when they're related in story form, and we also feel a rapport with the person telling the story. Increasing affinity with customers and co-workers is certainly one of our goals as professionals, and this book will explain exactly how to do that.

First, it's important to understand why it's worth our while to tell stories. I've been a proponent of storytelling for so long, it never occurred to me that some professionals feel it is inappropriate in business situations. After my encounter with the following doubting Thomas, I realized I shouldn't assume I'm "preaching to the choir" and take for granted that every reader is already sold on the enduring power and appropriateness of storytelling in business.

So, I'll share this story about my run-in with a resident skeptic, and then I'll identify seven specific reasons why it's in your best interest to make "SHOW and TELL" a part of your everyday workplace interactions.

Is Storytelling Really All that Important?

> *"Someone's boring me. I think it's me."*
> — poet DYLAN THOMAS

I was delivering a training program on "How to Use Strategic Storytelling in Business" for a group of hotel employees, when I noticed a woman fidgeting in the back row. It was obvious that this woman (who I had been told was Pat, the rather crusty HR Director) was taking exception to my statement that, "We're not finished speaking — until we've told a story."

Pat continued to fuss until I opened the floor for questions. Her hand shot up immediately. She said challengingly, "You keep suggesting we use stories in speeches, presentations and meetings, but I don't have time for that. Our meetings run late as it is."

I knew I needed to handle this delicately. "Can I ask you something?" She nodded. I said, "If you cover 10 agenda items in a thirty minute meeting, does that mean your employees heard, understood, and remembered all 10 of those items?"

Learn Why Storytelling is so Powerful

Pat thought about it for a moment and replied, "They better; that's their job. That's what they're being paid to do."

"That's true," I replied, "but just because a speaker shares important information, does that mean everyone in the room 'gets' that information and acts on it?"

"I guess not," she reluctantly agreed, "but what am I supposed to do when I have a lot to cover in a short amount of time?" Pat's exasperated tone revealed the frustration she was feeling.

"I take it you are tasked with chairing meetings and giving instructions. Would it be fair to say your employees don't always *follow* the instructions?"

"Yes," she admitted rather begrudgingly, "that would be fair to say."

"Perhaps they're not 'getting' the information and they're missing the *why*," I suggested.

"The *why*?" Pat responded, getting agitated. "All the *why* they need is that the boss says so!"

We all chuckled, then I said, "When people are given instructions, and they're not given a clear *why*," I continued, "they often express their confusion through resistance — through sub-standard performance. It's a manager's job to communicate information in a way that employees 'get' it and are motivated to 'act' on it. That's why we're not done speaking — until we've told a story."

"You've lost me," Pat said, shaking her head. "What do silly little stories have to do with motivation?"

"Silly little stories have nothing to do with motivation," I agreed, "But strategically chosen, well-told stories frame a situation or instructions in a personally meaningful way that turns on the light-bulb in their mind ('I see'), the compassion in their heart ('I relate'), and the inspiration in their soul to act ('I do.') Can I give you an example why it's worth the small investment of time to include a well-crafted story?"

"Sure," she said with some reluctance.

"Well," I said, "I know you're preparing your staff for the busy holiday season and that your hotel will be 100% occupied for most of that period. Perhaps you're explaining to your staff that it will be necessary to enforce the 3 p.m. check-in — with no exceptions — because housekeeping will need the extra time for cleaning the rooms. Perhaps you caution your employees to be ready to receive complaints from unhappy guests who may be upset about not being able to get into their rooms early — and then you move on to the next agenda item.

"Now, your staff members have just been given important information, but that doesn't mean that everyone in the room 'gets' that information and will act on it. You've been clear in sharing the information, but they don't have a personally relevant 'aha' associated with it. That means they probably won't remember it, and even if they do remember it, they have no incentive to act on it. We need to bring this 'dull' part of our information to life with a personal story so employees are motivated to enforce the policy compassionately and patiently when encountering these unhappy customers."

I continued, "Imagine instead that you took a couple minutes during your meeting to tell the following story, which actually happened to a friend of mine. You'll want to use vivid detail and dialogue of what took place, so your staff members can picture what you're saying."

Learn Why Storytelling is so Powerful

A friend told me about a man and his wife who recently traveled to Hawaii for a well-deserved vacation. Their flight from the east coast had been delayed due to bad weather.

They arrived at the hotel, appearing very disheveled and tired. They seemed to bump into each and fumble with their luggage, trying to be helpful to the porters. Finally, they had everything out of the rental car and handed the keys to the valet.

They finally drug themselves up to the front desk and presented their credit card and reservation number. It was noon. The front desk clerk announced, "I'll be glad to enter your information into the computer, but check-in isn't until 3 p.m., so it'll be a few hours before your room is available."

"What?" the gentleman squawked. "We haven't slept for 24 hours. We missed our connection because our first plane was late, then we were jammed into middle seats on the five-hour flight from California, and then we had to wait in line because the car rental agency ran out of cars. We're dead on our feet. All we want is someplace to lie down for awhile."

The hotel clerk looked at them sympathetically and then she said, "Tell you what I can do. We have a hospitality suite where you can change into comfortable clothes and freshen up. I'll give you complimentary tickets to our lunch buffet, and then you can take a nap on the chaise lounges by the pool. By that time, we ought to have your room ready for you."

They both let out a sigh of relief and were so pleased they wanted to give her a kiss. What could have been a perfunctory brush-off ("Sorry, we don't have any rooms available") turned into a positive experience. Instead of continuing their odyssey of bad luck, that savvy employee turned it around with her caring offer.

"Then," I told Pat, "you simply segue that story back to your employees and the challenge they are facing. Tell them, 'I know it can be hard to be compassionate when you've got someone yelling at you because they can't check into their room. However, please remember my friend's story. Put yourself in the shoes of your guests and imagine that *you* haven't slept for 24 hours and *you've* just been told it will be another 3 hours before you can get into your room. Please take the time to empathize with their frustration. We may not be able to give them what they want; however, we can *at least* give them our concern.'

I looked at Pat. "Stories increase our connection with the listener and help them the see the *why* of our message. Can you see how that 'little' two minute story would personalize your instructions so your employees would be more likely to remember them and act on them?" I said.

"Yes," she said, "I can see how it would make a difference," and then chuckled upon realizing that the story had also helped her to 'get' it.

The Nine Benefits of Strategic Storytelling

> *"Reality leaves a lot to the imagination."*
> — Songwriter JOHN LENNON

Like I mentioned before, you may already be convinced of the value of storytelling. After all, you bought this book. However, it's worth clarifying these nine benefits so that, from now on, you are absolutely clear that if you want to capture and keep the imagination of your audience — you've got to tell a story.

Learn Why Storytelling is so Powerful

Benefit #1: Stories Engage the Left and Right Brain

Please think back to a boring speaker you've heard recently. (Sorry, I know this is painful.) Was it an executive who droned on and on at the annual meeting — almost as if he were talking to himself? Was it a politician at a community meeting who "read" her speech, never once looking up from her notes? Was it a co-worker who took thirty l–o–n–g minutes to deliver a budget report?

The speakers who bore us to tears talk to our left-brain. They think their job is to organize their material and present it in a structured way, (i.e., "Just the facts, ma'am!") Wrong! A speaker's job is to deliver information in a way that motivates people to listen, remember, and act. Boring speakers talk to *your* left-brain from *their* left-brain. What they don't understand is that your left-brain doesn't make decisions, it simply collects data and feeds it to the right-brain which is where you "make up your mind."

You may be thinking, "What's this about our left and right brain? I thought I had one brain, not two." Well, here's a Cliff Notes explanation of what I'm talking about.

Your brain is divided into halves — the (logical) left-brain and the (emotional) right-brain. Your left-brain is linear; it deals with facts and data. Your right-brain is non-linear; it deals with feelings and creativity. (Or, as my son likes to put it, "Your left-brain is like a scientist; your right-brain is like an actor.) As you can imagine, it's more complex than this, but this brief explanation will work for our purposes.

Your audience member's right-brain is where the action is. It watches the speaker's body language, listens to vocal tone, feels energy (or the lack of); and then, in a split second (much like a Pentium Ten Thousand processor) — interprets it all and decides

Make Your Business Presentations Capture Attention, Inspire Action, and Produce Results

whether it likes, believes and trusts the speaker. If the answer is NO — the speaker is toast. It's Jamaican vacation time, baby!

Once and for all, we need to understand that intellectual stimulation (appealing to the left-brain with content only) is not enough. Likewise, emotional stimulation (appealing to the right-brain only) is not enough. Communicating to *both* sides of the brain is best. That's why we need to back up our stories with facts and statistics and illustrate our facts and statistics with stories. That's another reason why we shouldn't stop talking . . . until we've told a story.

Benefit #2: Stories Appeal to the Different Learning Styles

Research on how individuals process data and information has shown that there are three predominant learning styles. The three styles are auditory, visual, and kinesthetic.

AUDITORY LEARNERS process information primarily with their sense of hearing. They pay particular attention to the sound, quality, and inflection of your voice. They appreciate a good vocabulary and assimilate material best by listening to your words. They respond well to poetry, music, and lyrical language. They can't stand speakers who talk in a monotone because it's offensive to their sensibility. Their internal processing is also auditory. Chances are, they're having a two-way dialogue or debate with you in their head while you talk.

VISUAL LEARNERS need to *see* what you're saying. They respond particularly well to "SHOW and TELL" because they process things through their eyes rather than their ears. They appreciate handouts and often take copious notes. They like speakers to use PowerPoint presentations, overhead transparencies, poster pads, or chalkboards because these visual aids help them comprehend what they're hearing. They notice what you're wearing and want you to make eye contact. Their internal processing is also visual — they are picturing what you're saying in their head while you talk. Since visual stimulation is appealing to them, they respond warmly to speakers who "take up the whole stage," use dramatic gestures, and demonstrate open body language.

KINESTHETIC LEARNERS are more sensory and tactile. They learn by doing and like to be involved. They respond well to role-plays, exercises, and Q & A's because they enjoy participating. They want learning to be a two-way street in which they contribute to the process, instead of being forced to sit quietly and be a passive recipient of the process. They can't wait to add their "two bits." They also place a high value on the "vibe" of the audience, the "feel" of the surroundings, and how "in touch" the speaker is with the group. They like "hands-on" learning experiences where they get to accomplish, build, or create something — instead of just sitting there and being talked at or lectured to.

The good news is that Strategic Storytelling addresses ALL the preferred learning styles. You can have 500 different professionals in the same room at the same time — engineers, artists, Realtors and repairmen of different ages, ethnic, and educational backgrounds — and a well-selected, well-told story will resonate with every one of them. Why?

- Stories are inherently auditory because storytellers have multiple opportunities to change volume, tempo, inflection, and pitch as they "play" the different characters.
- Stories are inherently visual because good storytellers don't just "tell" the story — they act it out. The audience gets caught up in picturing the imaginary reality of the story.
- Stories are inherently kinesthetic because great storytellers don't simply narrate a past event — they re-live it so everyone in the room is experiencing that event and feeling the emotions of the moment.

- Stories work the left-brain because a well-crafted story flows forward in a logical and linear progression.
- Stories work the right-brain because it is stimulated by the sights, sounds and emotions triggered by strategic stories.
- Stories move people from their head to their heart and back again. If you can connect emotion to information, you can motivate your listeners to change their behavior.

In short, Strategic Storytelling using The Story Theater Method is a recipe for "communication charisma." You take a pint of important information, add a dash of organization and logic, include a cup of genuine emotion, provide two chances for meaningful participation, and Viola!, you've created a concoction of longed-for connection that engages everyone in the room.

Of course, we have the option of depriving our audience of 90% of the multi-sensory stimulation they need to be captivated, educated, and motivated. We could stand stock still behind a lectern, grip its sides with our tightly clenched fingers, and read from index cards. But why be boring when we can be fascinating?

Benefit #3: Stories Give Us Opportunities to Be Original

Let's face it — professionals in today's workplace are sophisticated. They've participated in dozens of annual conventions, self-improvement seminars, and continuing education classes. They've read all the latest business books and industry journals.

What does all this mean? People are *yearning* for someone to tell them something they don't already know — that's education. At the same time, they want speakers to captivate their attention and make it interesting. That's entertainment. And if the speaker is really good, people will feel better about themselves and their current circumstances when s/he's done. That's motivation and inspiration.

The problem with having to teach something, what I call the dissemination of data and information, is that it's usually as boring as a drive across Nebraska in January on a cloudy day. It's just not very interesting and — as I said before — there's the danger that people will check out on you and start daydreaming about a Jamaican holiday. Even if your audience is intent on paying attention, their brains are struggling to keep up with you. You've got to do something to captivate their attention before you can teach them what you're charged to teach.

This can be a bit of a challenge though, because you've probably heard that "There's nothing new under the sun." How then, can we share original thoughts?

Would you like to know the definition of "original?" If we haven't heard, seen, or read it before . . . it's original. That's *another* reason stories are so powerful. They *aren't* common knowledge. Audiences can't wait to hear what comes next because everything that's being said is *new*. Stories have the power to make familiar information fresh. People are compelled to concentrate because they're hearing this for the *first time*.

Benefit #4: Stories Can Give You Instant Credibility

"To be persuasive, we must be believable.
To be believable, we must be credible.
To be credible, we must be truthful."
— journalist EDWARD R. MURROW

The words that Webster's Dictionary uses to define credibility are "trustworthy, likeable, believable and authentic." Well-selected, well-told stories convince us that the speaker knows what s/he's talking about.

Although stories are not a magic elixir that will instantly make you all of the above; they certainly have the power to increase your credibility and heighten your impact. A shining example of this was a CEO who I had the privilege of seeing in action several years ago.

I was standing in the back of an auditorium, preparing for my turn to speak, as 300 people filed in for the second half of a day-long annual meeting of a nationwide company. As soon as everyone was seated, the Emcee called the meeting to order and then, with a lame attempt at a joke, and I do mean lame, proceeded to introduce Bob, the owner of the company.

Bob, a tall gray-haired man in his sixties, walked to the lectern and looked out over the audience. They were restless because they'd already sat through two dreary speeches that morning; one about a new 401k benefit plan and another about the acquisition of two new locations. You could tell they were bracing themselves for another long, lifeless litany of facts and figures.

Bob seemed to have anticipated this because he did something different. In a break with tradition, he walked away from the lectern and, without any notes in his hand, started telling us a story about the beginning of the company and how things had changed over the years. He reminisced about the good old days when they only had two stores in Salt Lake City and nine employees. Then, he explained how the company had grown to forty-two stores in twelve states.

As he moved around the stage, I could feel the energy of the audience shift. As Bob became more animated, the employees became more animated. Now, instead of slumping in their seats, they were sitting up and leaning forward. Bob began moving back and forth across the stage. His gestures were simple and honest. His voice was soft and tender one minute, jovial and fervent the next. It was obvious that he was speaking from his heart.

At one point, he "pulled an Oprah." He stepped down off the plat-form and walked right up to people in the front row. Then, he climbed back up on the stage to demonstrate the size of his first office and to show where his secretary Marge had sat, right outside his door.

He had our total attention. People were smiling and nodding as he recalled the names of those first few employees and talked loving-ly of his father, the founder of the company. I was impressed with how good he was. He had us laughing one minute and close to tears the next. At the end, he made a powerful point about the need for everyone in the company to persevere through the cur-rent expansion. He said they'd done it before, and they could do it again. I'll never forget his final words. "Stay the course," he plead-ed quietly, yet firmly. "Stay the course."

When he finished talking, there were a few seconds of amazed silence. Then, everyone rose as one and they filled the room with their heartfelt applause. Bob had done his job as a speaker and as a leader. He had captured and held everyone's attention, and he had gotten his message across authentically and persuasively. Most importantly, we had "bought into" his message. He had established credibility with his eloquent story. He had tapped into the employ-ees' collective history and reminded them that they had stayed the course before and they could do it again.

Benefit #5: Stories Establish Involvement

Have you ever been "swept away" by a speaker who told a story so well you were transported? For that moment, you were complete-ly mesmerized? As demonstrated by the CEO in the preceding story, when speakers get "into" their message, they make us hear, see, feel, and experience the message too.

When you "embody" a story and immerse yourself in re-living it, you bring everyone in the room along. Instead of being preoccupied, distracted, or bored, people can't help but listen with every fiber of their being. They are caught up in the spell of the story and are "one" with the speaker.

Benefit #6: Stories Create a Bond and Bridge of Commonality

Stories have the ability to humanize authority figures (whether that's a supervisor, union leader, or officer) because they establish that you've had the same kinds of things happen to you. Audience members start seeing you as *one of them*. Instead of a divisive "us versus them" mentality existing between the speaker and audience, stories bring us together so we are no longer separate.

Instead of thinking, "S/he doesn't know what it's like for us," people in the audience feel you understand them. Instead of a *side against side* conflict, the speaker and audience are now *on the same side*. Well-selected, well-told stories remove a label or title from you and make you common — not common in the sense of average, but common in the sense of shared experience.

A principle requirement of connection is our willingness to be vulnerable. Stories let us let our guard down. They let people in the room know we are willing to self-reveal. Wisdom is the accumulated knowledge of our life. It is by sharing this wisdom through first-person stories that people relate to us.

Are you wondering, "Why would people be interested in me? I'm not special?" Are you thinking, "I don't want to come across as stuck-up. It seems egotistical to talk about myself."? One workshop participant confessed, "I'm afraid that if I tell about a mistake I've made, co-workers will lose respect for me."

To the contrary. The very nature of stories is that they serve as a *bridge for bonding*. Their purpose is *not* to establish superiority; it's to establish affinity. Affinity is defined as "kinship, sympathy marked by community of interest." When you talk about your first sales call, a complaint from a client, or an error of judgment; it triggers a sympathetic response. It causes listeners to think about *their* first sales call, a complaint *they* just handled, or an error *they* made. Now, they're receptive (instead of resistant or resentful) because they feel you're a kindred spirit.

Later in the book, I'll ask, "What's your story?" What have you learned from life? What are the lessons you want to pass on to save people "trial and terror" errors so they won't have to make the same mistakes you did? What are your epiphanies, your regrets? What do you wish someone had told you way back when you first started out? Those are the stories you must tell.

Don't be concerned about coming across as conceited. You won't be standing there bragging about your accomplishments and puffing out your chest like some egomaniac that has to compensate for his/her insecurity by boasting how great s/he is. The stories you're going to be sharing all contain a challenge and a lesson learned. You're going to use your real-life examples to explain how you encountered and overcame obstacles.

Have you ever struggled? Have you ever made a mistake and learned from it? Have you ever made the same mistake multiple times and learned from it? See. I knew you had some good stories in you. Those are the ones we'll focus on. Those stories make you just like everybody else who's struggled. The difference is, *you're* the one who's extracting the value, telling the tale, and *sharing* the resulting wisdom. Which brings us to our next benefit of Strategic Storytelling.

Benefit #7: Stories Can Establish You as a Respected Expert

Here's how I approach this whole business of being an expert who speaks while using my life as a template for wisdom. I'm certainly not the smartest guy on the block — never was. I know who I am, and I'm fine with my average IQ. I'm a common-sense kind of guy who sits around all day (kind of like a bargain basement Galileo) contemplating the meaning of life. My life.

When something happens to me I ask myself, "What was that all about?" I take the resulting lesson, apply The Story Theater Method in this book to craft it into a story, and then stand in front of my audience with the intention to share what I've just learned. I'm *not* coming from arrogance; I'm coming from service. My approach isn't, "I'm smart and you're not — so pay attention and learn something so you don't mess up!" My approach is more like, "Hey you guys, I just figured something out, and I'd like to share it in case it might be interesting and useful for you."

I challenge you to assume the mantle of expert when you communicate in business situations. That doesn't mean being a jerk who "lords" it over other people. It means being a *teacher* who shares your expertise (what you've learned from first-hand experience) in the hopes it might positively influence those hearing it. There is nothing as compelling as the truth. Instead of relying solely on outside sources or anonymous experts, *you* be the authority on the topic by demonstrating how you have personally and professionally survived this trial-by-fire.

Benefit #8: Strategic Storytelling Gives You a Competitive Edge

> *"Once a human being has arrived on this earth,*
> *communication is the largest single factor*
> *determining what kinds of relationships he*
> *makes with others and what happens to him."*
> — psychologist VIRGINIA SATIR

Please think back to the last professional conference you attended.

Learn Why Storytelling is so Powerful

Where was it? How many keynotes and breakout sessions did you attend? Which speaker do you remember most? Why?

If you're like many people, you attended ten or more sessions in a three-day conference. You took notes, kibitzed with colleagues, and collected handouts. And, if you're like most people, you stashed those notes and handouts ... who knows where? If you're lucky, you may remember as many as *two* or *three* of the dozens of ideas you heard during the course of that event.

I'm going to project that the speaker who came to mind shared a "real-life" example that caused you to reflect on what you're doing and decide to do things differently. Speakers who incorporate well-crafted stories into their presentations almost always stand out because they're so *rare.*

Simply said, if you want to catapult your career; if you want to be remembered and respected by your professional peers; if you want to make a profound, lasting difference and be a catalyst for meaningful change; start telling stories!

My favorite boss once told me, "When it comes to careers, you either communicate or you stagnate." He explained, "We've got to remember that *people can't read our mind.* We may have a brilliant suggestion, but if we're afraid to speak up at staff meetings because someone might challenge us, our peers will never hear our innovative ideas. We may be the perfect person to head up a project team, but if we're intimidated into silence by aggressive members of the committee, our supervisor won't feel like she can entrust us with that leadership position. We may be a fine department head, but if we have to deliver bad news and we aren't able to do that in an empathetic fashion, our effectiveness and impact will be compromised."

"Look around you," he added. "*Hard work, talent, and intelligence are not enough.* In an ideal world, the most qualified person would always get the promotion and always get the credit. In the real world, that doesn't always happen. The people who advance into positions of power are almost always the best communicators. They're the self-assured ones who are comfortable contributing their ideas. They're the articulate ones who can get their messages across clearly and convincingly. They're the ones who can develop and maintain positive relationships because they're able to communicate in ways that turn conflict into cooperation."

The good news is, strategically selected, well-told stories can do all the above. They increase our perceived value in the marketplace because excellent communication skills are so hard to come by. In a 2002 *USA Today* survey of one thousand executives, the vast majority rated "communication skills" as the number one factor that determined their rapid rise through the ranks. If you're serious about your career, developing your ability to craft and deliver insightful stories is one of the best investments you can make on behalf of your professional future.

Convinced? I hope so, because it's time for us to move on to the "how-to's." If you're ready to learn how to use The Story Theater Method to make your business messages come alive, let's go.

PART TWO

Use The Story Theater Method™ to Make Your Presentations Come Alive

CHAPTER 2

Realize that Great Stories Make Great Theater

W hen I began my speaking career in 1989, it was natural for me to tell stories because of my background in theater and comedy. With repeated practice, these stories evolved into "signature" stories that took on a life of their own. Audience members who had heard me before would often request a specific story, and meeting planners would tell me to be sure to include the Streaking Story or one of my other crowd favorites.

As you can imagine, I welcomed this "Play it again, Doug" response, and evaluated what I was doing to figure out what was producing these command performances. I realized I was bringing the disciplines of drama and comedy to my stories and turning them into short one-act plays. Or, as one of my participants called them, "dramadies." I wasn't just telling my stories, I was acting them out in such vivid detail they were coming "alive."

Story Theater Combines the Practical and Theatrical

Story Theater is a synthesis of the practical and theatrical. It is a methodology that allows you to teach without seeming preachy, entertain without being artificial, and inspire without being evangelistic.

I've had the opportunity to coach all types of individuals — from nationally known professional speakers who want to take their platform skills to the next level — to shy people determined to improve their public speaking skills so their self-consciousness doesn't compromise their career.

Here are a few assumptions I'm making about you. I'm guessing that you're not interested in becoming a movie or stage actor, right? You just want to make your presentations better? I'm also projecting that:

- You are open to innovative methods that will help you get your message across
- You want to be a better communicator and public speaker
- You want to utilize more of your unique personality on the platform
- You hate dull, boring speakers and don't want to be one of them
- You have experiences that have the potential to be fascinating stories
- You want your thoughts, ideas, and suggestions to be heard

If you agree with most of the above statements, you're in the right place because that's exactly what the Story Theater methodology helps you do. The first step is to start with a good story.

It All Starts With a Story

Back in the 70's and 80's, I spent thirteen years in Hollywood trying to break into movies and TV. In the process, I often played the sidekick, clown, or comic relief in a lot of plays. Everyone kept telling me I should try my hand at stand-up comedy. I finally took their advice and went to my first Open Mic night at the Comedy Store on Hollywood's renowned Sunset Strip.

Realize that Great Stories Make Great Theater

I'll never forget walking into that famous place where many comedians had gotten their start. On the walls were framed pictures of Eddie Murphy, George Carlin, Richard Pryor, Ellen DeGeneres, Whoopi Goldberg, Lily Tomlin, Lucille Ball, Jerry Seinfeld and Jay Leno. I fantasized how my picture would be on that wall some day too.

A veteran comic from Canada had the spot before me and performed a hysterically funny ten minutes. His material was sharp, well developed, and he was masterful at working the crowd. Then, they called my name. I was up.

I still remember standing behind that mic, looking out into the hot lights, as sweat trickled down the inside of my shirt. I started into my Streaking Story and within seconds it was clear that it was not funny. The audience stared at me politely and waited for me to get to the funny part. It never happened. I felt like a particle of dust, and every member of the audience was a vacuum cleaner. I could feel my energy being sucked out of me with every supposedly funny line that didn't get a laugh. After five excruciating minutes, I wrapped up with a mortified thank you and slunk off into the darkness ... without my dignity.

I thought I had a funny story. Actually, it *was* a funny story — I just hadn't learned how to deliver it in a funny way yet.

Nine years later, and a million miles removed from that humiliating Hollywood experience, I was presenting a program on presentation skills for the Pikes Peak Library in Colorado Springs.

I'd been speaking professionally for about a year at that point, and was starting to find my own style. I had become more comfortable on the stage and had honed my ability to deliver material in a way that captured and kept interest. Without even thinking about it, I asked the audience if they'd like to hear a funny story. Of course, they said yes. I spontaneously started into my Streaking Story. I forgot about my traumatic experience at the Comedy Store and just tore into the story with reckless abandon. As a result, I had a blast and so did everyone in the room.

The Streaking Story

Are you curious about the Streaking Story? Here is a brief synopsis of it. It's a good example of a signature story.

Back in 1974, I was a member of an avant-garde theater company in Los Angeles. About forty young actors and actresses came to this theater five nights a week and did crazy theater exercises. This one particular Wednesday night, the exercise was called "Outer Theater." We were instructed to go out into the community with a partner and do something we would never do. It had to be something risky that was outside of our comfort zone.

This guy George and I decided we would go "streaking" in Westwood, a well-trafficked college neighborhood and shopping district near UCLA. George and I got into my (what else?) 1962 Volkswagen bus and drove around, looking for the ideal place to go streaking. We finally located a parking spot and surreptitiously got undressed in the back of the van.

(Dear Readers: Remember, I'm pantomiming all this for the audience. I'm pretending to drive the VW bus with my head on a swivel looking for the perfect place to "streak." I'm acting out what it was like trying to get my clothes off in the back of that crowded van with this guy George that I didn't really know.)

After agonizing over our decision, we leapt from the van and ran down the street hollering and screaming as we passed a line of people waiting to see a movie. As we rounded the corner and

Realize that Great Stories Make Great Theater

approached the end of the alley, a cop car came flying around the corner and ordered us to freeze and put our hands up over our heads. As we stood there buck-naked with our hands above our heads, a crowd of people gathered around screaming in hilarious delight. The cop handcuffed us, threw us in the back of the squad car and, after letting us put on our underwear, took us to the West Los Angeles police station where he checked to see if we had prior records as perverts.

In the end, he gave our clothes back and said we were free to go. Back at the theater, we were the hit of the evening, and I learned an important lesson. When you take a risk, you expand your comfort zone. I was now more "free to go" anywhere and do anything than I had ever been.

I'll never forget the audience reaction that day in the library. As I pretended to run down the street with George right behind me, the audience was laughing so hard, tears were streaming down their faces. The laughter got so loud that other people in the library started peeking in from the hallway to see what was going on. It was an amazing experience.

The same story I'd told so poorly at the Comedy Store was now a hilarious re-enactment that elicited howls of laughter. What was the difference? At the Comedy Store I stood still and "told" the story. At the library, I re-enacted it. I didn't talk about the time I went streaking — I streaked, albeit fully-clothed! The audience in the library became the crowd in the movie theater line watching us run past. I had used Story Theater techniques to make the story come alive.

Story Theater Blends Physical and Emotional Action

How do we make our material come alive? We move around! The

word "acting" implies action, which is why Story Theater features *both* physical and emotional action.

Many speakers just stand still and talk. They're not moved emotionally, so they don't move physically, which means they don't have the power to move their audience to new visions or behaviors. Their intention is just to get through the darn speech, often as quickly as possible. They just want to get it over. Talk, talk, talk! The world doesn't need more talk; it needs more action.

I've always been fascinated by the fact that the word "motivation" is derived from the Latin word *motivus* which means "to move," and that the word "emotion" is derived from the French *emouvoir* — to "stir up." If we want to stir up our audience, we've got to stir things up by NOT standing in one place. If we want to *move* our audience intellectually and emotionally from here to there, we must move physically here and there.

That's one of the reasons my Streaking Story worked so well with that library audience. Instead of being petrified (defined as "inert, lifeless, inactive, wooden, or stone-like"), I acted out the story. My physicality helped them visualize the scene, which engaged them emotionally. I had a good time telling it, so they had a good time hearing it. Back in Hollywood, I had the foundation, but I hadn't spiced it up with action.

My wife, who has seen me speak many times, likens it to making spaghetti sauce. You may start out with tomato sauce, but that's not enough by itself. Nobody would ever mistake plain old tomato sauce for tangy, savory spaghetti sauce. Tomato sauce is a good foundation, but you need to add oregano, basil, green peppers, garlic, (at least in our family!), and onions to make it fulfill its potential. Then it needs to simmer for a while. After all the ingredients mix and mingle, *then* you've got full-flavored spaghetti sauce.

Realize that Great Stories Make Great Theater

Your story is like that. It's a good place to start, but you need to add garlic and onions, which in story terms are the equivalent of a substantive point and a solid organizational structure. Then, you need to spice it up with acting techniques that help audience members SEE what you're SAYING. Then, the story needs to simmer over time, which is the creative process in which you write, re-write, rehearse, practice, and polish. Finally, you've cooked up a mentally and visually delicious story, which has the power to move people to laughter and tears, and which will be remembered long after you're gone. That's the power of Story Theater.

CHAPTER 3

Recognize that the Messenger is as Important as the Message

S ome presentation skills experts say you should alter your presentation style based on the makeup of the group. They say you should tone it down for one audience and enlarge it for the other — that you should speak slower in one room and faster in another. That's a bunch of ... baloney!

While professional actors are experienced at altering themselves to fit a particular role, non-actors have a hard enough time being themselves when they give a speech. I think the suggestion that people should change their presentation style for every audience is ludicrous because it flies in the face of what works.

Be True to Yourself and Your Message

The key to becoming an effective speaker is to be *authentic*. The goal is not to change who you are; it's to remain true to who you are. To do otherwise is to lose your power. Your power lies in your unique personality and style. Your gift to your audience is quite simply — you.

When you allow fear, lack of preparation, or some misguided

notion that you need to take on a different persona to morph you into something you're not, you send a mixed signal to your audience. They literally don't know who you are — and if they don't know who you are, they can't and won't trust you. Furthermore, they'll either lose interest because they've concluded you're a fake, or they'll be so preoccupied trying to read between your lines they'll miss half your material.

I witnessed this when I was keynoting a meeting for a company at a fancy downtown hotel. The company was rolling out a new customer service initiative and they asked me to deliver an inspirational message that could motivate their employees to step up to the challenge. No expense was spared.

The breakfast meeting was scheduled to get under way at 8:30, so I arrived at 7:30 a.m. to check the room and get comfortable. The first few attendees started to trickle in for breakfast around 8:00. The CEO of the company arrived a few moments later and walked over to say hello.

He greeted me with a smile and a firm handshake. He was in a good mood and it showed. After welcoming me, he made his way around the room, saying hello to as many people as possible. I watched him as he laughed and joked good-naturedly with his employees. Everything about his body language communicated poise and confidence.

Will The Real Speaker Please Stand Up?

According to the agenda, he was supposed to open the meeting with some brief opening comments, and then it would be my turn. As the clock ticked closer to the starting time, I watched this seemingly gregarious executive transform into a different person. As we waited in the wings together, his smile disappeared. One of his legs was jiggling, and he was nervously rolling a quarter around in his hand.

Recognize that the Messenger is as Important as the Message

By the time he was introduced, he was a fraction of his former self. He walked to the lectern as if it were a guillotine. He took his notes out of his jacket pocket, set them down, and fiddled with his glasses for a moment. They were the kind that sat down at the end of his nose, and they made him look like a stuffy professor. He took a sip of water, looked up, and began.

Whatever oxygen was in the air was immediately sucked out of the room. It was as if a cloud of gloom and doom had rolled in. His voice was flat, his language was stilted, and his body language was stiff. The self-assured CEO who, only moments before, had made the rounds joshing with his employees was gone. An imposter had taken his place — one with absolutely no power.

As he plodded along, reading from a dry script that sounded as if someone else had written it, (because someone else had!), everyone fell into a kind of dazed state. We were trying to listen — but it was hard work. What little eye contact he made was perfunctory at best. His brief remarks seemed to drag on endlessly.

After the meeting ended and people were leaving to go back to their office, I noticed him talking with a small group of people. His smile was back. The stiffness was gone. The evil spell had been broken. He was "himself" again. He had miraculously regained his power.

Bring Yourself to the Platform

Where did the "real" man go? Good question.

Please abandon the belief that you have to be "different" on the platform. The person you are *in front of* the group and the person you are when you're *with* the group ought to be one and the same. You don't have to pretend to be anybody — just be yourself.

Understand that you, the messenger, are the vehicle through which your communication is transmitted to the audience. If you are not comfortable with yourself, the transmission of the message will not be successful. That's why our first step in The Story Theater Method is to strengthen you, the messenger. Once we do that, we go to work on strengthening the message. They both must be equally strong.

When you become an accomplished speaker, you and the message become one. The two are completely congruent. You embody the message and become its perfect vehicle.

Many inexperienced speakers pay a disproportionate amount of attention to their content and not enough on their delivery. They spend all of their time creating a fabulous product (their presentation) and then give it to their customer (the audience) in a broken down vehicle badly in need of a tune up.

A fellow professional speaker confessed she had done just that. She had been contracted to deliver a public seminar on leadership for a respected university's Extended Education program. Several days before the full day seminar was to be held, she received the registration list. Much to her delight, she discovered that several senior training directors for large corporations were going to be attending. She knew this would be an incredible career opportunity so she spent many extra hours putting together a detailed workbook and mailed 100 copies to the hotel where the program was going to be held.

She flew into the city the night before the program, checked into the hotel, and asked that the workbooks be delivered to her room. Yikes. They hadn't arrived. Panicked, she asked the front desk clerk if she could use their office computer and copier to reproduce the workbooks, promising to take good care of their equipment and offering to pay for the paper. The hotel employee graciously agreed.

Recognize that the Messenger is as Important as the Message

She spent half the night regenerating and collating her materials and finally went to bed, exhausted, at 4 o'clock in the morning. Two hours later, the alarm rang. It was time to get up. She sleep-walked through getting dressed and dragged herself downstairs to the meeting room by 7 a.m. She normally used the night before and an hour in the morning to mentally prepare, however she never got around to it this time because of the crisis with the handouts.

The program went okay, but it wasn't anything special. She was so tired; she didn't have her normal enthusiasm, clarity, or confidence. She wasn't able to think on her feet and provide stories illustrating how her suggestions had been applied in the real world. She rambled (which she never did) and forgot several important points because her mind had been so scrambled and ill prepared.

In retrospect, she realized it would have been a better use of her time to rehearse her presentation and get a good night's sleep — instead of spending hours producing workbooks that provided content but not connection.

Connect IN to Connect OUT

One of the primary differences between an actor in a play and a speaker in front of an audience is their focal point. Actors focus inward on the thoughts and feelings of their character. Their actions and reactions are based on their inner world. While they are responsible to the other actors on the stage and to the playwright — they have no responsibility to connect OUT to their audience. Rather, they connect IN to connect OUT. By connecting IN — by bringing their imaginary character to life — you, the audience member, make the connection.

That is one of the many phenomenons associated with story-telling. Audience members play an active rather than a passive role in relating to the storyteller. They are invited — through the the-atrical device of storytelling — to follow what is being said and make their own associations. They, in fact, perform a type of multi-tasking — they experience their *own* story while the actors are portraying the story from the platform. In other words — the audience member has a sympathetic experience.

Stories Set Up a Sympathetic Experience

Sympathy is defined as a relationship wherein whatever affects one, affects the other. Therefore, when the storyteller acts out receiving bad news and shows shock and disappointment — audi-ence members feel a similar emotion. They don't feel it for the sto-ryteller however — they feel it for themselves.

J.R.R. Tolkien, the author of the *Lord of the Rings* trilogy says, "What really happens is the story-maker proves a successful "sub-creator." He makes a Secondary World, which your mind can enter. Inside it, what he relates is "true," it accords with the laws of that world. You therefore believe it, while you are, as it were, inside."

Have you ever cried in a movie theater? Why? The actors were not even in the room. You knew you were watching a movie, yet you allowed yourself to be swept up in the story. The same thing hap-pens to an audience watching a play. You cry for the plight of the character — but the tears are your tears — the emotions are your emotions.

Luckily, the same thing happens when a masterful communicator breathes life into a story. Time and space disappear. Any sense of separation between the actor/speaker/storyteller and his or her audience disappears. For all intents and purposes the audience members are IN the story. They see things from the point of view of the storyteller. They walk down the same crowded street — hear the same voices — and smell the same aroma of bread wafting from a nearby bakery. They're not just passively listening to words being spoken, they are actively experiencing what is being said as if it were really happening right then. The story is hitting them where they live.

Strategic Storytelling Sets Up Experiential Learning

"We learn best through self-discovery."
—philosopher SOCRATES

Would you agree that experience is the best teacher? You can tell children not to touch a hot stove — but it's often not until they burn a finger that they "learn for themselves" the wisdom of that advice. It is the same with adults; we learn best through experience. This is actually called the "Socratic Method." We need to involve all of our senses — to experience this ourselves — in order to completely integrate and truly learn a new task or concept.

So how can you as a speaker, trainer, or leader accelerate the learning curve and help people experience something that they have yet to experience? How can you get them to understand why something is so important without them having to learn it for themselves — quite possibly by making mistakes and wasting time and resources?

The answer, of course, is with strategic storytelling. Well-chosen and well-crafted stories create a sympathetic experience. Rather than telling people what you want them to do and hoping that they intellectually understand the instructions enough to do it —

you can take them on a storytelling journey where they experience what you're saying for themselves. That is the connection that needs to take place for them to really learn it and choose to do it.

The shortest distance between you and your audience is not in the physical space between you and your audience. It is in the short space between your head and your heart. By connecting IN to how you feel about what you're saying, you will connect OUT to them. By tapping into your passion and conviction, you will reach beyond their brains and into a place inside of them that can only be reached emotionally and spiritually. It is the place where everyone is the same, where we are one.

Become One With Your Audience

I like to explain this concept with the following visualization. There is a space between you and your audience every time you speak to a group of people. The space is more pronounced if you don't know them and they don't know you, however it exists even when you know each other because we must prove that we're worth listening to every time we speak.

Imagine you're standing on one side of a river and your audience is on the other side. The water is meandering past in between you and there are boats and fisherman out on the river having a good time. Somehow, you're supposed to bring them over to your side of the river. You're supposed to get them to come over to your point of view — to see things the way you see them so you can all move forward in life and be happier, healthier, and more productive.

So there they are. They're sitting there in their chairs on the other side waiting for you to say something or do something that will stimulate them. Some want to come over and be with you. They're

Recognize that the Messenger is as Important as the Message

cheering you on. Some are resistant because they don't know or trust you yet. They're bored and complacent. They need convincing. Some are just plain apathetic. They could sit there all day and not care about a word you say.

So, the people in your audience range from being receptive to resistant — however they share one thing in common — they're a captive audience and yours to win over.

Then, you hear a voice from somewhere off in the distance; or is it in your head? It's hard to understand what it's saying because of the competing sounds of the river, boats, and what not — but you can just barely make it out. "Convince me," it says. It's the collective voice of your audience and it's ringing in your ears. "Convince me. Persuade me. Make me a believer."

The combined voice of the people in the room says, "What are you going to do to hold my attention? Are you going to be stiff and boring? Is this going to fun and entertaining? Are you going to be creative, or just tell me the facts? Did you care enough to prepare? Do you have any interesting stories I can relate to?"

It's your job as a speaker to build a bridge of connection across that space and connect with them. If you build it, they will cross over to your side.

It's not an easy task. Audiences can drive a hard bargain. As mentioned earlier, professionals in today's corporate world are often a jaded group. You're not the first speaker to stand before them and make a case for your position. But they will cross that bridge if you present a strategically selected, carefully crafted, and well-delivered story. Your audience members will leave the space they're in and enter into your story space. They will momentarily forget themselves completely and become one with you and your story.

But I'm Not an Actor

You may be thinking, "I'm not sure about this Story Theater stuff. I'm not an actor and I'm not into this Zen 'become one with the audience' stuff."

Rest assured. I'm going to show you how to channel your unique, *natural* personality into your presentations. I believe there is an actor inside you waiting to get out. Offstage, during private moments surrounded by friends, family or co-workers, your behavior is filled with emotion. You laugh, cry, and rage against the absurdity of life. You get loud when you're angry and soft when you're sad. You may even gesture extravagantly as you share a funny story with everyone at the dinner table.

Notice that there is no faking involved when you act out your feelings sincerely. You are "one" with your emotions because you are experiencing them in the moment. All we're going to do is take that honest emotion to the platform so you can be equally authentic (and interesting to watch and listen to) when you're in front of a group.

You can act with integrity — if you give it a chance. Maybe all you need is a good director to bring out your innate acting ability. Will you allow me to be your director? Lend me your talent, and I will help you learn how to be yourself on stage while giving a naturally entertaining and enthralling performance.

And if you're thinking that "acting" doesn't belong in business presentations, ask yourself this: "What good is information if employees don't listen to it? What good are instructions if co-workers can't follow them? What good are recommendations if customers don't buy into them?" The acting methods involved in Story Theater and Strategic Storytelling make your material come alive so your audiences are motivated to listen to what you're saying, follow what you're saying, and act on what you're saying. Still not convinced?

You Can Be Brilliant

Did you go to summer camp when you were a kid? Did a camp counselor gather you around the campfire at night and tell you scary stories? Do you remember jumping out of your seat or off the log when the counselor got to the "good part?" If you got completely caught up in what s/he was saying, that counselor was a good storyteller.

You have the same ability to hold an audience on the edge of their seats. You're the author, teacher, and performer of the stories of *your* life. And the beautiful part of this is — the message I want you to hear right now — you *already* have all the skills, talent, and creativity to do this work. Perhaps you haven't learned how to focus them yet, but they're there waiting for you to learn how to use so you can connect with people and get your message across eloquently and persuasively.

The techniques you're about to learn are like dance steps, and they're the same steps for everybody. All you have to do is believe in yourself and follow the directions. Now, I know some of you are better at following directions than others, but if you follow this formula — storytelling can be a snap. You don't have to be Bill Cosby or Robin Williams to do this. It takes more time than genius. And if you carve out the time to develop this ability — the payoff will be tremendous. People will respond to you with admiration and respect for your newfound skill. They'll notice.

Do you believe you have something special to share? Mahatma Gandhi said, "Man often becomes what he believes himself to be. If I keep on saying I cannot do a certain thing, it is possible I may become incapable of doing it. On the contrary, if I have the belief that I can do it, I shall surely acquire the capacity even if I may not have it at the beginning."

Are you willing to work at this? Are you ready to embrace the gift of all you are without apology and let others watch? That's what people want from you. They want your humanity, your spirit, your soul, and your uniqueness. They're looking for a spark, a light, a ray of hope — and you are that spark, that ray of hope.

Once and for all, please understand: *it's not just your content.* Quit hiding behind your content. Audiences expect you to have content. What they're hoping for is someone who knows how to make the content come alive. They don't just want a message — they want YOU at your joyous best.

One more chapter on how we can be the best messenger we can be — and then we'll go on a story safari.

CHAPTER 4

Connect with Your Audience Via Non-Co-dependent Speaking

M any speakers tell me they critique themselves while they're presenting. It's as if a sadistic Roger Ebert-like reviewer is living in their head, screaming into their subconscious mind, monitoring their every word and move; whispering in their ear with directions, "Slow down. Move around. Say something funny. You're losing them!"

All the while, words are coming out of their mouth that make no sense because at the same time they're talking to the audience, they're talking to themselves. They have what amounts to a schizophrenic experience in front of the audience. No wonder so many people are afraid to give a speech or presentation. They are their own worst critic.

Enter the Critic

I suggest you become a self-coach instead of a self-critic. A self-coach has self-awareness, which is a good thing. It means monitoring and objectively observing our behavior so we can make necessary adjustments. A self-coach does not demean or disparage his or her performance; a self-coach notices what's working and what's not and makes appropriate suggestions. The inner-voice of a self-aware coach might say, "Oops, I've gone off on a tangent. Time to get back on track."

A critic is self-conscious and notices everything you are doing wrong. It compares, judges, and sees only the negative. This constant voice of disapproval acts as a distraction while you are speaking because it sets up a conflict of focus. The critical, self-conscious voice might say, "I've blown it. Why can't I ever stay on track? I'm probably not making any sense. Everyone in the audience looks confused. I'm a terrible speaker. I don't belong up here."

Get Out of the Audience

Self-conscious speakers watch their audience members' faces and body language and interpret it while they are speaking. Their insecurity as a speaker causes them to be hypersensitive to the perceived mood and reactions of the group. "That women over there looks bored; she doesn't like me. Oh no. The vice-president just yawned. I'm losing him."

It's insanity. How can you possibly know what is going on in anybody else's mind? Consider this: the guy who looked at his watch just remembered he forgot to pick up the dry cleaning. The woman who looks bored IS actually bored because she was forced to attend this mandatory training and is determined not to listen to a word you say. The vice-president who yawned didn't get any sleep last night because his daughter broke her ankle playing soccer and they were at the emergency room until the wee hours of the morning. It's entirely possible that none of the audience's reactions have anything to do with you.

I am here to skewer the notion that as a speaker you must try to

Connect with Your Audience Via Non-Co-dependent Speaking

please your audience and vie for their acceptance. Balderdash! Trying to please everyone in your audience is as pathetic as trying to please everyone in your life. I call it co-dependent speaking.

Deliver Yourself from Co-dependent Speaking

> *"If you feel your life is like a see-saw,*
> *perhaps you're depending on other people*
> *for your ups and downs."*
>
> — slogan on coffee mug

Co-dependency occurs when you are more concerned with what other people think of you than what you think of yourself. Co-dependent people have a hard time making decisions because they fear offending someone or hurting someone's feelings. They want everyone to like them. Co-dependent speakers make safe choices and HOPE everyone agrees with what they say. This makes them weak and wishy-washy. Co-dependency is a dead end street in a ghost town. It leads to failure in life. It is dangerous one-on-one and deadly as a speaker.

Building a bridge of connection and inviting your audience to cross over to your side is very different from running back and forth across the bridge and carrying them — one-by-one, on your back — to your side. The way you build a bridge of connection with your audience is by connecting IN to connect OUT. Become passionately committed to your content and its delivery, and they will be *compelled* to cross over to your side.

Non-co-dependent speakers like themselves and invite others to do the same. They choose their material based on what they want to say, not on what they think the audience wants to hear. They earn the audience's respect by having the courage to speak their mind.

While we want the audience's acceptance, we cannot gain it by appealing to the safest common denominator or by trying to be all things to all people. If we avoid saying anything controversial because we're afraid someone might take offense, we compromise our message and ourselves. Our goal is to become brave. To do that, we must take a stand and have confidence that our opinions and insights matter. It's our job to prepare such wonderful material that our audience is drawn to our point of view.

Powerful Speakers Have the Courage of Their Convictions

I've witnessed some of the best and most sought after speakers on the planet and I can tell you this: they do not change who they are and what they came to say based on their audience. They know who they are — they speak from their heart and stand in their power. They command the attention of their audience by having the courage of their convictions.

By no means am I suggesting that the makeup of your audience is irrelevant. Researching your group's needs is critical to your success as a speaker. Before I speak at a convention or for a company meeting, I always conduct pre-program interviews to understand the group's interests. I then carefully choose material that will meet those needs.

I do not however, use that pre-program information to make myself crazy. I don't throw out my entire speech and start over based on my perceived judgment of what they've requested. I don't redesign myself for engineers any more than I do for salespeople or nurses. I can't. My only shot at success is to be the best and most powerful me I can muster. If they hire Doug Stevenson — they're expecting Doug Stevenson to show up — not some toned-down version I created just for them.

Please understand — it is important to customize your content based on your audience's needs. Based on who they are and what challenges they're facing, it's appropriate to add certain content elements and delete others. Go ahead and develop stories that are appropriate to their specific situation; just don't change your style or major content elements. Making subtle adjustments for your audience is one thing. Changing the essence of who you are and what you say is another.

How Do We Appeal to Diverse Audiences?

Consider this. Your audience is made up of a variety of individuals. Although they may all be in the same profession or association, they are still unique and different. There are males and females and various age groups from baby boomers to Generation X and Millenials. Add to that the diversity of races, ethnicities and religions.

Now I ask you, how do you speak to an audience that diverse? How do you alter your speech to connect with an audience that includes Hispanics, Whites, African Americans, Arabs, Asians and a variety of other ethnic groups? Who do you speak to? It's an insane paradox.

The audience I've just described for you is not unusual. They're not their titles of salespeople or executives or construction workers — they're PEOPLE and deep down inside, everybody bleeds the same red blood and feels the same emotions. They all understand the language of storytelling.

Your job as a speaker is to do your speech — not to get everybody to like you. You can't possibly please 450 people at one time. In any audience, a certain percentage of them WILL NOT like you. It's a given. The moment you walk on stage somebody may conclude you're a pompous know-it-all and resent you because you remind them of their least favorite boss. Someone else won't like your hair or outfit. Someone else will have a religious difference of opinion or a philosophical objection to your viewpoint. You can't please them all.

The best you can do is know you have something important to say and that you've done everything in your power to prepare so it can be delivered in an interesting, useful way. Then, tell the stories the way you've rehearsed them and get into your talk so you're living and breathing it. You do your job and let the audience do theirs.

You Be The Speaker — Let Them Be The Audience

One client looked at me in disbelief when I shared the above suggestion. He asked, "Are you telling us we're not supposed to care about the audience?" I told him, "I'm not suggesting you ignore them. I'm suggesting that the time to be concerned about them is when you're at home writing, researching, and practicing your material. *That's* when you should think about their needs to make sure you're selecting and delivering content that will be appropriate for them."

Do your homework in advance and you won't have to sweat whether they find your information beneficial. Your success as a speaker is directly proportionate to the time you spend in preparation. The harder you work at home, the easier you'll have it when speaking because you'll be confident that the audience will find value in your remarks.

Remember, truly effective speakers focus IN to connect OUT. They are self-aware without being self-conscious. They are coaches, not critics. They are more concerned with how *they* are doing than with how their *audience* is doing. They've learned that the one

Connect with Your Audience Via Non-Co-dependent Speaking

thing they can control is themselves and their presentation. What they can't control is how the audience reacts. They leave that job to them.

Once you stand up in front of that audience, it's time to let 'er rip. Trust in yourself, and you'll know how to speak. It's too late to worry if material is going over with them. Focus 100% of your attention on being the best "you" you can be — and you will be.

PART THREE

Choose
the Right
Story

CHAPTER 5

Go on a Story Safari

I'm like the little kid in the movie *The Sixth Sense* who sees dead people everywhere. The only difference is, I see STORIES everywhere. Okay — I'm also older and taller than that kid. And I've never acted in a big budget Hollywood movie with Bruce Willis. But other than that — I'm like that little kid.

Once you understand the formula for building a story from the ground up, you'll see stories everywhere too. They happen all day long. They happen at the grocery store, in your backyard, driving your car, in sales meetings, in restaurants, and believe it or not, while you're making dinner.

It's not so much the story that's important; it's what you do with it. Later on, you'll read a story about a time I missed a shuttle at the airport. Has that ever happened to you? Probably. The only difference between you and me is that I've learned how to take those stories and craft them into compelling presentations that have the power to educate, enlighten, and entertain. Pretty soon you will too. The first place to start looking for stories is in your own backyard — your rich and fascinating life. Storytellers call it "mining the past" for story ideas.

Don't Minimize Your Life Experience

If there is one question I hear more than any other in my retreats and workshops it's this: "Why would anyone want to hear about stories from my life? They're so ordinary."

It's a good question. Why would anyone be interested in hearing about your ordinary life? Perhaps it's because most of us lead pretty ordinary lives and we find it fascinating when someone else with an ordinary life can make some sense of it for us. Once again — it's not so much your story as it is what you do with it.

Stories as Metaphors

The word metaphor is defined as, "A figure of speech in which a word or a phrase literally denoting one kind of object or idea is used in place of another to suggest a likeness or analogy between them." Whew!

What that means for us is that *our* stories are metaphors for everyone else's stories. Because they are based on relatable events — our stories act as a catalyst for our audience members' sympathetic experience. That is all our story needs to do — strategically make a point and teach a lesson that catalyzes audience members to think about how this relates to their own personal and professional situations.

That's what it's all about. Trust me on this: Your audience will get involved with your ordinary story because they've "been there — done that" — or at least they've "been there — heard, seen, or read that."

Five Criteria for Choosing Personal Stories

> *"Draw your chair up to the edge of the precipice, and I'll tell you a story."*
> — novelist F. Scott Fitzgerald

Go on a Story Safari

So, where do we start looking for stories? All of your stories will come from one of two places: 1) events, or 2) relationships. The events that you draw from will be in the past while the relationships may be past or present. With some events, the relationships are integral to the story. With other events, the relationships are peripheral to the story. Here are additional criteria to keep in mind when selecting your stories.

Criteria Number #1: They must feature vivid details.

You must be able to remember the event or the relationship in colorful detail. I call these events "Polaroid memories" because you can clearly see them in your mind's eye. When you recall the event or relationship; the time, place and specific details such as how it sounded, looked and felt come back easily and vividly.

Criteria Number #2: There must be a lesson learned.

You need to have gained insight, experienced an epiphany, or ascribed a lesson or meaning to the event or relationship.

Criteria Number #3: The story can be used in a business context.

For our purposes, the story must make a point about sales, customer service, innovation, leadership, communication, teamwork, productivity, or other topics related to the work world.

Criteria Number #4: The story must call people to a higher standard.

The world is full of obstacles and challenges. Our audiences are counting on us to deliver a redeeming message. They need us to remind them that life is good, that people are good, and that — in the end — everything usually works out for the best. They need a reason to get up tomorrow and believe that they matter, that they can make a difference and positively influence outcomes.

Criteria Number #5: You must enjoy telling the story.

The story's got to be fun for you. Regardless of whether it's heavy or light, you need to have good energy presenting it. You must look forward to telling your story if you want it to positively impact your audience.

Here's an example of something ordinary that happened to me that I've been able to use in a business context. This is the actual working script for the story.

> **Note**: In the following example I refer to a Story Theater technique called Stepping OUT and Stepping IN. You'll learn more about this technique in Chapter 18, but let me briefly explain these concepts. When you are OUT, you are speaking in the past tense narrative and are addressing the audience directly. When you turn IN, you often shift to the present tense as you re-enact a moment in time. You cease behaving as a speaker in a meeting room and begin to act out a moment in time from your story. You become like an actor in a play who is SHOWING rather than TELLING.

> (OUT to audience)
> One glorious September afternoon, my wife Deborah and I were driving through the Rocky Mountains of Colorado. The air was crisp, the sun was shining, and a gentle breeze was rustling through the trees. We were on a winding two-lane road surrounded by Aspen and Pine trees. It was gorgeous.

> (IN moment — shift eye focus from audience to the mountain environment)

Go on a Story Safari

As we drove around a curve, the scene changed dramatically. On both sides of the road was the blackened devastation (see it and react) from a forest fire that had swept through the area two days earlier. One minute we were in paradise, the next minute we were in a visual hell. (Feel the emotion of the moment)

It was eerie. It was totally silent (listen for a moment) — no sounds — no animals — just charred stumps and charcoaled earth. I'd never seen anything like it before and it made me deeply sad. I pulled over to the side of the road and we just sat there for a minute staring out the window. I turned to my wife and said, "Isn't this terrible? Look at all this damage."

It took her a moment to respond and then — in a logical and enthusiastic voice that contradicted everything I was feeling — she said, (Assume her vocal quality) "Oh no honey, it's not terrible. In the life cycle of a forest it's a natural occurrence. It's actually a rebirth of sorts — rejuvenation. Beneath the forest bed are seeds that have been lying dormant for years and because of the overgrowth they didn't have a chance to sprout. Now the warmth of the sun will touch the forest floor, the rains will come, the dormant seeds will sprout, and the forest will come back stronger than ever. See honey, this isn't terrible at all. It's a necessary part of the process of life. This is good for the forest. It just looks bad right now."

(Back OUT to audience — react sarcastically to her positive point of view in the midst of this negative situation)
Are any of you married to someone like that? Her relentlessly positive attitude compels me to look on the bright side of things, for which I am eventually grateful. Well, as we drove home my creative process began. My artistic instincts always kick into high gear when I have an emotional reaction to something. For me, that's where it starts, with emotion. Then,

the analyst in me tries to make sense of it and I wonder, "What was that about?"

(IN moment — talking to self)
What looks like a bad thing is actually a good thing? What looks bad now will look better later on. What feels like devastation is actually a rebirth — an opportunity for a new beginning. What's that like in my life? When have I felt destroyed by a metaphorical forest fire?

(OUT to audience)
Carole, one of my first girlfriends, burned me by being unfaithful. That almost destroyed me. Getting fired from my sales job and failing to become a movie star, were also devastating experiences. At the time, I couldn't see how anything good would come from them. It was years later before I understood that those experiences were each an opportunity for a new beginning. In retrospect — Carole was a jerk! That sales job was terrible and they treated me poorly, and if I hadn't failed to become a movie star, I never would have become a professional speaker. If my other relationships had not failed, I never would have met Deborah.

I went on like this for several hours just ruminating and letting the creative process wash over me. I let my brain wander, all the while looking for the point. When it finally came clear, this is what I discovered: It's all about faith and trusting the process.

If a forest fire, which appears to be total devastation, is a natural part of the process of life, then I need to have faith that those moments in my life that feel like devastation are also natural parts of my life. At those times, I need to trust the process.

Go on a Story Safari

> How about you? Have there been times in your life when you got burned? Have you had setbacks and disappointments that felt devastating? Looking back, can you see how they cleared the way for new opportunities that wouldn't have been available to you without that cataclysmic event?
>
> The moral of the story is, the next time you face a disappointment or setback — have faith and trust the process.

That's the end of the script. Let's analyze it for the five criteria I listed earlier.

1. **Vivid detail.** I can still see that spot on the road to this day. It's branded in my mind and memory.
2. **The lesson.** It took a little work to find the metaphorical insight, but I eventually did.
3. **Business context.** In today's rapidly changing corporate climate of mergers, acquisitions, and bankruptcies — people need to understand that the cataclysmic event they're experiencing today can actually lead to better opportunities.
4. **Higher standard.** Having faith and trusting the process are both higher standards of behavior.
5. **Enjoy telling the story.** I love telling that story because it's so real and because it has enormous insight for putting things in perspective. Instead of getting caught up in the misery of the moment, it helps us see that we may have a brighter future in store for us.

Which Comes First — The Story or the Point?

You may be wondering, "Which comes first, the story or the point?" The answer is, "It depends." First, let's talk about **when the point comes first**. When you're developing a new speech, you first decide what points you want to make. If you have three points to

Make Your Business Presentations Capture Attention, Inspire Action, and Produce Results

make, look for three stories to match those points. If you don't already have a story in your repertoire for a particular point, go on a story safari. Put on your metaphorical safari hat, pull on your most creative jodhpurs, and take a trip down memory lane into your personal history. You'll find that every story you need is waiting for you to harvest it.

The Step-by-Step Process for Going on A Story Safari

The first step for going on a story safari is to find a comfortable place where you can sit down and write. Have plenty of blank paper and a pen handy so you can record ideas as they occur to you. Then:

- Close your eyes and relax. (If you are a visual learner — you may want to do this exercise with your eyes open so you can mind-map ideas on a large piece of easel paper.)
- Ask your mind the following questions:
  - "What do I want an answer for?"
  - "Where in my life did I learn about _____ ?
- Let your thoughts roam — give your unconscious mind time to search.
- Narrow your search by picking a specific period of time (i.e., your high school years, when you lived in the Midwest, or your first job.)
- Move through different periods of your life. Think of friends, family, challenges, disasters, relationships, trips, apartments, cities, vehicles, hobbies, etc.
- Each time you get a story idea, jot down trigger words that briefly describe and bring back that event or relationship.
- Before you develop the story further, be sure it matches a point you want to make. Is it a natural fit or are you trying to force it? The fit must be effortless.

Go on a Story Safari

- Make sure the story "passes" the five necessary criteria for choosing a good story.

Can't Think of A Personal Story that Makes Your Point?

If you can't think of a personal story that makes your point, check out your favorite bookstore or library. I love my local library. It is a great place to conduct story research. In a few hours, you can browse through dozens of different types of books, magazines, newspapers, trade journals, and other resource material — all for free.

Before you go on a story safari using outside resources, ask yourself the questions so you have clarity about what you're looking for:

- *Identify the purpose of your presentation.* Are you speaking at a board meeting? What will the tone of that meeting be? Are you celebrating a record-breaking year or are you announcing cutbacks and a pay-freeze? If the mood of the group is celebratory, feel free to look for and use funny stories. If the mood is going to be solemn, it's wiser to use a philosophical story that's in keeping with the group's frame of mind. Look for stories that, when spoken, have the power to make your audience hear, feel, and see.
- *How much time do you have?* If you have a jam-packed agenda and only a few minutes for your presentation, it's important to select a short vignette that will illustrate your point but not overwhelm it.
- *What are the demographics of the group?* Is it a mixed audience, predominantly male, or predominantly female? Please don't take this as a sexist remark, however I've found that a predominantly female audience responds well to emotional

and humorous stories, while all-male audiences tend to be more reserved. That doesn't mean I don't use humorous stories with an all-male audience; I just don't expect as many laughs.

- *What is your intent?* Are you building your skills and ready to stretch and try new material — or is this a high-risk occasion where you need to go with what's tried and true?

Once you've thought through the above questions, seek out the following resources to find just the right story for your purposes:

Story Source #1: Anecdote Books

I found the following vignette in an anecdote book that had been left behind in a cabin that I rented one summer. Books like this are an excellent source of inspirational stories because they're in the public domain — which means you can use them without worrying about infringing on copyrights. As you read the following story, think about what it means to you.

> As Mahatma Gandhi was boarding a train, one of his shoes slipped off and fell on the track below. Since the train was already moving forward, he was unable to retrieve it. To the amazement of his companions, he took off his other shoe and threw it back on the track close to the other one. When a fellow passenger asked why he did so, Gandhi smiled and said, "The poor man who finds the shoe lying on the track will now have a pair he can use."

What lesson did you extract from the story? Would you use it to trigger a discussion on how you can turn a loss into a win for yourself or someone else? Would you use it to point out that an action that seems to make no sense — could make perfect sense if we just dig deeper for the meaning? Take a moment to write out how you could use this story about Gandhi to illustrate a point you want to make in an upcoming presentation.

Story Source #2: Newspaper Articles

The newspaper features human-interest stories every day in the Business, Money, Lifestyle, Sports, News, and Local sections. Speaking to your city's Chamber of Commerce? Look for a profile of a local business owner who did something noteworthy. Presenting a breakout session at your professional association's annual conference? Read that month's issue of their national news-paper and reference a story that addresses a current trend in your industry. Giving a short twenty-minute talk for your town's Rotary Club? Read last month's newsletter and refer to an event the group is particularly proud of.

Story Source #3: Biographies

If you want to make a point about leadership, I suggest you "walk the biography shelves" in your local library or bookstore and keep your eyes open for a book that captures your imagination. If you're going to be delivering your presentation to an international group, be sure to include stories from several world leaders so you have a balanced perspective of leadership in different countries. If you're speaking on sales, look for a book that tells the story of a sales manager who tripled his company's profits in a short amount of time. Biographies of Anne Frank, Winston Churchill, Colin Powell, Anne Morrow Lindbergh, Nelson Mandela, Mary Kay Ash and John Fitzgerald Kennedy are rich with stories of courage, per-severance, independence, and self-determination.

Story Source #4: Quotes and Quote Books

Remember the definition of "original?" If you haven't heard, read, or seen it before, it's original. Incorporating funny, profound, and provocative quotes into your stories is a wonderful way to add originality to your presentation. Keep your eyes and ears open and your "quote antennae" up whenever you read business magazines, periodicals, and quote books.

A good rule of thumb is, "If you read or hear a quote and it causes a visceral response — it makes you laugh out loud, stop and think, or immediately disagree — it will also cause a visceral response in your listeners." Those are the kinds of quotes you want to use — ones you haven't heard before. If you use common quotes that everyone has already heard, your audience will mentally roll their eyes and tune out because they'll conclude your presentation is going to be "same old, same old." Here's one of my favorites. This quote is from the book *The Way of Life According to Lao Tzu.*

> *"Fail to honor people, they fail to honor you;*
> *but of a good leader, who talks little,*
> *when his work is done, his aim fulfilled,*
> *they will say, 'We did it ourselves.'"*

Assume that you discovered this quote and liked it because it represents a style of empowered leadership you want to champion. Your next step is to develop a story to go with it. Follow these steps to find and/or develop that story:

- Make a list of people who role model this quality. Think of teachers, friends, coaches, ministers, relatives, parents, managers, and co-workers who have demonstrated this trait.
- When you have someone in mind, think of a specific time

they honored your skills and talents and guided you to a victory or accomplishment without taking credit for it.
- Craft that story using The Nine Steps of Story Structure in Chapter 11.

Think Metaphorically, Not Literally

Please keep this important caveat in mind: I've come to realize that too many people think *literally* when they're trying to find a story to match a point. They think a story that makes a point about customer service has to have a customer in it. They believe a story about leadership must have a supervisor in it. Not so.

The best stories are often metaphorical messages, non-literal illustrations that require a creative stretch to make the link. For instance, in one program I wanted to make a point about commitment, so I crafted an amusing vignette. The vignette was about the time when a cashier at my local grocery store asked whether I wanted "Paper or Plastic?" bags. I did this ridiculous Woody Allen impression of a guy who panics at the very thought of having to make a commitment either way. I pantomimed alarm at having to choose one over the other. "Paper or plastic?" became a running metaphor in my talk for an aversion to commitment. Can you get any more non-literal than that?

The World is Your Material

You can find these metaphor-rich stories by simply paying attention on a daily basis to what happens around and to you. If your life is anything like mine, it's full of ridiculous situations, humorous moments, and complicated relationships that provide more stories than you could ever possibly use. Mel Brooks says, "Life abounds in comedy if you will but look around you." You'll find life abounds in good material if you'll just look around for it.

Most professional speakers keep notes on the interesting events and people they encounter because they know they're rich with potential. In fact, some professional speakers actually welcome bad customer service experiences because they know they'll turn into great material. When something interesting happens, your first thought ought to be, "How can I make a story out of this?" Your next thoughts ought to be, "What was the point of that? What lesson did I learn? Is there a metaphorical message? What insight could be extracted from that experience?"

One of my students told a story about scuba diving and panic attacks. She talked about the time she was cave diving off the coast of California. After wending her way through a labyrinth of twisted turns, she switched to her second tank of air, only to discover it had a leak and contained less than ten minutes of air. She did such a good job of acting out her terror about this discovery that she had us in the cave with her. She explained how she kept her presence of mind because she knew if she didn't, she'd never make it out alive. She mentally retraced her route into the cave and then calmly (so she wouldn't hyperventilate and use up all the oxygen) swam back out and to the surface.

She then segued her experience back to the audience and asked what they did when they faced daunting circumstances. Did they panic and make things worse, or did they keep their head and think their way through? It was a memorable story and point about the importance of staying calm under pressure.

Another student told about the time she was on her way to a job interview when she got a flat tire. She was newly divorced after fifteen years of marriage and was re-entering the workforce after ten years of being a stay-at-home mom. There she was, in her best suit, heels, and nylons on the side of the road. She spent the next fifteen minutes trying to flag down someone to help her, but it seemed everyone was on their way to work and they weren't about to stop.

She finally realized she was going to have to fix the tire herself. She told us how, with tears of frustration streaming down her face, she struggled to get the equipment out of the trunk, jacked up the car, and changed the tire (for the first time in her life). As she wrestled the flat back into the trunk, bloody knuckles and all, she vowed to herself that she would never again wait for someone to rescue her, that she would do whatever it took to become independent and strong. She then asked audience members if there had been a pivotal event in their life when they had decided they would do whatever it took to become self-sufficient and resourceful — no matter what. Her story really drove home her point about the importance of developing the resolve to make it through hard times, instead of waiting for someone to come along and rescue us.

When the Story Comes First

As long as you can uncover the lesson and make a useful point, anything can be a story ... as long as it makes sense for the audience. The more bizarre the situation, the better. Here's an example.

> One time, while traveling, I decided to take a commuter train from New York City to Philadelphia instead of flying. Not being from New York, and not having taken a train in a million years, I had no idea what I was getting into.
>
> I arrived at Penn Station at 5:30 PM in the midst of the Manhattan rush hour. It was insane. There I was, dragging three pieces of luggage through this crowded hustle and bustle of people trying to catch their trains to go back to the suburbs, or wherever. As I looked around I realized I was the

only one with luggage. The rest of the station was filled with commuters.

They knew the ropes. I didn't. But, I soon caught on. Since my train wasn't leaving until 6:30 p.m., I got to watch one of the most bizarre phenomenons I'd ever seen.

Penn Station can easily hold a thousand people in the main waiting area at one time. The commuters would come in waves. They'd fill up the waiting area and then disappear down the escalators to their trains. Each wave that disappeared was promptly replaced by a new wave of commuters coming in the door.

Hundreds of people would stand together looking up at the huge schedule boards, which listed the train numbers, departure times, and gates. This throng of people would stand there like a bunch of zombies until the board flashed their train's gate number. Instantly, they all sprang into action and stampeded to a single file escalator that took them downstairs to their train.

Then, it would be calm until the next stampede. This happened over and over. I felt like I was watching a scene from the *The Night of the Living Dead*, only I was one of the zombies. It was the ritual dance of the New York commuter.

For forty-five minutes, I observed this bizarre ritual, waiting for my turn to join the mad dash. After six of these episodes, I knew my train was next. I knew what was about to happen and I was ready. My luggage was locked and loaded.

At 6:25 PM the board flashed my gate number for my train to Philly. The crowd surged forward and I plunged into the fray with my three clumsy pieces of luggage. I now knew what it was like to be a cow being loaded onto the truck for the ride to the slaughterhouse. Starting from an unruly mass of people fifteen feet wide, we pushed and shoved our way until we were in a single file line boarding the narrow escalator down to Gate 11.

Inch by inch, shoulder to shoulder, we moved forward. I couldn't see a thing. People were bumping into my luggage and giving me dirty looks. More pushing and shoving and then I finally reached the front of the line at the escalator. It was my turn to go down. I stepped onto the escalator dragging my one largest piece of luggage behind me and — it stuck. My big fat green fiberglass suitcase got stuck. The stairs were moving under my feet. I was now walking up the down staircase trying to get my luggage free. I yanked it harder. It got more stuck.

People began yelling from the back of the line, "Move it!"
"Make way."
"What's the problem?"
"Some moron got his luggage stuck in the escalator."
"What kind of moron has luggage?"
"A stupid moron, that's what kind."

As the escalator stairs kept going down, I kept trying to dislodge my bags. I was working up a sweat by this point. Somebody called for help. Meanwhile I kept pulling on my suitcase, which had now become wedged so tightly that three men couldn't pull it free. A lady in high heels started kicking at it and another woman joined in. No luck.

I was on the treadmill from hell while my other luggage piled up in all directions and fifty, one hundred, seemingly ten thousand people all looked at me and thought the same thing — "Idiot. You idiot."

They were right. I was the moron with super-sized luggage running up the down escalator making everyone late for their train. Children in Philadelphia would not see their parents tonight. Not as long as the jerk with the big fat green luggage stayed stuck in the escalator.

It took about six interminable minutes of me running up the down escalator before the maintenance guys turned the damn thing off and we finally freed my luggage. The people behind me had finally realized I was going nowhere fast and found another escalator to get down to their train.

In the end, I turned my culprit of a suitcase sideways (Who would have thought that a train station would have such narrow escalators?!) and rode the escalator down to the train ... all by myself. I was the last person to board and the last one to find a seat.

How about you? Have you ever messed up because you weren't paying attention to the details? Did you learn from your mistake and move on or did you beat yourself up about it for days, weeks or months? Because, that's what's important in business and in life — not avoiding mistakes — but learning from them and moving on. When I make a mistake, I remember the big, fat, green suitcase. Instead of getting down on myself, I simply **learn from it and move on.** (That is the Phrase That Pays for this story. More on that in Chapter 12.)

Whatdya think? Is that a good story? Immediately after it happened I knew I had to craft it into something I could use. Can you see its comedic potential? It's perfect for my style of broad physical humor. When something like that happens, *use it*!

In that case — the story came first and then I searched for the point it could make. So, which comes first, the story or the point?

Go on a Story Safari

Both methods work equally well. When you want to make a particular point, search for just the right story to illustrate it — and when you experience something fascinating, harrowing, or triumphant, search for the moral of the story — the salient point.

Lifelines and Turning Points

In his wonderful book, *The Power of Personal Storytelling*, Jack Maguire provides an exercise for discovering story "seeds." These seeds, when developed, provide the storyteller with profound and powerful stories.

Maguire suggests you chart your lifeline from birth to the present looking for turning points — times you chose between two alternatives or times when the choice was made for you. By investigating these pivotal incidents and thinking about why you chose one way or the other, you can glean insights and develop thought provoking stories that cause other people to reflect on their life choices. This is what that process stimulated for me:

I instinctively went back in time to 1972 when I made the choice to leave Chicago and hitchhike to Los Angeles to take the next step in my acting career. That was the first major turning point in my life. There were a myriad of decisions that had to be made before taking action:

- To leave Chicago or to stay put and build a stronger acting resume
  - The scary option versus the secure option
- Going west to Hollywood or east to New York
  - TV and movies and Palm trees versus the theatrical stage and traffic
- Waiting until I had enough money to fly or leaving now and hitchhiking with $250 in my pocket

- ○ Getting on with my life now versus waiting for some unknown later date
- ○ The bold choice versus the safe choice

In each case, I made a strategic and brave choice, the ramifications of which set in motion the rest of my life. I chose to go to Hollywood and to hitchhike rather than wait for perfect circumstances. Investigating what I did and why gave me multiple opportunities to craft a variety of stories that I still use today, more than 30 years after the fact. This demonstrates an important point. *The messages of stories are timeless.* We can plumb events that happened decades ago, yet the moral of those stories can be quite timely and relevant for today's circumstances.

Thirteen years later I reached another turning point when I chose to leave Hollywood and start over somewhere new. At that point in 1985, as in 1972, I made a choice to change my life and everything about it. By going back in time to those critical junctures, I found story "seeds" that led to stories about:

- Change
- Perseverance
- Believing in myself
- Overcoming adversity
- Strategic planning
- Pursuing a dream
- Doing whatever it takes

How Do I Find My Turning Points?

When looking for turning points, look for times you had to choose between fear and confidence. Look for the crossroads in your life where you either held back and stuck with what was safe, or moved forward and embraced opportunity and your higher self. Consider the following:

- Changes in geography — moving from address to address, city to city, state to state or country to country
- Changes in relationship — marriage, divorce, falling in and out of love, losing a friend due to a geographic move, falling out with relatives, gaining new in-laws
- Changes in job or career — job changes, status changes, relocations, getting fired or laid off, getting an advanced degree that leads to a job change, switching career fields
- Changes in responsibility — becoming a parent, boss, business owner, Big Brother or Sister, stepparent, legal guardian, landlord, or homeowner
- Vacations, trips, and business travel that changed your perspective
- Accomplishments — receiving an award, running for office, finishing a marathon, getting your pilot's license, building your own house, publishing a book
- Deaths, tragedies and personal injuries

In the next chapter, you'll learn about the different types of stories, so you can select just the right story for your purpose.

CHAPTER 6

Choose from the Seven Types of Stories

A re you ready to take your storytelling to the next level? The reason I refer to *"Strategic Storytelling"* is because we are deliberately selecting stories that will help us accomplish an identified goal. This isn't a random process where we say, "Oh, this is a fun story. I'll tell it." The story must fit the specific circumstances of the speaking engagement for which we're preparing and fulfill some predetermined purpose.

The following seven types of stories can be used for almost any business audience. Think about the next presentation you're going to give, and which of these types of stories are most appropriate for that upcoming speech.

Story Type #1: Vignettes

More often than not, when business speakers tell me they love to tell stories, they're referring to a type of story called a vignette. A vignette is defined as a short illustration; a brief, descriptive incident or scene. In other words, it's a mini story. It usually only takes a minute or so to tell, and it isn't as crafted or developed as a full story. The vignette, also known as an anecdote, is the simplest and most common form of business story and has less impact on an audience than a carefully structured story. Here's an example:

I was in O'Hare airport in Chicago on my way to a speaking engagement when I discovered my connecting flight had been cancelled. The only option that would get me to the location of my program, 150 miles away, was to rent a car. I went to all the rental counters, but no one had any cars available. So, I walked ten feet away from the counters, got on my cell phone, and started calling the 800 numbers of those same rental companies. Interestingly, they suddenly had cars to rent, but they were socking it to me on price, tripling their normal rates. That wasn't what I wanted to hear. I was determined to not only find a car, but a reasonable bargain as well.

My last call was to Budget. The employee listened to my plight and suggested a solution. He asked, "Do you mind driving a Ford Ranger? It's a small pickup truck, and I can give it to you for $19.99 a day." Since everyone else had been quoting me prices of more than $100 a day, any car sounded pretty good, so I quickly agreed, "Let's do it."

I hopped on the shuttle bus to the Budget lot and walked up to the rental counter. The employee behind the desk looked at my order and said to me, "Do you really want a pickup truck?" "No, not really," I replied. Suffice it to say, ten minutes later, I drove out of the lot in a Mazda Protégé, a small economy car that worked just fine, for $19.99 a day. Just goes to show you what we can get with a little perseverance, creativity, and flexibility.

That vignette is an absolutely true story. If you fly a lot and rent cars like I do, you've probably had something similar happen to you. This takes a little over a minute to tell, and I use it with business audiences to show that it's often in our best interest not to take "No" for an answer. This little vignette reminds us that with a little resourcefulness, we can often go over, around, or under a wall instead of being blocked by it and giving up. Vignettes can be used anywhere in your speech. They can even be spontaneously recalled and related because they don't require the careful structure of a full story. And, after you've read Part Four on crafting your story, you'll be even more comfortable recalling and relating vignettes on the spot.

Story Type #2: Crucible Stories

A crucible is defined as a severe test. Crucible stories are stories of great loss, hardship, or pain. Olympic athletes, cancer survivors, and people who have overcome incredible odds tell crucible stories. They are often survivor stories that tell of near misses, encountering danger or severe challenges, and coming out alive. They are powerful because these "tests of the human spirit" are real, and because they reveal our human frailty and resilience.

Since crucible stories deal with "life-and-death" matters, they have the potential to move audience members to a deep level of vulnerability and take them on a roller-coaster ride of emotion from depression to joy. As a result, presenters who share these high-impact stories need to have courage, honesty and a willingness to be vulnerable. They must take responsibility for consciously crafting their story and delivering it with integrity. There can be no artifice or insincerity.

Sharing these stories is like being a circus performer walking a tightrope. The audience is metaphorically sitting on your shoulders as you tiptoe across the tightrope. They are so attuned to what you are saying, they are completely with you. Whatever you're feeling, they're feeling. If you fall, you take them with you. When you get across safely, they get across safely. That's why it's so important to know what you are doing — you have the audience's emotions in your hands.

A good example of someone with a powerful crucible story is LeAnn Thieman, the author of *This Must Be My Brother*, and co-author of *Chicken Soup for the Nurses Soul* and *Chicken Soup for the Christian Woman's Soul*. Her book recounts her miraculous adventure rescuing 200 Vietnamese orphan babies during the fall of Saigon at the end of the Vietnam War. I had the privilege of coaching LeAnn and one of her goals was to tell her story in a way that audience members felt they were "there" in the harrowing moments of that daring rescue mission. We also wanted to make sure she didn't gratuitously dwell on the violent parts of the story.

LeAnn is now a popular professional speaker who uses her crucible experience to show how ordinary people can do extraordinary things — if they put their minds to it. Corporations and professional associations welcome her message that shows how, when faced with a crisis, professionals can rise to the challenge — or run from it. Her inspirational story demonstrates what can happen when someone decides to be proactive in the midst of a high-pressure situation.

One of the most satisfying aspects of my business is having the opportunity to work with clients who have inspiring crucible stories, i.e., growing up black in the racist south, nearly committing suicide, surviving breast cancer, raising a severely retarded son, running in a marathon race, surviving a near fatal airplane disaster, learning to live with Lupus, and going blind as a teen. These clients decided they were going to share the story of how they triumphed over tragedy in the hopes their lessons-learned would save others pain, misery, or trial-and-terror learning.

I believe each of us has at least one crucible story. We have all felt pain and loss. We have each experienced defeat, overcome adversity, and prevailed over disaster A single mother of three who goes back to college to complete her Masters degree need not feel humbled by someone who has climbed Mt. Everest. They are both stories of a severe test.

Anyone who has suffered the loss of a child or spouse in a highway accident knows as much pain as a cancer survivor. There is no formula, no qualification, and no litmus test for what will make a powerful crucible story. There is however a vital requirement before you can step in front of a group to share it. You must have enough emotional distance from the event to share your crucible story without reliving it. It is not your right to do therapy in front of an audience. Assuming you have healed sufficiently, the goal is to plumb the depths of your experience for its profound personal truth, and to glean the lesson it taught you.

You may be wondering, "What is a profound, personal truth?" It is a universal truth that is broad enough for everyone to relate to, regardless of whether they have experienced your pain or not. Many who survive a traumatic event seem to find a depth of faith and understanding, a peace that comes from release. Ironically, the most intimate revelations can be the most universally relevant.

Champion athletes challenge us to believe in ourselves, work hard, and dream big. Accident survivors remind us to live for today, to count our blessings. These are profound, intimate, yet universal truths. The reason they are powerful rather than trite is because the story actually happened, which makes the storyteller credible. They aren't just mouthing rhetoric or sharing empty platitudes we already agree with. They have gone through this "trial-by-fire" and they know from personal experience how true it is.

Do you have a crucible story that taught you a profound lesson? If so, you have a responsibility to share it. For those of you who cannot sing, crucible stories give you an extraordinary voice. They enable you to create a blanket of intimacy that warms and comforts other individuals. When presented with delicacy and grace, stories of overcoming adversity are like medicine for the soul. They heal invisible wounds with the gentleness of a caress. Like time-release medicine, they work slowly, over time. You may not be present when the final healing takes place, but you can play an integral part in its process.

Performing crucible stories calls for two specific ingredients: humor and silence. Because crucible stories can be solemn and serious, the need for humor is even greater. In some instances, during a heavy moment in the story, it's appropriate to add a wry comment to add levity and perspective. This is not meant to diminish the power of the moment, however sometimes a little relief is needed. (I'll give specific ways to do this in Chapter 15: Incorporate Comedy so Listeners Laugh While They Learn)

Silence is another essential tool in crucible stories. Allow for silence during the most powerful moments, the moments where you are facing your mortality, the times your mind is filled with thoughts of whether or not you can go on. By filling the silence with thoughts and emotions during these pivotal scenes, you are SHOWING rather TELLING how momentous they were. You didn't rush through those crucial decisions, neither should you rush through their retelling. Your gravity while re-enacting those scenarios allows the audience to be with you and take time to process their own emotions. When you slow down and allow space between the different scenes, you give your audience opportunities to reflect upon and absorb what you're saying.

The placement of crucible stories is critical. In a sixty-minute keynote, it's important to give the audience at least ten minutes to get to know you before you launch into a crucible story. You wouldn't walk up to strangers on the street and tell them about what it was like being orphaned as a child. Neither should you do that right off the bat with a new audience.

Choose from the Seven Types of Stories

When addressing business audiences, you want to first establish your expertise and build commonality, then gradually reveal more private details. Instead of leaping right into a highly intimate story, start with a thought-provoking quote that frames your message or give background information that leads up to your crucible story so they can understand it in context.

It's equally important not to close with a crucible story. You don't want to end your speech on a somber note that sends everyone out the door sad or depressed. One of the features of a well-crafted crucible story is that it concludes on an inspiring note. Be sure to carefully craft the last three to five minutes of your presentation so it ends with a message of hope and a better tomorrow. You want people to leave energized and determined to apply your insights to their own lives.

Story Type #3: Imbroglio Stories

An imbroglio is defined as an acutely painful misunderstanding or embarrassing situation. Think of a time when you unwittingly found yourself in deep trouble, and you have the makings for an intriguing imbroglio story. Ironically, some of your funniest stories will come from your most humiliating moments.

My Streaking Story and Penn Station Story are both imbroglio stories. They feature self-deprecating humor and provide a pleasant change of pace and style in my presentations.

Audiences love imbroglios because they can relate to the awkward times we've lost face and made foolhardy choices. They recognize themselves in our stories and take vicarious pleasure in knowing that we have screwed up and lived to tell the tale. In a way, they're both laughing at us and with us.

Imbroglio stories allow us all to be comedians.

You probably don't have to look too deep into your past to find a moment where you made a wrong turn, got in over your head, or rushed into a hasty decision that backfired. Perhaps you're thinking of one right now. Did a family vacation turn into a fiasco? Did you ever try to impress a date and do just the opposite? Did a job interview turn into a comedy of errors? How about that home repair project that turned into a money pit? Identify what point that mortifying-at-the-time experience could illustrate, and then plan how you are going to insert it into your next presentation to humanize you so the audience identifies with you.

Imbroglio stories lend themselves to exaggeration. It's okay to slightly fudge the facts or, as I tell my students, to gently rewrite history. A little exaggeration can turn a mildly amusing incident into a highly absurd incident, which can make it hilarious. You will learn more about exaggeration in Chapter 15.

> **Caution**: It's never wise to get too fast and loose with the facts. You want your audience to trust you, and that means telling the truth on all the important details so they don't have to read between the lines to determine whether your stories are fabricated or factual.

In fact, if you are a journalist, elected official, public figure, or company spokesperson, it's best to NEVER fudge the facts for any reason. You may think it's not important that you tell a story as if it happened to you when it really happened to your brother; you may not think it matters if you say an experience happened in Washington DC when it really happened in a nearby Virginia suburb; but believe me — it matters to your constituents, editors, stockholders, and audience. As my mom used to tell me, "It's a good policy to always tell the truth. That way, you don't have to remember or worry about what you said."

Choose from the Seven Types of Stories

Before you invest too much time developing an imbroglio story, be sure to decide up front what lesson you learned and how the resulting insight can be applied to business. Then, and only then, will it be worth the time and effort to craft this story.

Imbroglio stories require lots of rehearsal. Comedy is so dependent on the nuances of what happens between the lines — on facial expressions, timing, and vocal inflection — that if you don't practice until you get it just right, you'll miss lots of laughs. While crucible stories don't involve much movement because of their solemn nature; imbroglio stories often feature lots of physical action because they work better when you SHOW what happened to you rather than just TELL. I'll give more specific tips on how to rehearse and deliver comedy so you can maximize laughs in Chapter 15.

Place imbroglio stories somewhere *after* the first ten minutes of your speech. Using your funniest material up front may not work because audiences usually need a few minutes to warm up to a speaker. I learned this the hard way by opening with my Streaking Story. It never worked there. I moved it to the halfway point of my presentation where it always works. Why? I think it's because, by the middle of my talk, people can hear that story in context. By then, they've concluded I have valuable information so they take the wild and crazy story of me racing through Westwood bucknaked on balance with my other, more professional, credentials.

Want to leave them laughing? It's okay to close with an imbroglio story, but be sure it makes the point you want to leave them with. You've probably heard that we don't get a second chance to make a first impression. We also don't get a second chance to leave a lasting impression. Make sure your final words are ones you want your audience to remember and apply.

Story Type #4: Minerva Stories

Minerva was the Roman Goddess of wisdom. When you have a story or parable that draws upon ancient wisdom, whether from the Bible or a traditional American folk story, that is a Minerva story. Other resources for Minerva Stories include:

- Native American Indian stories
- Greek and Roman Mythology
- African-American folk stories
- Celtic folk stories
- Traditional American folk stories
- Jewish, Muslim, Christian, Hindu, Buddhist, Sufi and other religious stories
- Mythological stories and folk legends

Developing Minerva stories usually involves research and memorization more than start-from-scratch-crafting because the stories themselves already exist in written, recorded, or visual form. Your goal is to interpret these legendary tales for modern day audiences so listeners clearly "get" how the accompanying insight is timeless and universal.

If your credentials or professional background are not as impressive as you would like (or the audience wants), you can use Minerva stories to add credibility. By incorporating enduring insights and wisdom into your message, you increase the likelihood that audience members of all ages and backgrounds will respect and appreciate the thoughts you share. Since, by their nature, Minerva stories appeal to a broad range of people, they can be used anywhere, anytime in your speech.

Choose from the Seven Types of Stories

Story Type #5: Credibility Stories

Credibility stories are any non-personal (meaning they didn't happen directly to you) stories you find from outside sources such as a book, article, radio show, or TV broadcast. They may relate to a current event, news story, or international incident that recently happened that "proves" a point you want to make in your presentation.

Corporate giants, Enron and WorldCom, both collapsed during the time I was writing this book. The huge accounting firm, Arthur Anderson, went out of business, and billion dollar companies, United Airlines and US Airways, declared bankruptcy. The stock market was in turmoil and the economy was in shambles. Unemployment soared, and our nation declared war on Iraq.

If you speak about ethics in leadership, all you had to do was look at the daily headlines to find plenty of "real-life" material. If your topic is Change, you could share a story pulled from the newspapers about an intrepid manager who was laid off only to rebound and use her severance package to start her own, now thriving, company.

Looking for an example of resourcefulness? You could use the awe-inspiring story of two teen-age girls who were stranded in the Colorado Mountains in January. These girls got lost skiing in the slopes around Aspen, and became disoriented in the whiteout conditions. As darkness set in, they realized they were going to have to spend the night in the backcountry without shelter, food, or warm clothes. Remember, this was 12,000 feet up in the Colorado Mountains in the middle of a harsh winter storm. People usually die when they make this kind of mistake.

Not these girls. They went to work saving themselves. The two carved out a snow cave so they would not be out in the freezing wind. They survived the bitterly cold night by huddling together for warmth. In the morning, they tromped outside and carved HELP in fifteen-foot tall letters in the snow so rescue helicopters could find them. They were picked up that afternoon, unharmed and in good spirits, thanks to their initiating efforts to help themselves survive instead of being helpless victims.

Do you see how using a story like this could lend credibility to a message about the importance of being resourceful in trying times? It doesn't matter if you personally haven't survived a winter storm, telling this story about how these girls did would still get the point across.

Another type of credibility story accesses the expertise of a recognized authority. Quoting respected industry experts and best selling authors such as Spencer Johnson, Ken Blanchard, Steven Covey, Margaret Wheatley, Jack Welch, Peter Senge, and Lee Iacocca can lend credibility to your points. Professionals are yearning to hear original, thought-provoking, leading-edge ideas. You may not be the one who conceived a profound insight into increasing capital gains; formulated a new management theory; or invented a technological breakthrough; however you *can* be the one who plays the role of messenger and introduces these concepts to your audience. When you read a fascinating bestseller by a CEO, keep your eyes open for stories that demonstrate leadership in action. Peruse the business magazines or the money section of the newspaper to look for timely, "real-life" anecdotes you could use to illustrate your points.

> **Caution**: Be sure to give credit where credit is due. It is NOT appropriate to "borrow" other people's intellectual capital without proper attribution or permission. It is appropriate to use a couple of lines or a brief vignette regarding another individual as long as you quote the source.

Choose from the Seven Types of Stories

Say, for example, you're talking about how to survive office politics. You might quote author Fawn Germer who said in her book *Hard Won Wisdom* (Penguin Putnam, 2001), "You know why I wrote this book? When I went looking for a source that would tell me how to deal with emotional battlefields in the workplace, all I could find were books telling me how to dress. I needed a book that would tell me how to survive." Then, segue her observation back to your audience and ask, "Some days, is it all you can do to survive the back-stabbing and behind-the-back gossip?"

Be sure to honor copyright laws. It is not appropriate to "lift" a story from someone else's spoken or written material and pass it off as your own. I know, high school and college students do this for term papers and call it research. In the professional world, doing this is called plagiarism and you open yourself to liability if you steal someone's intellectual property and claim it as your own.

Be sure to use credibility stories from other experts sparingly. If other people's insights form the bulk of your presentation, it's in your best interest to stop speaking on that subject. Audiences want to hear what YOU have to say on your topic, not what everyone else under the sun has to say about that topic. You have no reason to be speaking on a subject unless you have some personal experience, insight, or recommendations to offer. Remember, credibility stories from other sources are there to add authority to your own insights, not replace them.

Another type of credibility story is one about an individual who has accomplished something extraordinary. The person may not be well known, however his or her feat proves your point and showcases a characteristic you're discussing. In my keynote presentation entitled "Empowered Leadership — Pass the Power," I tell a story about Aaron Feuerstein. Heard of him? Probably not. However, I love to share his story with my business audiences because he's a walking-talking role model of an ethical leader who practices what he preaches.

I discovered Aaron in an issue of *Parade* magazine, the magazine that comes inside many Sunday newspapers. That week's feature story explained what the President of Malden Mills, a textile company in Massachusetts, did when the company's factory burned to the ground. Instead of taking the insurance settlement and retiring, this remarkable executive did something bold. Aaron paid his entire workforce *full* wages for three months while he rebuilt the mill from the ground up. As a result of his unprecedented benevolence, his workers were motivated to respond in kind. They rewarded his generosity by nearly doubling the monthly output of fabric, even though they were working on rented machines in a temporary facility.

It doesn't matter that I have never been the CEO of a multi-million dollar company with hundreds of employees. Aaron's story makes a powerful point about the fact that leaders reap what they sow. Audience members can learn from HIS example, it doesn't have to be my example.

Story Type #6: Pattern Stories

When stories cover a period of time (from days to months or years) or when multiple stories share a common theme, they are called pattern stories. Though the circumstances may change from scene to scene or over the expanse of time, the plot structure builds on the use of a repetitive pattern, which gives the story a resonant structure.

This is a sophisticated technique that the best professional speakers use. They know that a well-crafted pattern can build suspense, anticipation, and a satisfying sense of full-circle completion in

Choose from the Seven Types of Stories

listeners. The first time you introduce a specific gesture or phrase, your audience will simply notice it. The second time, they will realize that a pattern is emerging. The third time they will "get wise" to the pattern and begin to anticipate and enjoy it. You may even see a few smiles of recognition or titters. By the fourth time, especially if you add a little attitude and exaggeration, the group will laugh out loud because by now they are "in" on the joke.

Do you remember Johnny Carson's popular bit on *The Tonight Show* when he'd lament, "It was so hot today…" and then he'd pause to let the audience chime in with "How hot was it?" That's an example of a patterned line with a patterned response. By intentionally repeating a phrase in conjunction with the same gesture or posture (whether it's raised eyebrows, rolled eyes, or shoulders hunched up in a "why me?" pose), you can set up a second-level response in your listeners. They're aware of your technique and it adds impact to what you're saying. You can choose to use patterning subtly — so the group isn't aware of it — or use it overtly and purposely so the audience is cognizant of what you're doing and part of it.

I had the opportunity to coach an executive on a presentation she was going to give which featured the lessons learned from her entire 30-year career. First, she selected the five points she wanted to share — each gleaned from a different position on the corporate ladder starting with her first job and continuing to her current position. I suggested that each time she shared a lesson from a different job, she move to a different part of the stage. Five lessons, five job positions, five stage positions.

She started stage left and progressed across the platform ending at stage right. Her visual movement reinforced her verbal "journey." Each time she was ready to move on to a new lesson and a new job, she would move to "its" spot on the stage and the audience would have a clear transition from one part of the story to the other. It was a masterful example of how deliberate use of a *physical* pattern can heighten the impact of a presentation.

Her presentation worked on several levels because there was also an over-riding moral lesson. She described how, at each position, she plotted and planned how she could climb the corporate ladder. She admitted that she had been an extremely ambitious person, always striving for the success and happiness that always seemed one promotion away. It was only when she reached her current position that it dawned on her that she had spent her entire life working towards the magical day where she would be truly happy. To add the verbal pattern to the physical, I directed her to end each segment of the story by saying, "But I still wasn't happy."

As she shared this epiphany, she looked back across the stage shaking her head in remorse, gazing at the other spots on the platform that represented her past, looking at the original spot on the stage where she had naively started her journey. Then, she turned to the audience and spoke from her present position (in time and on the platform) about her revelation that the contentment we seek is available whenever we want — in the here and now. Her progress through life and across the stage were a visual and verbal metaphorical marvel — and it had been accomplished with purposeful patterning.

Would you like to use the patterning technique in your next presentation? You can use it in one of your stories, or you could do what this female executive did and craft your entire speech around a pattern. The key is to physically repeat the same movements and/or gestures each time you introduce a specific phrase or a new scene in your presentation. This creates a parallel connection between what you're saying and what they're seeing and hearing. The physical and verbal repetition will be linked in their mind and they will become highly attuned to it. Their alertness to your methodology will keep them on the edge of their seats. It will enhance their learning, heighten your impact, and create a type of intellectual satisfaction because they will appreciate the sophisticated level of craftsmanship that you've invested into your presentation.

Patterned stories work well at the beginning of your talk because they engage and tickle the minds of participants. They can also be introduced towards the middle of the talk, but be sure to allow enough time to reiterate the pattern so it "matures" and the audience "gets" the joke or receives the full value of the repetition. In some cases, your entire presentation may be one intricately crafted pattern story.

Story Type #7: Instructional Stories

Instructional stories rely heavily on narrative structure and often contain multiple points. While I teach that each story should only make *one* point, instructional stories break that rule. They must be crafted efficiently though so they don't confuse the audience.

Many of the trainers that participate in my Story Theater Retreats arrive with stories that contain a confusing garble of messages and lessons. It is often difficult, upon hearing their story for the first time, to know exactly what lesson we were supposed to learn.

Here's the problem: These trainers know their topic well because they've been giving presentations on it for years. They understand their subject on many levels because they've lived through the experience and have had multiple opportunities to contemplate its meaning over time; or they've been practicing this technique or skill for years and it's become "second nature" to them.

The audience, however, is hearing it *for the first time*. They're not only trying to keep up with the story that's being told, they're trying to absorb all the new information they're hearing. If a speaker gives them three lessons in one story, they can't grasp all those at one time so they're forced to choose one. It's not that they're stupid or apathetic — they just can't process all this new data at the speed at which it's being delivered.

It's the speaker's job to simplify the message so it can be easily assimilated upon first hearing. If you want your audience to make sense out of your message, the story must focus on *one* point in a logical and linear format — *except* in the case of instructional stories.

Instructional stories move back and forth from the story to the lesson. They look, sound, and feel different from other stories. First of all, they are more cerebral. The action in instructional stories is minimized and the narrative is maximized. In other words, there's more TELL than SHOW. Instructional stories exist to teach rather than entertain. It is not that they can't entertain. Because of my background in comedy, I'm convinced that almost any story can and should have humor. But in the case of the instructional story, the focus is on the clarity of the narrative.

An instructional story may also involve audience interaction. We've already discussed the importance of the Socratic Method in which participants learn best through self-discovery. Since the point of the instructional story is to teach, the more opportunities we give attendees to take part in the learning process, the more likely they are to "get" our point(s).

When you reach the part of the story where the lesson is conveyed — you might want to pause and ask the audience some open-ended questions. You could ask, "Has this ever happened to you? What did you do to handle that situation successfully?" Or ask, "What would you have said in that situation?"

Choose from the Seven Types of Stories

> **Note**: I think it is particularly important to ask questions of the audience when instructing managers and senior executives. They have often been in business for years and are accustomed to being in control. It's tough for executives to sit and listen to someone else because they are usually the ones doing the talking. They often have a lot of experience and expertise and are eager to chip in their "two bits." By asking for their advice and input, you move them from the passive, receiving state to the active, transmitting state. Not only will they welcome the opportunity to contribute, their insights will add variety and fresh perspective to your material and heighten its learning impact.

Imagine you're going to tell an instructional story that has three points or steps. It can help for you to announce that up front with "There are three steps to this process." By "warning" your audience in advance, they're mentally prepared to pick up the three points Tell the story that illustrates the first step, at which time you "come out" of the story and say, "That's the first step." Then, pick up the story where you left off until it reaches the next learning point. Once again, announce to the group, "That's the second step." Then, resume the story until you get to the final point at which time you say, "And that's the third step of the process."

Then, recap. It's essential to reiterate the points or steps you've just covered. Since the instructional story is the most complex of all the types of stories mentioned so far, it's incumbent upon us to make it as easy as possible for our audience to remember the information. The best way to do that is to actually say, "To recap, our first step was . . . ; the second step was . . . ; and the third step was . . ."

You've probably heard the military advice about how to give a briefing: "Tell 'em what you're going to tell 'em; tell 'em; and then tell 'em what you told 'em." I usually don't suggest that much repetition — however that advice is wise when it comes to telling long instructional stories that cover multiple points. It's our responsibility to make sure each point is illustrated logically; that it builds upon the preceding point; and that in the end, all three points form a contiguous body of knowledge. By following a clear, clean structure, participants will be able to concentrate on and follow what we're saying instead of getting hopelessly lost.

Recap What We've Just Learned

In our discussion of different types of stories, I hope you've found one that suits your purposes. Feel free to mix and match the seven types of stories — vignette, crucible, imbroglio, Minerva, credibility, pattern and instructional — in your presentation. Think of it this way: in a sixty-minute keynote, you'll want to incorporate all the different learning modalities. The left-brainers in our audiences like pattern and instructional stories and the right-brainers want the crucible, Minerva and imbroglio stories.

I suggest you stretch yourself by getting out of your comfort zone and trying new disciplines. If you've never attempted an imbroglio story and want to know what it's like to get big laughs, give it a shot. If you want to try out your new material in a safe workshop environment, consider attending one of my Story Theater Retreats or one-day workshops where you can receive one-on-one coaching and constructive, compassionate feedback from peers. If you've had a powerful experience that changed your life, understand that sharing the lesson you learned could change other people's lives. Get to work on your crucible story and take advantage of that opportunity to make a difference for others.

Choose from the Seven Types of Stories

Are You Up To the Challenge?

Does all of this sound like a lot of work? Well it is. But please read on. When I started speaking, all I had going for me was a ton of enthusiasm and a lot of natural performing instincts from twenty years of professional acting. I was not a writer and had no experience crafting stories. My storytelling was undisciplined and I got mixed results from one speech to the next.

Then I saw a man named W. Mitchell give a short presentation for the Colorado Chapter of the National Speakers Association. Mitchell is a living crucible story. Riding through the streets of San Francisco, he was blindsided by a laundry truck that had run a red light. The resulting fiery crash left him with a disfigured face and terrible burns over most of his body. Being an eternal optimist, Mitchell recovered from those horrific injuries and went on with his life, becoming mayor of Crested Butte, Colorado and running for Congress.

Then, in another cruel twist of fate, the private plane he was piloting crashed upon take-off. After helping his passengers to safety, Mitchell found he couldn't move his legs. He was paralyzed from the waist down. Many people would have spiraled into depression after these two life-shattering incidents. Not Mitchell. He has traveled to more than thirty countries and shared his inspiring message, "It's not what happens to you; it's what you do about it," with almost a million people. He is an inspiring example of someone who is taking responsibility for achieving his desired destiny.

I sat in the audience as he told his story, while wheeling himself back and forth on the stage in his wheelchair. I recognized two things simultaneously: 1) W. Mitchell is an amazing storyteller with a natural gift for comedy and drama; and 2) his story and delivery were meticulously crafted for maximum impact. I saw him present a keynote at our NSA convention a year later and his presentation was exactly the same ... and just as powerful.

I had an epiphany watching Mitchell. I realized that if I wanted to be as good as Mitchell, I was going to have to work as hard as he had. Excellence is within your grasp. All it takes is the desire, the knowledge of the process, and the discipline to apply and practice that knowledge.

William Jennings Bryan once said, "Destiny is not a matter of chance; it is a matter of choice; it is not a thing to be waited for; it is a thing to be achieved."

I'll give you the knowledge. What you do with it is up to you.

CHAPTER 7

Differentiate Between First-Person Stories and Third-Person Stories

T he next question is, "Should you use first-person stories or stories about other people?"

When making important decisions, I like to look to the experts in the field for guidance. In my opinion, the experts in the field of public speaking are professional speakers. Professional speakers are paid handsomely for their ability to share their expertise, day in and day out, in presentations delivered in a variety of challenging situations. They've studied and learned what works because their ability to earn a good living depends on it.

Professional speakers prefer to tell their first-person stories. If the audience wants to hear Tony Robbins, Tom Peters, or Spencer Johnson's material, they'll hire them to come in and speak to their group. Audiences come to hear YOU, which is why it's almost a point of pride with professional speakers to create their own intellectual capital. They occasionally supplement their stories with credibility and Minerva stories, however their goal is to develop signature stories that are theirs, and theirs alone.

Please don't tell me you have no stories, because you do. You don't have to climb Mount Everest, survive cancer, or win an Olympic

Gold Medal to have something interesting to share. I survived cancer on Mount Everest after winning a gold medal, and I don't even use that story because I've got better ones. Just kidding.

Moving Stories Don't Need to Be Manipulative

A recurring issue with many of my coaching students is their reluctance to share first-person crucible stories because they don't want to be perceived as manipulating their audience.

Please understand that the word "manipulation" has positive as well as negative connotations. You probably are already familiar with its negative definition, which is, "to control or play upon by insidious or unfair means, especially to one's advantage." Yikes. That is *not* what I'm suggesting.

The manipulation I'm advocating is defined as, "to skillfully or artfully manage, utilize, or move something from one place to another." Our goal as speakers is to move people from one place to another, intellectually as well as emotionally. If we don't move people by challenging them to change their opinion on a subject, if we don't stimulate them to feel differently than they did before we walked in the door, we have failed. So, manipulation is not something to avoid or be ashamed of. It is completely ethical to skillfully and artfully craft stories that manipulate your audience members — that move them from a state of resistance to a state of receptivity.

Using emotional stories to move an audience from thinking to feeling is also okay, as long as we're acting from integrity — which means we're doing this to benefit our audience, not ourselves. I was sickened one time when I heard a speaker brag, "I can make any audience cry whenever I want." That immature individual was, unfortunately, using negative manipulative tactics to control his

Differentiate Between First-Person Stories and Third-Person Stories

audiences' reactions — for his own ego gratification. That is never acceptable.

The fact is many people crave and appreciate mediums that cause them to tap into their feelings. They voluntarily go to movies like *Titanic,* willingly read books like *Bridges of Madison County* and *Message in a Bottle,* and eagerly attend presentations where they experience a gamut of emotions. What this means is, don't shy away from sharing private stories by using your audience as an excuse. People welcome stories that cause them to experience fear, love, joy, and sorrow — to feel alive. That's a fact that box office receipts prove again and again. The same people who bought tickets to every weepy romantic comedy starring Meg Ryan or Julia Roberts are sitting in your audience!

It can be life saving to hear a story about how someone else has resolved a problem we're facing right now. Are you going to deny your audience that opportunity?

Are You Worried About Appearing Conceited?

Are you afraid that people will think you're conceited if you tell stories about yourself? That is an old belief from childhood that doesn't fit into the speaker's role. Speakers are *supposed* to talk about their experiences. Otherwise we would call them reporters.

I'm not suggesting we drone on and on *only* about our own exploits, adventures, observations, and insights. It would be conceited to assume our audience wants to know EVERYTHING about us. I'm also not suggesting you share stories that only showcase your strengths and triumphs. Balance is the key. Blending in stories that reveal a weakness and building in quotes and credibility stories from other experts will insure a comprehensive combination of content.

One client had just the opposite concern. She wasn't afraid to come across as conceited, she was afraid she'd come across as boring. She felt she didn't have any life experiences that were special and worth telling. I told her, "Remember, your everyday stories are metaphors for everyone else's everyday stories. Your first-person stories don't have to be about profound, once-in-a-lifetime events. They can be as simple as taking a moment to listen to a child or compliment an employee whose good work has been overlooked. The simplest stories can serve as a spark plug that sparks thoughts and feelings in others."

What If I Make A Fool of Myself?

I believe another reason many speakers shy away from sharing their powerful first-person stories is they don't know how to craft and perform them. They lack confidence and skill and they're afraid of getting up there and making a fool of themselves. I understand. It's not easy baring your soul in front of other people. It's not something we do naturally. Hundreds of people have come to me and requested private coaching specifically for this reason. They have a story to tell, but they're afraid to tell it, even though they know it will benefit others.

That's where my acting training factors in. Actors bare their souls in front of audiences all the time. That's what acting class is all about — learning to express emotion through the playwright's lines. The actor's job is to use his or her emotions to bring the character he or she is portraying to life. For the speaker however, there is no character to hide behind. As a speaker, you *are* the character and the emotions are *your* emotions. Emotional vulnerability can be a slippery slope that some speakers avoid for fear of falling.

Want good news? The guidance in this book will teach you how to

Differentiate Between First-Person Stories and Third-Person Stories

stand on your own two feet and share emotions honestly in a way that is comfortable for you and your audience. I'll share specific ways to do that in Chapter 23, "Stand in Your Power."

The final reason I believe speakers avoid sharing personal stories is because they've seen inexperienced speakers butcher them. They've been in an audience watching a poorly prepared speaker ooze all over them with sloppy sentimentality, and they've vowed never to do that themselves.

How about you? Have you ever seen a speaker share a crucible story that was more than you EVER wanted to know about that person? Do you fear committing the same offense? It's true that a crucible story done poorly and without the proper intent can be an exercise in excess. However, a crucible story that is crafted correctly and delivered skillfully for the right reasons and with the proper placement can be a positive vehicle for connection, healing, and renewal.

Telling first-person stories doesn't mean you're selfish or self-absorbed. What matters is how well they are crafted and presented. If you've had a significant experience from which you learned a profound lesson, I hope you'll share it. My work and this book are based on the belief that the life experiences that are most painful and difficult to endure can and should be used as teaching moments. Don't do it for ego reasons. Do it to create an "aha!" that moves your audience beyond intellectual understanding to emotional impact.

Turn Reluctance into Resolve

I challenge you to look at your reluctance to share your private stuff. Are you intimidated because you've never done it before? Are you afraid to relive the experience for fear it will bring back the pain? Are you "hiding" from your audience by not self-revealing? Wait a minute. You've chosen to be a speaker. This is your chance to serve people by sharing what you've learned.

You must be brave and risk experimenting with your own life. How can you inspire people to do what you are afraid to do, to go where you are afraid to go? Trust me, the scariest and most powerful work is already done. You've already conquered the fear and survived the test. Your courage in the face of adversity has already been proven. The first real test was the experience itself. The second test is summoning the courage to share your insights so others can benefit.

Think of me as a member of your next audience. I'm sitting right in front of you and I need to hear what you have to say because I'm having a hard time right now. My life is challenging. I'm concerned about my future. I'm trying to believe everything is going to turn out all right, but I need reassurance and inspiration. Through your story of challenge and triumph I can see myself succeeding. You have the power to give me hope. Will you help me?

CHAPTER 8

Go Deep and Tell the Truth to Add Insight

The word "insight" is officially defined as "the act or result of apprehending and/or discerning the inner nature of things." To me, it means the ability to look deep inside yourself and make profound sense of the past. Insight leads to understanding. Understanding leads to transformation. That is what good story-telling does — it transforms the listener.

I have come to realize that when telling first-person stories, only the truth will serve. Experience has shown me that authenticity is the foundation on which we build our careers, our lives, and our stories.

All stories that have power must reveal true insight. But insight is elusive. Our mind sometimes runs from the truth as if it were a hot poker. We often avoid the pain of the past so as not to feel it again. In doing so, we live the pain daily. The only way to gain insight is to go through the darkness and into the light of understanding. Only then can we craft stories that mesmerize and transform. Once the truth is established, the words and images needed to express it arrive on schedule. Our stories leave the surface and dive down into an ocean of clarity.

That is the journey I speak of in The Nine Steps of Story Structure. It is a journey from safety to danger and back again. Without the danger, the story is safe; the listener is a mere observer rather than a participant.

Only one question needs to be asked. What obstacles did you overcome to get here? Let me hear that story. Tell me the truth and profound insight of your experience and I am compelled to listen.

Search for Universal Truth

Think of the events in your life that taught you a life lesson. The more that life lesson applies to everyone, everywhere, the better. That's why life lessons are called universal truths.

A universal truth transcends gender, race, religion or ethnicity. It is relevant for all people. It speaks to us at a deep level of humanity. "What goes around comes around" is a universal truth. When you use stories that have universal truths at their core, you impact the largest possible percentage of your audience. As stated before, these events may have had a life-changing impact, may have seemed silly at the time, or could have been a quiet, ordinary moment where you intuited what was really important. Want some examples?

Examples of Universal Truth:
- Honesty is the best policy.
- You get what you give.
- Change your thinking; change your life.
- You can't get to second base without taking your foot off first.
- You get better results with a carrot than a stick.
- People learn more from what you do than what you say.
- If you believe it, you can achieve it.
- Hate is like a cancer that consumes its host.

Go Deep and Tell the Truth to Add Insight

- In the end, everything works out for the best.
- Time heals all wounds.

W. Mitchell's story, told in the previous chapter, is wrapped around the universal truth that "It's not what happens to you; it's what you do about it." The reason his story is so compelling is that he can vouch for the veracity of that universal truth through his personal experience. Sometimes, universal truths are easier to *say* than *do*. We may believe a universal truth *in theory*, however it can be tough to follow when life deals us one blow after another. It's easy to get caught up in how unfair or undeserved our circumstances are, instead of brushing ourselves off, getting up, and doing something about them.

Look at the universal truths on the previous page and pick one that is particularly meaningful to you. Now, think about an experience you've had that "proves" how true it is.

A fellow speaker named Linda talks about a time she was unfairly fired from a job. She explains that she was so bitter it consumed her for months. She kept re-playing the events that led to the fateful day she had been ordered by her bully boss to collect her belongings and leave the office within one hour. In the following weeks, she went for several job interviews but didn't get any offers. Finally, a former co-worker brought her to her senses. They were having lunch and Linda was once again venting her resentment and ranting and raving about what had happened. Her friend decided to bite the bullet. She gently said, "Linda, I agree this was not your fault and you deserved better. Your behavior isn't helping you though. Look at yourself. Would you hire you right now?"

It was an epiphany for Linda. She looked at herself in the mirror behind the restaurant table and was shocked at what she saw. She saw a woman with pinched eyes, pursed lips, and a clenched face full of anger. Definitely not hiring material. She decided then and there she would put her resentment behind her, extract the lesson from the situation, and move on. Her story is a perfect illustration of the universal truths that "Hate consumes its host" and "Most people are about as happy as they make up their minds to be," (an expression coined by Abraham Lincoln).

Point Out the Exception to the Universal Truth

There's a caveat to this, as there is to almost any extreme statement. If ALL your stories have universal truths, the audience may conclude you're not telling them anything they don't already know. That's why you may want to occasionally share a universal truth and then point out the exception to it. Being contrarian and playing devil's advocate is a great way to stop listeners in their mental tracks and cause them to re-think their automatic way of seeing things.

Want an example? Instead of mouthing the commonly accepted corporate maxim that "the customer is always right," perhaps you could give an example of circumstances when the customer is NOT always right. Perhaps you could tell a story about a time you were dealing with a particularly cantankerous client. After doing everything in your power to appease this person, you realized she was determined to be unsatisfied no matter what you did. At that point, perhaps you decided to "fire" that client and take care of the other customers who had been patiently awaiting your attention.

Today's sophisticated audiences are fed up with speakers who give canned speeches. They are tired of hearing stories that have been featured in many other motivational talks and books. They want to hear original, real-life material and get to know the person speaking to them. As a storyteller, your job is to become a type of "lay" philosopher who makes profound sense out of the ordinary. So, before searching out other sources, be sure to mine your own.

Go Deep and Tell the Truth to Add Insight

Fact, Fiction, or a Combination of Both?

In crafting a first-person story, you may face the dilemma of what to put in and what to leave out. If you're telling a story that's not so flattering about people who are still in your life, you may be wary of offending them. You may be concerned with liability or slander if you depict someone in a less-than-favorable fashion. You may not remember all the salient details of something that happened long ago.

Thank heaven for "creative license."

The guiding principle of storytelling is that it is a story, not a report. A business story's purpose is to teach a lesson in an interesting format. As Sir Robert Armstrong pointed out, there may be times when it is in everyone's best interest to be economical with the facts. Please note, as stated before in Chapter 6, I am *not* suggesting you lie about critical elements. It is never acceptable to steal someone else's story and say it happened to you when it didn't. It is never acceptable to claim you've won awards, accomplishments, degrees, and honors when you haven't. It is never acceptable to fabricate a story and say it is factual.

It's important to understand that the audience isn't concerned with every little detail of your story. We grew up listening to bedtime stories, campfire stories, and family stories passed down through the generations. We don't expect them to be documentaries, perfect in every detail. In fact, you probably have a favorite birthday story, fish story, or family vacation story that gets more and more embellished (and fun!) each time a relative tells it. Therefore, feel free to expand a story, delete some details, or tweak your story JUST a bit to make your point as long as you follow these guidelines:

- Stick to the facts regarding:
  - The essence of the story
  - The event or situation
  - The people in the story
  - The obstacle you faced
  - The process you used to overcome the obstacle
  - The resolution of the story
  - The lesson you learned

- Feel free to embellish or re-write history with:
  - Timelines and locations that are irrelevant
  - Character names and descriptions
    - Exaggeration here can add humor (his legs were so bowed, a barrel could have passed through them without touching anything)
    - Change names when it's wise to create anonymity for characters
  - The obstacle can be exaggerated for dramatic impact (the wall must have been 20 feet tall)
  - Re-sequence the process for overcoming the obstacle
    - You may add or delete a step to make your point
  - Creativity is often helpful in communicating the lesson
    - You may create a Yoda like person to assist you (Dan Millman does this with his mentor/muse "Socrates" in his book *The Path of the Peaceful Warrior*)
    - You may re-language the lesson to make a more memorable point
    - You may choose a different lesson *as long as it is true to the story*

Go Deep and Tell the Truth to Add Insight

To Tell The Truth

Want a good litmus test? Ask yourself this question, "Would I be embarrassed if the 'truth' came out and the audience discovered that something I represented as being real was actually made up?" If you called a character in one of your stories Charlie, and his actual name was Roy, I don't think the audience would be upset. If you shared a story about launching your own business and didn't reveal the fact that you borrowed money from your parents to purchase your franchise operation, I don't think listeners would feel you've misled them — unless you told them *you* supplied all the start-up capital.

On the other hand, the audience would have a right to question your integrity if you claimed to have an MBA from Harvard, and the closest you ever got to Harvard was one summer day you drove by it. As stated before, if you are in a public position where it is assumed EVERYTHING you say is factual, then it is incumbent upon you to honor that presumption. If you want to share a great story that is not fully factual, refer to it as an "apocryphal" story or let your audience know in advance that you don't remember all the details and you're using your imagination to fill in the blanks. As long as you let your audience know which stories are 100% true and which aren't, they'll feel they can still trust you.

PART FOUR

Craft
a Compelling
Story

CHAPTER 9

Ask Yourself, "What's the Point?"

S trategic storytelling is just that — strategic. Business stories are verbal tools designed to be used in a specific situation for a specific purpose. Their utility is dependent on making a point that is congruent with the story and the audience's needs. If the point of the story does not address the issue the audience is facing, what's the point?

Most stories have the potential to make several points because most life experiences teach multiple lessons. It is your job to determine in advance which points a particular story can make, and then match the story and its point to the appropriate speaking opportunity.

As an example, a coaching client named Doug shared a story about going for a job interview and being talked into taking a job he hadn't applied for and wasn't particularly interested in or qualified for. After the employer sweetened the deal with a big salary and an impressive title, Doug agreed to work for the company even though he had serious doubts and his gut was waving red flags. He caved in to the high-pressure tactics of the employer.

He started regretting his decision almost immediately. He should have realized that the unpleasant style of the employer was only going to get worse once he was hired. His new boss piled on backed-up work and rode him mercilessly. Within three months, Doug started suffering from stress-related health problems. His stomach was giving him fits and he was putting in long hours doing work he didn't enjoy. Furthermore, the pressure at work was taking a toll on his family life, as he was often irritable and short-tempered with his wife and kids. After 18 months, he finally summoned up the courage to quit and search for a job that was much more suited to his talents. He also made sure his new employer was someone he could respect and enjoy working with. That experience provided him with a fascinating story that had several possible points and universal truths. Several of the messages he could derive from that story include:

- *Stress That Affects You Also Affects Your Loved Ones* — Hating his job was not only making him sick, it was also negatively impacting the people he loved. He had a choice. He could either improve circumstances at work so he was happier — or if that wasn't an option, then for the health of himself and his family, he needed to find other work where the stress wasn't taking such a toll. The lesson or point is: Do what you love or learn to love what you do. It's up to you.

- *It's Important to Understand Who's Controlling Your Life* — He began to realize that he had willingly given up control of his life when he accepted a job he didn't want. He could either be a passive victim of that decision or quit and take back control of his life. The lesson or point is: Take control your life.

- *It's Your Right To Question Authority* — He had allowed himself to be intimidated by his boss. Doug realized he had fallen back into a submissive pattern he'd had with his father who was a forceful, dominant personality. Even into his twenties, he had let his dad talk him into doing things he didn't want to do. He would then perform poorly and be chastised for his failure. It had been a vicious cycle. By having the courage to confront his boss, he had stood up for himself and made it clear that he was no longer going to allow authority figures to overpower him. The lesson or point is: Have the confidence to say no when something is not right for you.

Can you see how this story can be used in three different ways for three different audiences? All three are thought-provoking messages that could prompt audience members to reflect on their circumstances and determine whether they are healthy or unhealthy — and what they're going to do about it.

> **Caution**: Remember what I said earlier about matching your story to the situation? You might think twice before sharing the above story with a corporate audience. The company's executives might not appreciate your telling a story about someone who quit his job because he didn't like his boss. If this is a hierarchical bureaucracy, they might not like your suggestion that employees have the right to question authority and say no. That particular story might work better for college grads entering the marketplace. Each of its points would give young adults excellent criteria to consider before accepting that all-important first job.

A Story About Teamwork

Let's shift gears and see if we can find a story that would be suitable for a corporate group. Let's say an organization is having a difficult time with teamwork. Employees aren't getting along and it's affecting morale and productivity. You need a story that illustrates a way to get along with different types of personalities.

I often use this first-person story about my relationship with my stepson Bennett because it portrays a situation in which two very different individuals were able to bond together despite their differences.

> Anyone who knows me knows I'm kind of wild and crazy — very creative and spontaneous. I talk a lot. I think out loud. Bennett is a quiet kid — very internal and reflective. He's a man of few words.
>
> When Bennett was in his early teens, it was hard to bond with him because he was so private. He just didn't say much and all my talking drove him further into his shell. In trying to find a way to connect with him, I stumbled upon a quote by an anonymous philosopher that stimulated a new awareness for me.
>
> *"Make what is important to the other person as important to you as the other person is."*
>
> I realized that I'd instinctively done just that with my older stepson, Michael. When Mike was on the wrestling team, I went to his wrestling meets. When he shifted to playing soccer, I shifted to watching soccer. When he got interested in cross-country, I stood in the rain and mud at his cross-country races and supported him. When he joined the track team, I was in the stands cheering him on. I made whatever was important to Mike, important to me. In retrospect, it was easy with Michael. He was wild and crazy and verbal like me. Plus, he was always out there doing stuff I could show up for.
>
> Bennett was different. He came home after school every day and sat on the couch watching *Gilligan's Island* and *Star Trek*. Then he'd finish his homework and go right to the computer for hours of video games. I tried getting into video games with him, but I was so pathetically slow it didn't work.

Ask Yourself, "What's the Point?"

For a solid month, I kept observing Bennett — trying to make what was important to him important to me. All the while he kept playing video games and downloading new programs from the Internet. Then one day I found him down in the rec room taking apart an old computer just for kicks. He was curious about what was inside and wanted to figure out how it all fit together. A couple days later, he was online ordering parts to build his own computer from scratch.

I didn't know you could do that. I was flabbergasted. This kid was so different from me — so amazingly smart in a scientific way — it was no wonder I hadn't been able to connect with him on the deep level I craved. But I was starting to get a clue as to what he cared about. He was fascinated with everything about computers and the technology that made them work. Plus, he liked to build things. He was an engineer in the making!

Once I knew what was important to him, it was only a matter of time before I could figure out how to use that knowledge to bond with him. Then two things happened at about the same time. Bennett started looking for a job and I needed to build a website for my business.

There are very few job opportunities for a fifteen year old. Most jobs require you to be sixteen. But Bennett needed money for his new computer fixation and I needed a website. Although he didn't know anything about building websites, he did seem to understand computer programming. So I decided to make him an offer he couldn't refuse.

"Bennett," I said at dinner one night. "You need a job and I need a new website and eventually a web master to manage it. I'm going to hire someone to come to the house and build my new website. How would you like to earn $10 an hour to sit next to him and learn how to build and manage websites?"

$10 an hour was more than he could earn anywhere else and on top of that, he didn't have to leave the house. Such a deal. When I explained how he could make $25 an hour with his own website business within a couple of months — he readily agreed.

After one month, Bennett was handling the website. I watched as he became more and more excited and empowered with his new skill. We would sit at the computer and collaborate on the website. I'd tell him what I wanted and let him figure out how it could be done. I placed the responsibility for execution in his lap and allowed him to make creative decisions on my behalf. All the while we were bonding. Two very different people with different ways of seeing the world were starting to find common ground.

He went on to start his own web design business when he was sixteen. He designed his own company logo, created his own business cards, and learned how to create invoices and bill his clients for services rendered. To this day that experience will live on in his and my memory as a positive experience for both of us. It brought us closer together.

After telling this story in a presentation, I sometimes ask participants, "Do you have a talented employee who has a lot to offer — and you're just not connecting with him or her the way you'd like? Maybe, like me, you're verbal and he's not. Maybe she's organized and logical, and you're not. Could you identify what is important to that person and make it as important to you as s/he is? Have you worked with someone who was very different from you, and been able to find common ground? Would you be willing to share that story with us? What other insights did you get from this story?"

I then open it up for comments and contributions. It's fascinating

Ask Yourself, "What's the Point?"

to hear the different points participants get from that story. A sampling include:

- Empowerment — One supervisor said the story reminded her of the most important lesson she's learned as a manager — that her job is to give employees responsibility for a task and then get out of their way and let them do it. She confessed that early in her career she had a tendency to do the work herself instead of delegating — and that if she did delegate, she intervened too often with advice and corrections. Now, she's learned, like I did with Bennett, to Pass the Power instead of constantly looking over their shoulder.

- Job Compatibility — One business owner said what the story brought up for him was his belief that his success depends on his ability to match the right person to the right job. He's learned from trial-and-error experiences that administering aptitude assessments to insure that employees' abilities are being used effectively is the key to making sure workers are happy and optimally productive.

- Mentoring — A manager in one of my audiences said she thought my story about Bennett role-modeled the primary goal of a mentor — to discover what someone does well and then nurture it. She said the most satisfying aspect of supervising for her is to fan the spark of potential and guide people forward to their own success. She believes we give a gift when we create opportunities for people to develop their innate talents.

When Not To Make A Point

You may be wondering, "Is there any time you don't want a story to make a point?" Yes. You can deliberately stop short of making a point when you want the audience to derive the "moral of the story" themselves. If your goal is to stimulate discussion, then don't explain the point yourself; ask participants for their interpretation. Ask what the story meant to them or for examples of when they've experienced something similar in their lives.

A particularly effective time to do this is when you notice the audience's attention wandering. Perhaps you've talked too long and/or given too much information and their minds are full. Perhaps this is the second hour of a morning workshop and the coffee-drinkers need a bathroom break. Maybe this is a full-day training program and it's tempting for attendees in the lull of the afternoon to start studying the inside of their eyelids.

The average attention span is about 20 minutes. That's the normal length of a sermon in church (and we all know how long those can sometimes seem). Anytime you're speaking for longer than 20 minutes, it's at your own peril. If you have excellent platform skills and use several descriptive stories, you should be able to keep people on the edge of their seats for longer than that. Better yet, build in interaction by giving participants an opportunity to come out of the passive (listening) state and into the active (speaking) state. They will be more likely to stay attuned if you ask what they think instead of just telling them what you think.

> **Note:** If you want feedback, alert the group to that fact before you start your story. If the group is preoccupied and you ask for their opinions "without warning," they may not have any since they didn't know they were supposed to be formulating a response. Unless we tell attendees to be prepared to speak up, they won't understand that it is expected or wanted of them. If you tell the group up front you want them to pay close attention because you'll be asking for their opinions, they will.

CHAPTER 10

Write the Way You Talk — Talk Onto Paper

To take your stories to the next level, you have to accept one fact of life — you'll need to develop your writing skills. There is no way to throw a story together at the last minute, tell it off the top of your head, and expect it to have maximum impact. You may get lucky now and then, but you won't be as consistently excellent as you can be.

Writing forces you to create the linear progression of the story. You'll be challenged to make strategic choices about words and phrases. You'll recall important details of the story you've forgotten. Pieces of the story puzzle usually don't fall naturally into place. You'll have to wrestle with many decisions about what to put in and what to leave out. In short, writing out a story makes it better because you have invested the time necessary to make it better.

If you try to "wing" a story, the flow of events will probably be out of sequence. People will have a hard time following you because you'll be preoccupied with trying to remember what happened instead of being 100% focused on delivering the story that will lead your audience to a powerful conclusion. You will most likely blow it and everyone watching will know it.

Have I made myself clear? Any ambiguity about how I feel about this issue?

On the other hand, when you master the art of writing conversationally using The Nine Steps of Story Structure, you will be extraordinary. People will think you are better looking and more intelligent and will want to buy you a Martini. They'll ask your opinion and seek you out for leadership positions. You'll be invited to parties and be nominated for "Employee of the Month." You'll be given a raise and a corner office — with a ficus plant!

Talk Naturally — Onto Paper

There's a huge difference between writing a story that's meant to be *spoken* and writing a story to that's meant to be *read*. Books and articles are written logically with standardized sentence structure. They follow prescribed rules for grammar and punctuation.

Unfortunately, people who give speeches with that type of "formal" language often sound stilted or pompous. They come across as if they're reading a report in tenth grade, or worse, as if they're a stuffy bureaucrat speaking government gobbledygook.

Here's the secret to conversational writing. Just talk your story onto paper — write the way you talk.

The problem is — many of us don't really know how we talk. I didn't. I had to work hard to discover my own natural speaking style and language. The first time I tried to sit down and "talk onto paper" I could hear my high school English teacher, Miss Kornet, giving me a hard time because I wasn't using "proper English." I can *write* properly, but when I talk to audiences I speak with them (not down to them) with a natural conversational tone that doesn't always follow the rigid rules of composition. For example, here's how I would "talk on paper" about my feelings about Miss Kornet:

Write the Way You Talk — Talk Onto Paper

My problem with Miss Kornet, my high school English teacher — was that she stood over my shoulder and stared down at my paper as I wrote. She was such a pain — always correcting me when I could care less — proper English — who cares? She taught me how to write though and now I'm having a hard time getting her out of my head when I try to talk onto paper. It's not easy having Miss Kornet in my head. I have to tell her to shut up so I can do this — to talk out loud and write down what I say — whether it's perfect or not.

Notice that the above paragraph has partial sentences, run-on sentences, and some incomplete thoughts. That's how we talk naturally! Most of us don't speak in complete sentences. When we converse with people we stop, start, and change directions midsentence. That's because we're formulating what we want to say *as* we say it. We're thinking out loud. I call that "think speak" and it's an absolutely normal way of communicating.

In fact, our "normal" communication style is how we want to write-out our stories. We want to capture that everyday way we converse with people so our audience will connect with us on that realistic level. If we assume an unnatural voice in an effort to impress people, we'll probably come across as pretentious. We want to be authentic, not artificial.

An Exercise for Finding Your Natural Voice

Here's a bonus for you at no extra charge. I've developed an exercise that can help you "find" your natural voice. Follow the directions below. You can do this exercise with pen and paper, however it works best if you speak your thoughts into a tape recorder, then play back the tape and transcribe it.

Make Your Business Presentations Capture Attention, Inspire Action, and Produce Results

- Think of something interesting that happened to you lately — something you'd want to tell a friend. It doesn't have to be a big thing at all. It can be a trip to the grocery store, a walk with your dog, a phone call from a client. Just pick something.
- Pretend you're telling your friend what happened. Talk out loud and make sure you use all your normal gestures, vocal inflection, and facial expressions. Have fun with it.
- Notice how your mind leaps around in a nonlinear fashion as you're thinking. Don't stop to get back on track — say whatever comes out, regardless of whether it makes sense. Let it all flow into the tape or onto the page.
- When you're done — play back the tape and transcribe it word for word. Record every um, aw, and stutter, every mispronunciation, every mixed-up sentence. Transcribe everything.
- Study it objectively. Don't get all worked up about the way you speak. It's fine. It's gotten you this far, hasn't it? This will take about half an hour for one five-minute story, and it's well worth it.

Voila! You now have a writing sample (and a tape) that shows how you actually speak. Notice that you probably have sentences that trail off, abrupt changes in topics, and conjunctions (i.e., instead of saying *you will,* you say *you'll.*) Study your cadence and rhythm. If you've added any words you don't regularly use, go back and put in how you would *really* say it. *That* is your natural speaking style and *that* is the voice you want to use to write-out your stories from now on.

Here's another exercise that you can do frequently to get into the habit of talking onto paper.

- Power up your computer and, using a stream-of-consciousness approach, talk out loud about your day, typing what you're saying as the words come out of your mouth. Describe the day's events in detail. Don't stop to think, criticize, or judge what you're saying or how you're saying it. Keep your fingers moving on the keyboard as fast as you can.

Now that you've completed the Find Your Natural Voice and Talk Onto Paper exercises, are you ready to learn how to craft a story for an upcoming presentation? I've divided the process into four steps.

Story Crafting Step #1: Use the First Draft to Remember

Note: The first step is to set up your computer with the proper margins so your written story has enough space for you to make follow-up notes. In your word processing document, go into "Page Setup" in the file menu in the upper left-hand corner of the screen. Set up the page with a two-inch left margin. This will leave enough room on the left side of the page for you to make structure, comedy, and performance notes later on.

The purpose of this first draft is to simply remember the event you're going to talk about in your story. Don't worry about structure, time sequence, or making a point. Just talk your story onto paper as it comes back to you. Go into as much detail as you can remember. If you forget a detail or if something occurs to you *after* its proper place in the story, just write it down. You can go back later once you've exhausted your memory and insert it where it belongs.

A good way to reconnect with your story is to close your eyes and "relive" what happened. Jog your memory by using the five senses. What did you see? What did you hear? What did you smell or taste? What did you feel? What did you do with your hands? Were other people there? What were they saying? What were they doing? What was the weather like? Just get it all down. Talk Onto Paper. That's the first draft.

Story Crafting Step #2: Develop a Second Draft Using The Nine Steps of Story Structure

The purpose of the second draft is to clarify and simplify the story line. The goal is to make sure all the details people need to know are included and all the details they don't need to know — aren't. You accomplish this by going back over the first draft using The Nine Steps of Story Structure you'll learn in the next chapter. That process places events in their proper chronological sequence, edits out what is superfluous, and highlights what is essential.

A common problem many speakers have is they tell their stories in fits and starts. By that, I mean they're rolling along and all of a sudden they're off on a tangent. Digressing causes them to lose their forward progress and it confuses the audience because the story no longer makes sense.

It can be challenging trying to decide which details are relevant — and which are extraneous. I always go back to the spaghetti sauce analogy. There are certain ingredients that make sense in spaghetti sauce like onions and oregano. These are spicy details that add flavor to the story sauce; however, if you were to add cookie dough, (which happens to taste just fine on its own) it would spoil the sauce.

> **Example**: A coaching client told a story about her rebellious teen years. Her first boyfriend had been named Charles Smith but everyone called him Chickenhawk. She went into detail about him because he was her first love. Her next boyfriend was in a rock-and-roll band. As part of

her teenage insubordination, she defied her parents and ran away with him on the road for six months. She casually mentioned that his name was also Charles Smith. I kept waiting for her to "do something" with the fact that both boyfriends in her younger years had the same names, but she never did. Although the fact that these guys shared the same name was mildly interesting, it actually ended up being distracting because we kept waiting for the other shoe to drop. In our follow-up review, I suggested she drop that piece of information. It wasn't adding to the story — it was taking away from the story. It was cookie dough in the spaghetti sauce.

When trying to decide what goes in and what goes out of a story, ask yourself the following questions:

- Is the element or detail so important that if it was deleted the story wouldn't make sense? If the answer is yes, keep it in.
- Is the element or detail interesting, but if it were edited out no one would notice? If no one would notice, take it out.
- Does the element or detail add comedic or dramatic texture to the story? If the answer is yes, keep it in.
- Does the element or detail help the audience understand the character's motivation? If the answer is yes, keep it in.
- Does the element or detail support the point you are making? If it doesn't, take it out.
- Is the element or detail part of the forward progression of the story or does it take us off on a tangent? If it's a diversion, take it out.
- If the element creates a diversion, does the diversion add to the story without confusing the issue? If it adds to the story, keep it in.
- Does the element require a long explanation that's just not integral to the story? Either simplify it or take it out.

After the second draft, you should be able to read the story to someone and they will understand it totally. It may not be particularly funny or dramatic yet, but it will make sense.

Story Crafting Step #3:
Use The Third Draft to Embellish

Ironically, now that you've just edited your story to make sure it's sequential and tight, you're going to build it up again for entertainment value. With this third draft though, be sure to add details in the correct logical sequence so you honor the linear flow established in the second draft.

How do you embellish? Look for juicy details that will enhance the story. Don't hoard the sensory narrative that makes a story come alive. Lavishly re-enact what happened so the audience can see what you're saying. Do this by asking yourself, *"What Else?"* This marvelous question is a creative process that works on two levels. The first level is to find details that will make your story colorful, and the second level is to find the deeper truth your story teaches.

Here's how I helped a client use the *What Else?* process on his story.

David told our group about his job as Maintenance Manager for a large airline. He had been in charge of managing 150 people who overhauled the planes and kept them safe to fly. He described how he had been deceived by his bosses and eventually let go. He felt his firing had been politically motivated because of his active role as a union leader. When he was finished with his story, the group's feedback was that they didn't have enough information about his job to sympathize with him as much as they needed to. They understood his point intellectually, but he hadn't given them enough detail to cause them to buy in emotionally.

Write the Way You Talk — Talk Onto Paper

I thought the group had made an excellent observation and suggested that David elaborate about the deception he felt took place. Since the obstacle of the story dealt with his perception that he'd been lied to and laid-off by a ruthless employer, I felt we needed to understand more about his responsibilities and work history with the company. During the *What Else?* process, the following details started to emerge.

These were not just planes; they were the really big ones, the 747's with ten seats across that hold 400 people. Overhauling each plane took three months and thousands of man-hours. They had to be stripped down, every inch gone over with a magnifying glass, and then painstakingly reassembled. Every screw, bolt, wire, fuse, light bulb, and fixture had to be tested.

Here's the good part, the emotional buy-in part. As David recalled these details, he casually mentioned that he and a number of other workers had never used any of the months of sick leave they had coming because they had been so dedicated to keeping the airline afloat during the financial crisis. *That* was the missing link. The fact that he and his staff had continued to work so loyally despite current labor disputes gained our sympathy. What emerged from this exercise was a picture of an extremely dedicated manager with an exceptional work ethic who took his responsibility to his company and its customers very seriously.

This added information was not only pertinent to his point, it also made us care. That's a great example of how asking the question *"What Else?"* can help you find and add vital background information that makes the story more gripping. Now we understood and empathized with his outrage, whereas before, he was perceived as if he were just another disgruntled employee.

On another level, you can use the question *"What Else?"* to find other underlying truths in your story. Think about the critical moment in your story where you *learned the lesson.* Close your eyes and ask your self, *"What Else?"* Take the time to go deeper. Try to recall all the thoughts that went through your head, the emotions you felt. What *was* that situation all about? What was the lesson — the point? Once you have an answer, ask yourself, "What if it wasn't that, what if it was something else?" Don't be content to skim the surface and end at the obvious points. What is the secretive truth you're hesitant to share? Be brave. Reveal your inner beliefs, your most private revelations. Even when you think you have all the answers, ask yourself again, *"What Else?"*

Story Crafting Step #4:
Use The Fourth Draft To Polish

The fourth draft revision takes place while you walk and talk. Yup, you read right. You're going to get up on your feet and read the story out loud while you figure out when and where to move and when and where to stand still. Perhaps you're going to move to one side of the platform for your female character, and the other side for the male character. If you're telling a story about shoveling snow, you're going to pantomime picking up the shovel and throwing the snow over your shoulder (and holding your aching back!) Find a passionate place in your story where you're going to speed up and speak intensely — and a contemplative moment when you pause and share a quiet insight.

> **Note**: Write your performance notes with a colored pen in the margin next to each scene so you can easily differentiate between your story lines and your staging instructions.

The real windfall of the "on your feet" rehearsal process is that something magical happens. The walking and talking integrates your mind, body (and if you really get into it) soul. It energizes both hemispheres of your brain, and heightens your creativity because you're not just sitting at a desk trying to think.

Inventors, authors, and composers know the importance of going for a walk when they want to facilitate this exquisite flow state where their mind is working optimally. Beethoven used to talk fondly about the walks he took which caused symphonies in their finished form to burst forth in his mind. Champion athletes wouldn't think of stepping out onto the track or field without mentally and physically warming up and rehearsing their desired performance. Your "on your feet" rehearsal is the storyteller's equivalent. Walking and talking while you practice and polish is where the language, style, pacing, and humor of the story becomes organically yours.

Several of my professional speaker friends wouldn't think of delivering a presentation without going for a walk or run that morning. They agree with philosopher Soren Kierkegaard who said, "I have walked myself into my best thoughts." If you want to activate your mind and energize your story so it *breathes* life, generate it while doing some type of physical activity. You will eliminate lethargy and enliven your words so they have a forward pace that mirrors your purposeful movement.

Paint Vivid Word Pictures

> *"What's another word for Thesaurus?"*
> — comedian STEVEN WRIGHT

Your best friend in your pursuit of crafting your story, (other than your pen, paper, tape recorder, and walk-talk rehearsal) ... is Roget's *Thesaurus*. I've had mine since 1972. It's pretty beat up, but

Make Your Business Presentations Capture Attention, Inspire Action, and Produce Results

I use it more than any other book I own. Where do you think I came up with the word "imbroglio" for the imbroglio story? Roget's *Thesaurus*, thank you very much.

Some words just work better than others. For instance, in my Penn Station Story I describe the people waiting for their trains as, "This throng of people would stand there like a bunch of zombies."

Can you see the commuters just standing there like a bunch of zombies? I think the words "throng" and "zombies" add visual and verbal spice to that story. If I'd been lazy and just used the first words that came to mind, it would have sounded like this, "The people stood there staring at the schedule board."

Now I ask you, which is better, a "throng of zombies" or "people standing there staring?" It only takes a few extra minutes to search for words that paint a mental image in your audience's mind. And it's worth it. If listeners are picturing what you're saying, they're fully engaged.

There's another reason why Roget's *Thesaurus* comes in handy. If you keep using the same words, it sets up a sense of repetitiveness and the audience starts to feel you're saying the same thing (because you are!) Using synonyms, on the other hand, keeps your language fresh so your audience can't wait to hear what's next.

Author Anne Sexton says, "It might take me ten pages of nothing, of terrible writing, and then I'll get a line, and I'll think, 'That's what I mean!'" If it takes her that long, don't be concerned that you don't get it right the first time. Enjoy the discovery process.

> **Caveat**: Remember, I'm not recommending you use words that aren't normally in your vocabulary. As said before, if you reach for big words you don't regularly use, they'll sound unnatural. Want good news? You can easily access

Write the Way You Talk — Talk Onto Paper

a thesaurus on your computer. Just use your mouse to highlight the word you want to search. Then, click on Tools in your word processing program at the top of the menu bar and scroll down to Language and then over to Thesaurus. It's easy. Or, as my thesaurus just told me: it's simple, uncomplicated, straightforward, painless, effortless, and trouble-free!

CHAPTER 11

Follow The Nine Steps of Story Structure

It's no coincidence that Steven Spielberg and George Lucas have produced some of the top money-making movies of all time. These directors have mastered the art of storytelling. The *Star Wars* and *Indiana Jones* movies are textbook lessons in story structure. Now we've got *Harry Potter* mysteries and the *Lord of the Rings* trilogy, too.

In its most basic form, the classic story has a hero going off on a journey or a quest. Along the way the hero encounters an obstacle or test. Having succeeded in overcoming the obstacle or surviving the test, there is a happy ending.

For example, in *Star Wars*, Luke Skywalker is the hero. He goes on a journey where he has to battle enemy fighters and escape from danger, time and again. His journey causes him to cross paths with mentors like Obi Wan Kenobe and Yoda who teach him to use The Force. In the end, he must battle the dark side in the form of Darth Vader.

These same elements can help you craft a powerful business story that teaches a lesson. Would you agree that succeeding in business is occasionally like a dangerous journey? Do you, the hero, encounter obstacles along the way? When you overcome those obstacles, do you learn a lesson that leads to a happy ending?

Make Your Business Presentations Capture Attention, Inspire Action, and Produce Results

In this chapter, I'm going to introduce you to The Nine Steps of Story Structure and how they apply to strategic storytelling in business. They are:

Story Structure Step #1:   Set the scene
Story Structure Step #2:   Introduce the characters
Story Structure Step #3:   Begin the journey
Story Structure Step #4:   Encounter the obstacle
Story Structure Step #5:   Overcome the obstacle
Story Structure Step #6:   Resolve the story
Story Structure Step #7:   Make the point
Story Structure Step #8:   Ask the question
Story Structure Step #9:   Restate the point or Phrase That Pays

Steps #1–6 are the basic elements of classic storytelling. If you were simply telling a story to children or for entertainment purposes, these six would suffice. Steps #7, #8 and #9 specifically relate to storytelling in business.

The Script for the Airport Story

The best way I know to illustrate the practical application of these nine steps is with a fully developed script. This is the script for my "Airport Story."

> **Note**: A brief word about IN and OUT. When you are speaking to the audience in a past tense narrative voice — you are OUT. When you act out a moment as if it is happening in present time — you are IN.

> *OUT to audience.*

> I had the opportunity not long ago, to present one of my keynotes as an after dinner speech in Overland Park just

outside of Kansas City. The keynote is called, "The Positive Power of Change — GET OVER IT." I was scheduled to speak at 8 o'clock, following a sit-down dinner and a brief awards ceremony. Although I normally fly in the day before, I figured since I wasn't being picked up until 5:30, I could fly in the same day.

So, I booked a flight that would be on the ground in Kansas City at 2:30 in the afternoon, plenty of time if everything went as planned. The plane took off from Colorado Springs on time. It landed at O'Hare on time. So far, so good. When I got off the plane I walked over to the departure board to find my connection.

Step IN. (Turn away from the audience and act out looking at departure board — talking to myself.)

"Let's see. Kansas City, Kansas City, Gate B18. Delayed one hour! (Frustrated reaction — looks at watch). Okay, okay, my flight's delayed. Instead of landing at 2:30 I'll land at 3:30. My client's meeting me at my hotel at 5:30 so that still leaves two hours to get from the airport to the hotel. No problem. No sweat. This is going to work."

Back OUT to audience.

So I did what I always do when I have time to kill in an airport, I went to the Red Carpet Club. You know the fancy club frequent flyers go to, to escape the noise of the airport, where you can sit down in a comfortable chair and get a cup of free coffee. Of course it costs you $400 a year for free coffee, but hey...

So I set my luggage down, picked up a copy of the Chicago Tribune and started to read. About ten minutes later, I got the munchies, so I walked over to get a cup of coffee and see what kind of food was on the refreshment counter. Now, if you time it right, and you have good Karma you can get chocolate chip cookies. Well it must have been a good Karma day because there they were — chocolate chip cookies.

Step IN. (Act out picking up a cup of coffee and a couple of cookies and turning to walk back to my seat. Eye focus is IN while language is OUT.)

So I grabbed a couple of cookies and, as I was going back to my seat, I decided to check the departure board again just in case the flight times had changed. (Looking at the screen on the wall) "Delayed again!!!" (React in disgust by throwing hand with cookies up in the air.)

OUT to audience.

I got so upset I tossed my cookies.

Well, I finally got the flight out of O'Hare. As we land in Kansas City and pull up to the gate, I look at my watch. Yikes. The meeting planner had told me to catch the blue shuttle bus that runs every half hour because the cab service in Kansas City is notoriously slow. She's picking me up at the hotel at 5:30, and it's now 4:45. You do the math.

I'm sitting on the plane, row 38, window seat, and I've got fifteen minutes to get off the plane, find my luggage and get to the curb. What are my chances of making it? Next to none, that's what.

Step IN. (Act out being in the aisle of the plane trying to get off.)

Follow The Nine Steps of Story Structure

So finally the aisle clears, and it's my turn. (Moving like a turtle an inch at a time as people slowly depart the plane) I get off the plane and hustle through the terminal to Baggage Claim. (In the airport now looking for Baggage Claim — finding it) I have five minutes to spare. I can't believe it. So, I've got one eye on the luggage carousel and one eye on the curb outside looking for the blue shuttle bus. (Act-out in broad physical fashion alternating between watching the luggage carousel and looking out the window for the shuttle bus.)

My luggage still hasn't arrived and I'm looking for the shuttle.
"Four minutes left.
Come on luggage — (looking out the window) shuttle — three minutes left.
Come on luggage — shuttle — two minutes left.
Come on luggage — shuttle — one minute left"
(Luggage arrives — grab it and go)
and then — "Oh my gosh oh my gosh, here it is." I get my luggage and I'm heading for the door. (Nudging past slower people who are in the way) "Excuse me — excuse me." And I get to the curb just in time to see the blue shuttle bus (move head from left to right) ... drive ... right ... past me ... without ... stopping. (In shock)

"I can't believe this. Now I'm going to be late. I'm screwed, glued, and tattooed." (Frantic delivery — very tense and frustrated)

OUT to audience.

And then it hit me. Oh yes, this is rich. I'm about to do my speech called "The Positive Power of Change — GET OVER IT" and change just happened to me and I DO NOT

WANT to get over it. I want to find someone to blame. But there's no time, I have to get to my hotel.

Step IN.

So I'm thinking, "Okay Douglas, what do you teach people in this program on change? (Mental transition moment — from frantic to calm) Oh yeah oh yeah, change represents an opportunity for something better to take place in your life so when things don't work out the way you want, you don't focus on the problem — you focus on the solution." (Standing at the curb now. Change demeanor to happy-go-lucky. Smile — tension on the inside — calm on the outside.)

"All right, I'm standing here at the curb and I'm looking for the opportunity. (Looking back and forth — right to left) I'm focused on solutions. I'm looking both ways, I'm looking for the … (explode in anger) Oh for crying out loud, where is the damn opportunity?!?" (Freeze. Hold the moment. I see the solution sitting right in front of me.)

Back OUT to audience.

And then I see it. Sitting right in front of me. I had literally been looking over the roof of a long white stretch limo. I figured, what the heck. The driver, a short little stocky guy with chubby hands and a thick neck, was standing at the rear of the limo with the trunk open.

Back IN. Talking to the limo driver in a frantic sprint.

"Excuse me sir, are you by any chance going to Overland Park? I just missed my shuttle and I've got to get there right away to give a speech. It's an emergency. Can you give me a ride?"

OUT to audience.

He looks at me. He looks at this empty trunk. And then he says,

Step IN.

(Become the limo driver — change voice) "You're in luck, my friend. My other ride missed his flight and I was about to deadhead back to the garage. Yeah sure, hop in." (React in amazement. I do a little dance of joy from side to side — lick my index finger and make a sizzling sound as I touch my backside as if to indicate I think I'm hot stuff.)

OUT to audience.

I'm thinking to myself, "I am so hot. I mean, I teach people that change represents an opportunity for something better to take place in your life … and I tried it … and it worked." So we're riding along having a conversation when he says,

Back IN. (Act-out the driver with hands on the wheel talking to me in the back of the limo.)

"You know buddy, if you *had* taken that shuttle, you would have been late. That shuttle has nine hotels on its route and yours is number nine. If you'd caught it, it would have taken at least an hour and fifteen minutes to get there. But, I'm going to get you there on time. So the next time you come to the airport, don't look for the shuttle, look for the limo."

Step OUT.

He dropped me off at my hotel at exactly 5:29. The speech that night went great.

Change represents an opportunity for something better to take place in your life — if you're flexible and if you focus on solutions rather than problems. You've got to Look for the Limo.

I find it fascinating that as long as I was angry and frustrated about missing the shuttle — the limo didn't exist. It was right there in front of me, the solution was right in front of my face, but it was invisible — until I shifted my focus from the problem to the solution. As soon as I did that, the limo appeared.

How about you? Do you ever miss the shuttle; get left behind, left out, or just plain messed-with by life? Do you ever feel screwed, glued and tattooed? Look for the Limo. Change represents an opportunity for something better to take place in your life — but the opportunity only appears when you switch your focus to answers rather than anger.

In life, you get what you focus on. So focus . . . on solutions. Look for the Limo.

That's the end of the story. Now we're going to go back and dissect it, and see how I used each of The Nine Steps of Story Structure.

Story Structure Step #1 — Set the Scene

The first of the nine steps is to "Set the Scene." The purpose of this step is to create context — to frame the story with enough information so people understand where you're starting. This is how I began...

> I had the opportunity not long ago, to present one of my keynotes as an after dinner speech in Overland Park just outside of Kansas City. The keynote is called, "The Positive Power of Change — GET OVER IT." I was scheduled to speak at 8 o'clock, following a sit-down dinner and a brief awards ceremony. Although I normally fly in the day before, I figured since I wasn't being picked up until 5:30, I could fly in the same day.

That's the end of Step #1 in this story. In order for the story to work, you needed to know that it was an after dinner speech at 8 p.m. because time plays a crucial role in this story. You also needed to know the title of my speech because it ties into the dilemma I face at the curb. And you needed to know I was flying in the same day, because that sets up the tension and drama that is created when the flight out of O'Hare gets delayed.

Story Structure Step #2 — Introduce the Characters

The second step is "Introduce the Characters." The only other character in this story is the limo driver. To tell the truth, I couldn't remember exactly what he looked like when I was writing this story later on, so I gave myself creative license to rewrite history. The image that came to mind for me was the actor Danny DeVito, so this is how I described him.

> The driver — a very short little stocky guy with chubby hands and a thick neck.

That's it. That's how easy it is to introduce a character. A little descriptive language and the character becomes real to the audience. They can picture him and associate him with someone they know or have seen.

Even though this is listed as the second step, I don't mean that you have to introduce all your characters up front. They will arrive in the story in their own sequence. The concept of introducing the character means that when a major character enters the story, you create a visual picture the audience can see and feel. Paint a picture with words and actions. My description of the limo driver was only 14 words long but it did the trick. To complete the picture I changed my posture and gave him a character voice when I spoke his lines. Here are some guidelines for introducing characters:

- Start with the visual. Describe the physical characteristics of each person. In addition to height and weight, look for idiosyncrasies such as the way they walk, dress, talk, eat, etc.

- Look for personality quirks and behavioral traits like a woman who smacks her gum or a man who fiddles with his tie. My lovely wife Deborah has a habit of having to turn off all the lights in the house and close all the cabinets before she walks out the door. It takes us fifteen minutes to get out the door to go grocery shopping. See what I mean?

- Describe your relationship whenever applicable. For instance, comedienne Phyllis Diller used to joke about her husband ... Fang. A lot of her one-liners were about her relationship with him. All she had to do was say FANG and you started laughing because that one word description set up a comical image. Use adjectives to describe your relationship, i.e., contentious, loving, competitive, stimulating, strained, or effortless — and then say that word with a matching vocal delivery so the audience "gets" the picture.

- Describing a person's clothing is often a good visual insight into their character. Picture a grandmother with her apron, a father with his ratty old slippers, a boss with a huge belly whose shirt is straining the buttons, a child with big round eyes.

As an actor, it's second nature for me to create characters physically as well as verbally. I often shift my posture to distinguish between the other character and myself, even if it's only for one or two lines. If you're sharing a story about your six-year-old daughter coming home from school unhappy, you may actually look up with a beseeching expression and talk with a higher voice when you're talking as her, and then look down with a concerned look on your face and a soothing voice when you're portraying yourself. "Playing both roles" helps the audience get lost in the story because they're picturing your dialogue and one-act play as if it were really happening.

You may not initially be comfortable doing this, but I encourage you to try it for several reasons: 1) Putting yourself into the different roles helps you re-live the event so you embody the story; 2) it will become more natural and fun with practice; and 3) audiences love it because it's so much more involving than the one voice, "talking head" style of lecturing.

Tips for Creating Characters Physically

Remember my Streaking Story from earlier in the book? When I perform this story, I act out the different characters. I pantomime my friend and myself running down the street. When I describe sprinting by the line of theatergoers, I actually change characters and become a person in line applauding as he sees us streak past. I "surrender" and put my hands up when the policeman comes around the corner. All the gestures and physical acting make the story even funnier.

Use these tips to give your characters shape and form so audience members see them in their minds. Start by assuming their real physicality and then add on from there.

- Change your stance and posture to indicate the emotional state of the character
  - Lean forward slightly and shift your weight to the balls of your feet if you're talking as someone who is eagerly looking forward to something.
  - Lean away and hold your head back if you're indicating someone has knocked you off balance or is coming on strong.
  - Shift your weight to one side and place a hand on your hip if you're pretending to flirt with someone.
  - Cross your arms in front of your chest and jut your chin out if you're portraying someone who's belligerent or stubborn.

- Change the width of your feet. When they are close together you appear prim and proper. When they are shoulders' width apart in a more athletic stance, you are loose and flexible. When they are spread wide, you are powerful, "taking up space," and holding your ground.

- Change the angle of your head and expression on your face. Looking down can signal scrutiny or defeat. Gazing up and off to one side signals reflection or trying to recall. Cocking your head to one side can indicate you're quizzical or puzzled. Holding you chin up can mean resolve or a determination to see things through.

- Change the motion of your hands and arms. Almost every character you will portray uses their hands when they converse. Try different elbow positions and play with the range of motion for the entire arm.

A friend who also speaks on presentation skills likes to say, "Let your armpits breathe." Why? Gestures within the plane of the body tend to become repetitive because there are only so many things you can do in that restricted area. When you move your hands and elbows away from your body, your gestures have much greater potential for emphasis. These bold gestures help you "own" the stage so you look as if you belong there (instead of giving the impression you rather be any-where but there.)

Note: Always strive to make your choices from the inside out. Start with the character's motivation. Let the charac-ter's movements and gestures flow from their intention. For comedy you will go broad and mimic — to the point of creating a caricature of the real person. In a dramatic exchange with another character — keep it real. Make your adjustments subtle.

Story Structure Step #3 — Begin the Journey

The journey begins when you leave the comfort and safety of the known and step out into the unknown. Do you remember where that happened in my Airport Story? Here's where the journey began.

> So, I booked a flight that would be on the ground in Kansas City at 2:30 in the afternoon, plenty of time as long as every-thing went as planned. The plane took off from Colorado Springs on time. It landed at O'Hare on time.

That was it. When I left home, the comfort and safety of the known, and went to the airport to hop a plane for O'Hare, I stepped into the unknown. The journey is always that jumping off place where you accept a challenge, begin a project, or initiate an activity. It's the knight in shining armor riding out of the castle to slay the dragon and rescue the damsel in distress. It's accepting the promotion to be Vice President of Marketing for the east coast region of your company and relocating to Baltimore. Great stories have a journey.

Story Structure Step #4 — Encounter the Obstacle

During the course of the journey, the hero of the story (that's you) encounters an obstacle. The obstacle can be anything. It can be a person who plays the role of the bad guy or gal. The bad gal? Is that proper? I can see it now — the good guy is seated at a table in the saloon eating his steak and drinking a beer when ... da da dummm ... we hear the sound of boots approaching and then ... the saloon doors burst open and the bad gal enters, guns a blazin'. It just doesn't sound right, does it? Now, if that bad gal was Sharon Stone ... but I digress.

The obstacle can be a person, a difficult decision, a physical problem, a personal challenge, or a psychological obstacle. In the Airport Story, the obstacle is anything that prevents me from meeting my client at 5:30 p.m. If all the flights had been on time and I arrived on schedule — we'd have no story.

Encountering the obstacle is one of the juiciest parts of your story, so make it dramatic. This is where the rubber meets the road, where all of the drama begins to unfold. Focus your writing on this critical moment and invest the time to describe it vividly. Make sure you paint the picture.

I encountered the first obstacle when I went over to the departure board and discovered that my connecting flight had been delayed. This is how I described it:

> As soon as I got off the plane, I walked over to the departure board to find my connection. "Let's see. Kansas City, Kansas City, Gate B18. Delayed one hour! (Frustrated reaction — looks at watch). Okay, okay, my flight's delayed. Instead of landing at 2:30 I'll land at 3:30. My client is meeting me at my hotel at 5:30 so that still leaves 2 hours to get from the airport to the hotel. No problem. No sweat. This is going to work."

The Magical Effect of Piling On

Remember when you were a kid on the playground and everybody would jump on someone and make a big pile? We called it piling on. If you can do that with your obstacles, by all means, do it. Don't stop at just one thing going wrong. Pile it on — the more the better. Three obstacles are better than one. Think of Harrison Ford in the *Indiana Jones* movies. As soon as he gets out of one mess, he encounters another.

In the Airport Story, the flight got delayed a second time, which made for a better story. The first delay created tension; the second delay created panic. Then I got to Kansas City and encountered the third obstacle by missing the last shuttle that would get me to my hotel on time (or so I thought). Now I had a catastrophe.

> "Come on luggage — shuttle — one minute left" (Luggage arrives — grab it and go) and then — "Oh my gosh oh my gosh, here it is." I get my luggage and I'm heading for the door. (Nudging past slower people who are in the way) "Excuse me — excuse me." And I get to the curb just in time to see the blue shuttle bus (move head from left to right) ... drive ... right ... past me ... without ... stopping. (In shock)

How you *react* to the obstacle makes all the difference in your story. It's not just what you say or do at that moment, it's *how* you say it or do it that gives your story emotional impact. Be an actor. "Portray to convey." Don't just encounter the obstacle matter of factly and keep on talking. Stop. Experience the frustration or anger you felt at that moment before continuing. Why is this so important? If *you* don't re-experience the feelings you had at the time — the audience won't experience the feelings *this* time. In this case, no angst in the speaker, no empathy in the audience.

Story Structure Step #5 — Overcome the Obstacle

In overcoming the obstacle, we plant the seed for the point to be made or the lesson to be learned. This is the teaching step — for you trainers out there — the How-To step.

The point I chose to make with this story relates to how we deal with adversity. For me, the lesson was about shifting my focus from what was wrong to what could be right — the *opportunity* the situation offered. Since one of the main messages of my keynote is that "*change represents an opportunity for something better to take place in your life,*" I use this story to illustrate *how* an opportunity can present itself.

We pick up the story after the plane has landed in Kansas City, and I'm standing at the curb watching helplessly as the shuttle drives past without stopping.

> "I can't believe this. Now I'm going to be late. I'm screwed, glued, and tattooed." (Frantic delivery — very tense and frustrated)
>
> And then it hit me. Oh yes, this is rich. I'm about to do my speech called "The Positive Power of Change — GET

Follow The Nine Steps of Story Structure

OVER IT" and change just happened to me and I DO NOT WANT to get over it. I want to find someone to blame. But there's no time, I have to get to my hotel so I'm thinking, "Okay Douglas, what do you teach people in this program on change? (Mental transition moment — from frantic to calm) Oh yeah oh yeah, change represents an opportunity for something better to take place in your life so when things don't work out the way you want, you don't focus on the problem — you focus on the solution." (Standing at the curb now. Change demeanor to happy-go-lucky. Smile — tension on the inside — calm on the outside.)

"All right, I'm standing here at the curb and I'm looking for the opportunity. (Looking back and forth — right to left) I'm focused on solutions. I'm looking both ways; I'm looking for the ... (explode in anger) Oh for crying out loud, where is the damn opportunity?!?" (Freeze. Hold the moment. I see the solution sitting right in front of me.)

Back OUT to audience.

And then I see it. Sitting right in front of me. I had literally been looking over the roof of a long white stretch limo. I figured, what the heck. The driver, a short little stocky guy with chubby hands and a thick neck, was standing at the rear of the limo with the trunk open.

Back IN. (Talking to the limo driver in a frantic sprint.)

"Excuse me sir, are you by any chance going to Overland Park? I just missed my shuttle and I've got to get there right away to give a speech. It's an emergency. Can you give me a ride?"

> *OUT to audience.*
>
> He looks at me. He looks at this empty trunk. And then he says,
>
> *Step IN.*
>
> (Become the limo driver — change voice) "You're in luck, my friend. My other ride missed his flight and I was about to deadhead back to the garage. Yeah sure, hop in."

Overcoming the obstacle was twofold. I first overcame the obstacle mentally when I made the decision to shift my focus from the problem to the solution. I then overcame the obstacle actively when I asked for the ride from the limo driver. I am switching my focus from the problem to the solution with both my body (action) and mind (phrase) to "Look For The Limo."

The How-To process of overcoming the obstacle is scripted as an IN moment, a conversation that I have with myself, out loud.

Story Structure Step #6 — Resolve the Story

In step six, you need to tie up all the loose ends. Make sure your audience knows how everything worked out. Beginning speakers sometimes leap from the obstacle right to making the point and leave listeners with unanswered questions. In this story, my audience wants to know if I got to the hotel on time to meet my client. They want to know if the speech went well. Here's how I resolved the story.

> He dropped me off at my hotel at exactly 5:29 and the speech that night went great.

Follow The Nine Steps of Story Structure

If you don't resolve the story, you can create confusion in your audience. They may be so preoccupied trying to figure out what happened to a character they cared about, they could miss the point altogether. Here's a perfect example.

At a Story Theater Retreat, a former fireman told a story about a time he responded to a bizarre 911 call. He rushed to the house and knocked loudly on the front door. A female voice shouted, "Come on in." He opened the door and there was a woman without a stitch of clothes on, sitting in a big stuffed chair, staring straight at him. A handgun sat on the tray table next to her. Without saying a word, she picked up the gun, pointed it at him, and fired off a round. He dove into the bushes on the side of the porch for cover and felt the bullet whiz past his head. At this point he went on and told another story about an even crazier emergency call he'd handled.

Even though he had moved on, we were still wondering what happened to the naked woman with the gun. He had failed to tie up the loose ends and give us a sense of completion. We had unanswered questions like, "How did you get the gun away from her? Did she surrender and get arrested? Did she wear a satin nightgown to jail? Is that what the phrase 'I dodged a bullet' really means?"

Attend to the details, my friends. Resolve the story. By the way, after we begged him for details he finally wrapped things up by explaining that the naked lady did get arrested, no one got shot or injured, and she wore a blue terrycloth robe to jail.

Every once in awhile you'll encounter a left-brained, analytical, some would say — anal-retentive — individual who will obsess about the tiniest details. S/he will come up to you after your program and say something like this:

"Hey, uhmmm, in that story, you said you started shampooing your poodle when the tornado hit your house, tore your roof off, sucked you up into the air and carried you from Oklahoma to Texas where you landed in a swimming pool. Ummmm, what kind of shampoo were you using?"

Don't be frustrated with them. Be grateful they were paying such close attention.

If you were writing a novel, making a movie or telling a story at the local library, the first six steps of story structure would be all you'd need. The hero met the challenge, overcame it, and everything is resolved. However, as a business speaker, you need to do three more things: make the point, ask the question and restate the point or Phrase That Pays.

Story Structure Step #7 — Make the Point

One of the main points of my keynote about change and of this Airport Story is to *focus on solutions*. It is crucial to phrase the lesson succinctly. "Focus on Solutions" is clear and to the point. It is also a call to action. The entire story leads up to overcoming obstacles in life by focusing on solutions. When I finally clarify the "moral of the story," it flows logically from the content.

> Change represents an opportunity for something better to take place in your life, if you're flexible — if you're able to focus on solutions rather than problems. You've got to Look for the Limo.

Don't try and force a point onto a story that isn't congruent. The point or teaching lesson must flow organically from the story for it to work. This story had a shuttle and a limo in it. The shuttle represents what we expect from life and nothing more — and the

Follow The Nine Steps of Story Structure

limo symbolizes moving up to something nicer. If change represents an opportunity for something better to take place, what better symbol than a limo? My point is "Focus On Solutions" and my catch phrase, my Phrase That Pays (Chapter 12) is "Look for the Limo."

> **Note**: I've said it before, and I'll say it again. I believe you should only have only one point per story. While your story may contain other points you *could* make, it's your job as a speaker to discipline yourself to narrow it down to the best one for this presentation. If you are greedy and try to make several different points, your audience's minds will be wandering all over the place. Trust me on this. Their brains are overloaded as it is and they're doing their level best to keep up with you as you move from story to story. Have mercy on them by being clear. One point per story. The cleaner you keep it, the more they'll remember it. Less is more.

Story Structure Step #8 — Ask the Question

Up to this point, the story you're sharing has been about your experience, not the audience's. While they may have had (hopefully had!) a sympathetic experience, it's still about you. In this step, we transfer the lesson back to the audience with a "you" question. By asking, "How about you?," "Has something like this ever happened to you?," or some variation of that type of question, every person in your audience has an opportunity to personalize the lesson.

> How about you? Do you ever miss the shuttle, get left behind, left out, or just plain messed with by life? Do you ever feel screwed, glued, and tattooed?

The word "you" is very important in this follow-up question. "Are *you* spending too much time being angry and frustrated?" I know that others teach that we should use "we" or "us" instead of "you", but I disagree in this case. There are times to be inclusive and there are times to directly and intentionally engage each audience member with the specific word "you." I want to engage my participants and challenge them to take personal responsibility right then and there for answering the questions that the story poses.

- How about you?
- What about you?
- When will you?
- What will it take for you?
- How will you?
- Is it time for you?
- Are you ready to?
- Have you ever?

After you ask the question, either 1) give them a few seconds to answer the question in their heads; 2) open it up for discussion; or 3) if this is a hands-on workshop, give them a few minutes to write their responses in their workbooks.

Story Structure Step #9 —
Restate the Point or Phrase That Pays

After you've asked the question and given them a few moments to ponder their response — you want to give them a call them to action. Do this by restating the point or Phrase That Pays with an authoritative delivery. You have now moved from asking a question to making a statement and giving guidance.

> In life, you get what you focus on. So focus ... on solutions. Look for the Limo.

CHAPTER 12

Brand Your Message with a Phrase That Pays

O ne of the most important lessons I've learned as a professional keynote speaker is that my audience members will seldom take away more than one or two ideas from an entire speech. At first, this realization was kind of depressing. Regardless of how many amazing ideas we share, people focus on the one or two that have special significance for them at that time.

It's different in a training environment where people have more time to discuss and digest the ideas being put forth. In a keynote however, everything moves very fast. As the speaker makes one point after another — the audience grabs on to whatever hits them where they live.

I discovered this by asking people who came up to me after a speech, "What is the one message you're taking home from my program today?" Time after time they'd say, "Look for the Limo" or "Get Over It." It didn't matter how many points I'd made, their answers confirmed to me what wise men and women have known since ancient times. People remember what hits home for *them*, not necessarily what hits home for us.

Everyone who walks into your presentation has issues. If one of your concepts helps them with one of their issues, that's the concept they'll remember. The way I figure it, if they're only going to remember one concept, it better be the one we want them to remember. If I succeed in getting them to remember *my* main point, I can brand my story and my speech or presentation with that one point and supplement it with printed materials. If I want to take it even further I can create a logo around that point and design a website and business cards and books and tapes and bookmarks and posters and balloons and . . . well you get the idea.

Remember, this is about strategic storytelling to accomplish a specific purpose. If you want people to buy in to a new idea, embrace a new philosophy or purchase your product or service — your message has to stick. Think of a Phrase That Pays as Velcro for the brain. Do this right and your listeners will be thinking about you and what you said for a long time.

Have you ever found yourself humming a catchy jingle you heard on the radio? It just kept replaying in your mind? If the answer is yes, it's because some advertising genius created a clever phrase, put it to music, and sent it out over the airwaves with the specific intention of making you hum it all day. And it worked!

One of the best is Nike's ubiquitous slogan, "Just Do It." Chevy advertises its trucks with "Like a Rock" sung by Bog Seger. I bet many of you actually *sing* that phrase just like Bob does in all those ads, right? That's an effective jingle!

Let's employ the genius behind those advertising slogans to create a literary jingle our audiences can't stop thinking about. I call this story slogan a Phrase That Pays. How does it pay? Let me count the ways. Perhaps most importantly, a Phrase That Pays sticks in people's minds. They remember it and, better yet, they act on it.

My approach to speaking is founded on the belief that we want our audience to change their thinking or behavior as a result of hearing us speak. If they don't, we've failed them. The following ten criteria can help us create succinct sound-bytes that resonate in our participants' minds and hearts for days, weeks, and months after they've heard us speak.

The Ten Criteria for a Memorable Phrase That Pays

Criteria #1: It must summarize or convey the point of the story.

The Phrase That Pays needs to encapsulate the message of the story. If we coin a catchy phrase but it doesn't quite fit the moral of the story, people will miss the point (so to speak.) It may take some time for you to come up with the perfect Phrase that Pays — but it's worth it because that one phrase will capture your message in a nutshell. Just keep asking yourself, "What's the point?" The reason I didn't choose "Focus on Solutions Rather Than Problems," as a Phrase That Pays is because it's not catchy. "Look for the Limo" is stronger because it is alliterative, succinct, and has a double-entendre meaning.

Criteria #2: Use only one Phrase That Pays per story.

There can be too much of a good thing. You don't want to baffle your audience by having several different points. Pick the one that does the best job of capturing the essence of the message for this group. If you want participants to be clear, you've got to be clear.

> **Caveat:** Many of my students like to start every story with their Phrase That Pays. I try to dissuade them, because it gives too much away up front. Good stories create mystery and allow the audience to discover — along with the storyteller — the meaning of the story. It's to your advantage to delay the introduction of your Phrase That Pays so you can maximize drama and suspense.

Criteria #3: Make it short and sweet — the fewer words the better.

Clint Eastwood hit it big with "Make My Day." Arnold the *Terminator* is remembered by "I'll Be Back." Any of you out there remember Crosby Stills and Nash's song *Love the One You're With*? The Beatles had *Let It Be*. You get the idea. These are all five words or less — and we remember them years (many years!) after the fact. Strunk and Whyte said in their classic book, *The Elements of Style*, "Every word must tell." Prune every word that isn't necessary so the language is tight, tight, tight.

Criteria #4: Make it musical and rhythmic.

Think back to your early school years when you were learning your ABC's. Do you remember the little sing-along chant, "A, B, C, D, E, F, GEEEE..., H, I, J, K, LMNOPEE".... Think also about "Jack and Jill went up the hill ... to fetch a pail of waaaa–ter.... Jack fell down and broke his crown...."

Do you hear the syncopated beat when you repeat those? That rhythmic cadence is called Iambic Pentameter and it gives the mind a hook on which to hang a memory. If you want to increase the likelihood that people will repeat your key message long after you're gone, be sure to craft your words so they fall into some form of rhythmic tempo. Practice saying your phrase until it has a musical lilt to it so people say it just the way you said it.

A good way to develop an ear for these rhythmical patterns is to study commercials on TV and the radio. Listen how they catch your ear.

Criteria #5: Use words that are organic to the story.

A few years ago I had the privilege of coaching a talented young man who was launching his career as a motivational speaker. At that time his Phrase That Pays was rather generic. I think it was something like "Believe in Yourself" or "Live Your Dreams." Those are certainly valid and worthwhile thoughts, however they're not very original. So we went back to his story to search for a more distinctive phrase. His story was about the time he was playing hockey and got body-checked up against the sideboards. He got hit so hard that by the time he landed on the ice he couldn't move. In that instant, he had become a quadriplegic.

Your Phrase That Pays often reflects what's unique about you and your story. Since this was a story about a hockey game, I asked if his hockey coach had a favorite phrase he used a lot. Without hesitation my client replied, "Skate with Your Head Up." That was it. The perfect Phrase That Pays for his story. It captures the essence of his message and articulates his inspiring philosophy that we should move through life with our head up, looking forward in the direction of our dreams. With the proper syncopation, it is also musical. Best of all, it is an honest, integral part of his history. You and I couldn't use that phrase. It's a one-of-a-kind original, just like him.

What's unique about you and your story? If it's a fishing story, find your phrase in the world of fishing. Maybe it's "Fish or Cut Bait" which could mean stop complaining and start acting. If you've survived a tornado, perhaps you could find a weather analogy such as "Weather the Storm" or maybe you could riff off *The Wizard of Oz* and say, "We're Not in Kansas Anymore."

Criteria #6: Make it alliterative.

Alliteration is defined as the repetition of the initial consonant sound in two or more neighboring words. "Make Your Move" is good because of the M's. Others include: "Take Your Time," "Watch Your Words," "Send a Signal" and so forth. Deliberately selecting words that have the same first sound makes a phrase that would otherwise sound flat — *pop*. For example, say the words, "Are you a teacher or a critic?" Flat. Now say, "Are you a coach or a critic?" Better, right? The two C's make it "pop."

Criteria #7: To rhyme is sublime.

"Walk Your Talk" is a good one. Here's one for you Mensa members — "Evolve and Solve." My fellow author/consultant, Sam Horn, who helps people get their books out of their head and into the world, was working with a client who was searching for a better sub-title for her book *Read More, Faster* — a book that explains how we can increase effectiveness by speed-reading computer communication. Sam interviewed her client and mind-mapped her responses, keeping an eye out for words that captured the essence of her message. Their first stab at the sub-title was "Increasing Productively On-line While Saving Time, Paper, and Frustration." Yuck. Doesn't sound too tantalizing, does it? Wait a minute. They simply re-arranged the words and it became "Increasing Productivity *On-Line* — While Saving Paper, Frustration, and *Time*." Say that sub-title in its Iambic Pentameter cadence and emphasize the words "on-line" and "time." All of a sudden, it ends on a rhyme, which makes that boring sub-title sublime. That's what you want to do with your Phrase That Pays.

Criteria #8: Turn it into a call to action.

I agree with the adage that says, "The object of education isn't knowledge; it's action." If we want our audience to ACT on the lessons they've learned, we need to start our Phase That Pays with a verb. "Seize the Day" is a classic call to action. "Think Big" is another. "Walk," "Start," "Begin," "Master," "Capture," "Run," and "Take" are all vivid verbs that inspire people to follow up on their intentions and apply their lessons-learned.

Caveat: That doesn't mean a Phrase That Pays can't start with a word that has a negative connotation. "*Never* Give Up" and "*Don't* Sweat the Small Stuff" are calls to action — with a twist. You may have heard that some people are motivated by fear and others are motivated by love. What drives some people to action is the desire to avoid pain — what drives other people to action is to add value. The title of this book — *Never Be Boring Again* — is a title that focuses on unwanted pain and how we can avoid it. Sometimes, Phrases That Pay that focus on a problem are more compelling than ones that focus on a solution. Which book would you rather read, or which presentation would you rather hear: "Be More Confident" or "Never Be Shy Again"?

Criteria #9: Use words that end in a consonant.

Advertisers and direct mail marketers will tell you that the word "get" is more memorable than the word "grab" because of the T. Consonants stick! Vowels evaporate. "Just Do It" works because of the hard consonants in "just" and "it." The same goes for "Get Over It." The K's in "Walk Your Talk" make it incredibly powerful because they give it punch. "Kick Start" is excellent. That's another reason why I liked my client's "Skate with Your Head Up." "Skate" has a K and a T.

Criteria #10: Make it memorable.

Want your Phrase That Pays to resonate in their memory? Remember this little jingle — *repetition aids retention*. Say your phrase up to six times in a 60-minute speech. Weave it into the theme at crucial points and have your audience say it with you. You can either ask them to repeat it after you, or you can build up to your point, pause, look at the group with your head to one side and your eyebrows raised as if asking them to finish your sentence, and the group will often say the phrase on their own. You can even cup a hand around one ear and lean towards the group so they know you want them to "fill in the blank." You know you've imprinted your Phrase That Pays when the group voluntarily feeds it back to you with the same cadence you use when saying it.

Studies of how adults learn show that when adults verbalize what you're telling them, *their retention goes up to 75%,* whereas when they just listen to what you've said, their retention is only 10%. This is why it's smart to give participants opportunities to say your message out loud. Doing so imprints your Phrase That Pays so you and your message become synonymous. That means when some-one asks a member of your audience what your talk was about, they'll repeat word for word your Phrase That Pays. That's what I call branding your message!

Book-End Your Speech

There's another way you can make your significant points stick. Book-End your speech with your Phrase That Pays and use it sev-eral times in its related story. Let me define "Book-Ending." Just as bookends are identical and go on either end of the books on a shelf, using a phrase or sentence identically at the front and back of a speech is called Book-Ending.

Want an example? I gave a talk on leadership to a room full of Fortune 500 executives. I began my speech with the words "Pass the Power." Notice I didn't start with small talk, no "It's nice to be here today in Tampa. What beautiful weather we're having." Perfunctory remarks cause our audience to roll their eyes and think "Stop wasting my time."

I walked to the center of the room, looked out over my audience, paused and then said in a strong, distinct voice, "Pass the Power." I used that phrase again in the story I included earlier in this book, about my stepson Bennett developing my website. The story illustrated the concept of empowerment and the action I wanted them to take as leaders, which is to Pass the Power. The last words out of my mouth were "Pass the Power." I blended them into my closing sentence at the end of my speech like this:

> So my friends, my challenge for you today is to empower your people to be their very best and the way to do that is... Pass the Power.

Do you see how this works? The Book-Ending Technique and The Phrase That Pays Technique, used in concert in a pre-determined fashion, produce even more drama. You start strong, you weave in the phrase, and you end strong. It's clean, it's crafted, and it works.

Make Your Message More Memorable and Marketable

In addition to repeating my Phrase That Pays throughout my talk, I go a step further and make branding cards. On the front of the card is my Phrase That Pays in big bold block letters. The **IMPACT** font is my favorite. Just below the phrase, in smaller letters, is my name and contact information. Many attendees take this card back to their office and place it somewhere they'll see it frequently. It becomes their daily affirmation card. Often, other employees or customers see it and ask about it. That leads to a discussion of my presentation and message. Next time that individual needs a speaker, my name and number are right there in front of them. I have now translated my Phrase That Pays into a marketing piece, a win–win advertisement that stays "in-sight — in-mind" instead of "out-of-sight — out-of-mind."

I know you may be thinking, "That's fine for you, Doug. You're a motivational speaker and you need to market yourself when you speak. But I'm not selling anything." Yes you are. No matter what business you are in you are always in the self-promotion business. If you don't toot your horn, the next promotion may go to the person who did. The marketing tips I am sharing with you now will help you stand out in your workplace, on the platform or wherever you need to stand out.

Could you have your Phrase That Pays printed on a bookmark, poster, coffee mug, or calendar? What is a product that business people would appreciate receiving? What is a product they'd continue to use in the months ahead? For a small investment, you could keep your motivational message in front of these people. Isn't it worth it?

Before we move on to our next chapter, please think about this: If you could summarize your entire talk in one literary slogan, what would it be? If the guy in the back row didn't remember anything else but this one idea, what would you want it to be? Now, take the time to craft that idea into an adage that is short and sweet, musical and rhythmic, and a call to action — and you're well on your way to being memorable, marketable, and remarkable. Hey, maybe I have something there. That was short, sweet, and alliterative. Maybe that's my next Phrase That Pays!

CHAPTER 13

Link Your Openings, Closings, and Transitions

N ow that you've invested time in crafting your stories, it's time to think about how you're going to get in and out of those stories. You could say, "I want to tell you a story about..." That's definitely an option. What if you have more than one story though? Are you going to keep saying the same thing every time? I don't think so. Too predictable.

You have already arranged your content so it flows in a sequence that makes sense. Now, you need a sentence or two that wraps up what was said before and introduces your next idea. It's important to have a clear division between points so your material doesn't get all jumbled up.

Chapter 11 featured the script of my Airport Story that is a pivotal part of my keynote on the topic of change. The opening line of the story is, "I had the opportunity not long ago..."

To lead up to that story, I ask the audience to participate in a survey where I ask them to add up how many places they've lived, how many jobs and/or career changes they've had, and how many major romantic relationships they've been in.

The point I am making with this survey is that everyone has experienced changes in their lives, some more than others. I then ask audience members if any of those location, job, or relationship changes were traumatic at the time but turned out to be "for the best" in the long run. There are always a lot of heads nodding. This simple survey causes people to understand that events that are initially awful can turn out to be the proverbial "blessing in disguise."

I then say, "The challenge of this philosophy is to be able to recognize the opportunity for change when it happens. For instance, I had the opportunity not long ago…"

By setting up the premise of being able to recognize the opportunity at the moment the change is happening, I insinuate where the story is going without giving the point away. I don't want to say, "Look for the Limo" up front because that would dilute its power later on. I don't want people to know there's a limo in the story yet because that's the surprise. The limo is the unexpected opportunity.

To find your transition sentence, simply link a word or phrase from your previous point to your next point. Your entire speech can progresses seamlessly from one story to the next by chaining together these word links.

Transition With Verbal Bridges

Want to know how to transition out of a story? Simply de-brief the point of your story, and then lead into the next content piece with a verbal bridge. The bridge can be a question, reflection, or segue of a particular word that you carry from one point to the next. If you're a trainer, it can be as simple as saying, "Now that we've learned how to greet our customers, let's move on to how we can identify and meet our customers' needs."

Link Your Openings, Closings, and Transitions

See how you summarize what you've just covered in a few words and then introduce what's next? Other transitional phrases you can use to link your points and stories are:

- "Speaking of _____, let's talk now about we can apply that idea in the workplace."
- "That reminds me of the time_____"
- "You may be wondering what that story has to do with you. Well, _____"
- "Are you thinking, 'I agree with that but what about _____?'"
- "Now that you know how to _____, let's address what to do when _____."
- "Here's another way you can _____."
- "Want to know another technique for _____?"
- "Did you notice how _____? You can do that in your career by _____"
- "Now, on to the second step: _____"
- "The next part of the process is to _____"

Open With A Story To Pleasantly Surprise Your Audience

Want to know what to put first in your presentation? Start with a story. Don't preface it with any explanation. Just jump in. POW! Grab them from the get-go by eliminating the obligatory remarks most speakers use to start their speech. You know, the "When Joe called to ask if I'd be your luncheon speaker..." or "I'm proud to be here today..." or "I want to thank Jan for giving me this opportunity to kick-off your conference." In those first few precious moments, your audience is deciding whether you're going to be worth listening to. Don't blow your opportunity to win them over by sharing dull perfunctory information.

Make sure the first words out of your mouth pleasantly surprise them by being different than what they expect. If you start right into a story, i.e., "I was walking through the San Francisco airport when I noticed a very tall man walking toward me. I'm sure he was at least 7 feet tall. I couldn't believe it. There were people in front of me laughing and pointing at him. I thought, 'How rude.' Then he got closer and I could see why they were laughing. He had on a t-shirt with big letters that said…" See? Wouldn't you want to know more? Wouldn't you already be on the mental edge of your seat? Do something similar with your audience and I guarantee they'll love it.

Close With A Story That Sends Them Out The Door Inspired

Make sure your presentation ends on a note of hope or inspiration. It should lift people's spirits and make them feel optimistic about the future. Choosing the right story for this moment is critical to how you and your message will be remembered.

Once again, we must go back to the context for the presentation. Why are you speaking and what needs to be accomplished? Your closing story must speak to one of the main issues your audience is facing. Are people uncertain about their future? Tell a story about a transition with a happy ending? Is your audience being asked to do more with less? Share a story about a creative solution to an insurmountable challenge.

Lou Heckler, a talented keynoter and fellow member of the National Speakers Association, is known for his ability to craft spellbinding programs that leave audiences begging for more. He believes we should introduce a concept in the first minute of our talk and include that same concept in the final minute of our talk

Link Your Openings, Closings, and Transitions

so participants have a satisfying sense of completion. Audience members feel as if they've come "full circle" — because they have. This sets up a sense that you've delivered what you promised and they got what they came for.

One device that accomplishes this nicely is to begin your speech with a story and only take it half way. Stop the story just after the main character (you?) encounters an obstacle but before s/he overcomes it. Let your audience know you will finish the story later and then, at the end, pick up the story where you left off. With just the right story and the right closing message, this theatrical device is a surefire winner.

Customize Your Story to the Occasion

Have you been asked to tailor your presentation? You can research the issues facing your audience by asking the meeting planner what challenges the group is facing. You could also ask to briefly interview three to five of the participants in advance via phone to get their ideas on what would make this presentation worthwhile for them. You may prefer to send a pre-conference questionnaire.

Some sample questions you could ask to elicit important background information about your audience include:

- What are employees gossiping about around the proverbial water cooler?
- What are workers grousing about over beers after work?
- What changes have taken place that are affecting everyone's mood?
- Why are they having this meeting? Does this meeting have a specific theme?

Make Your Business Presentations Capture Attention, Inspire Action, and Produce Results

- What other speakers are part of the program? What are their topics?
- What did speakers present at last year's meeting? Who was well received and why?
- What are the demographics of the group? Average age? Gender balance? Educational level? Length of time with the company? Union, non-union?
- What topics do they want you to address — and which do they want you to avoid?
- What terminology and industry trends should you be familiar with?
- What are a couple real-life challenges they deal with on a daily basis?

> **Note**: Please understand that most meeting planners are extremely busy juggling the myriad of logistics involved with putting on an event. Be sure to acknowledge their demanding schedule and let them know you'll honor their time restraints by keeping your questions brief. If you do send out a pre-conference questionnaire or if you do interview program attendees in advance — *be sure to include their input in your presentation*. A pet peeve of program coordinators is when speakers send them an extensive questionnaire or keep them on the phone for hours — and then don't even *use* the input they solicited.

Thank these individuals in your presentation by saying, "Al from the Virginia office had a great suggestion about how we can create a welcoming climate for customers. In their office, they _____." Or, "Barbara, VP of Sales for the Southeast region, has a wonderful story about how their sales team actually increased profits this past quarter. She said the reason they were able to pull this off, despite the economic downturn, was because _____."

Link Your Openings, Closings, and Transitions

You've probably heard the saying, "They won't care how much you know, until they know how much you care." That observation may be trite, but it is true. Taking the time to customize your content lets your audience know you care enough to make your comments relevant for them. It's a worthwhile investment.

CHAPTER 14

Create a Cast of Characters Your Audience Will Care About

T he movie *Star Wars* could have been a very dull picture if Luke Skywalker hadn't encountered friends, allies, and enemies along the way. On his quest for enlightenment, he partnered with Han Solo, R2D2 and C3PO and the sage Yoda. Darth Vader personified the Dark Side and Princess Lea played the spunky heroine. The *Harry Potter* series, *The Lord of the Rings*, *Indiana Jones*, *Star Trek* and James Bond's *007* movies are all classical versions of the hero's journey.

The characters in your stories provide opportunities for comic relief, dramatic tension, and words of wisdom. Classical character types fall into the following categories:

- The ally representing partnership and teamwork
- The antagonist or enemy representing danger and evil
- The wise man (or woman) or teacher representing learning and wisdom
- The sidekick representing loyalty and friendship
- The lover representing romance and love

In this chapter we'll discuss how to introduce characters your audience can relate to. The objective is to give such vivid, visual and visceral cues; your audience sees your characters as real human beings in their mind's eye.

How To Make Characters Come Alive with Words

When we meet people in person, we have the advantage of experiencing them through sight, sound, touch, smell and aura. We not only see them — we feel their energy, their vibe. When telling a story, our goal is to help our audience members experience our characters as if they were meeting them in real life.

Generic descriptions don't have the power to make us picture someone. To make our characters come alive, we must use words that describe them so vividly it's like they're standing in front of us. Imagine I'm telling a story about leadership and I say, "My boss Loretta called me into her office." You have no idea what Loretta is like. You don't know (because there was no word picture of her) whether I'm dreading that visit to her office or looking forward to it. A better description might be:

> My boss Loretta is a very small woman with a very big heart. She's a redhead in her mid-fifties who has the energy of a twenty year old. She doesn't just walk from place to place, it's more like she falls forward, like she's tripping along. Her office looks like a complete disaster with papers everywhere, but she is in complete control and knows where everything is. She has never once forgotten to get me a birthday card. As long as you do what you say you're going to do, she's on your side and will stick up for you to the very end. But let her down and you'll hear about it.

Were you able to picture Loretta as you read this portrayal? Did you notice my portrayal had a combination of tangible and intangible descriptions? There's a purpose to this. The more aspects you

Create a Cast of Characters Your Audience Will Care About

address when describing your character, the more your audience will be able to visualize that person. Identify a character you'd like to develop for your next presentation. Consider the following elements when you're crafting their introduction:

- Physical descriptors like height, weight, posture, coloring, wardrobe
- Emotional descriptors like heart of gold, short fuse, happy go lucky, hair-trigger temper
- Personality traits such as impatient, paranoid, generous, courteous, sneaky, friendly
- Energy descriptors like how someone walks or talks, drives or competes
- Metaphors: he was a Pit Bull of a man, she was as graceful as a cat, he was like a hand grenade with the trigger pin removed, he was a fast food kind of leader — more interested in quantity than quality
- Relationship descriptors like big brother, second aunt, stepmother, boss, youngest daughter

In the case of Loretta's introduction, did you notice how I gave hints as to what kind of a boss she was while weaving in details about her looks and behavior? Those hints tie back into the overall purpose of a story I tell about leadership, in which Loretta appears. The point of the story is "Little things make a big difference." Those little things about Loretta become big things when I explain, later in the story, how she mentors the main character Emily through the challenge of planning and coordinating a regional meeting.

We are all multi-dimensional beings with distinct personalities. When you are in the initial planning stages of developing your characters, write down everything that comes to mind. You can always go back later and edit them but it's helpful to have a range of words from which to choose. Pull out your old buddy, the thesaurus, and let it stimulate your mind with imaginative words that capture the essence of that person — not just how tall he is or what color hair she has.

Embellish Your Descriptions with Vocal Inflection

If you love and respect someone, your regard for that person will be communicated in your vocal tone when you talk about him or her. Likewise, if you loathe someone, that will come across as well.

Think about Loretta. Let's say she's your boss and you really like her. Although she's a hard taskmaster and expects a lot of you — you respect her. Say the following line out loud with that sentiment in mind.

> My boss Loretta is a very small woman with a very big heart.

Now, imagine you don't like Loretta. She's always on your case and she expects more from you than you're willing to give. Say the following sentence out loud with that sentiment in mind.

> My boss Loretta is a very small woman with a very big mouth.

Do you see how word choice and inflection play a major role in clueing others in to your relationship with her? You have only changed one word in the sentences above, however there is a world of difference in how your listeners perceive this woman. It seems obvious that we should include this type of vocal interpretation when describing our characters. Unfortunately, many speakers rush through their material and introduce different characters with little or no emotional context. They never reveal the subtext that is churning underneath — the underlying relationship with their characters — that makes them live and breathe in our minds.

Think about it. If you were talking to someone over a cup of coffee about your supervisor criticizing you in front of your peers, you wouldn't have to think about vocal inflection — you'd do it naturally. Vocal animation when we're conversing is as unconscious and natural as breathing.

As soon as people get up on a stage though, their minds and mouths freeze up. What is normally done unconsciously must now be done consciously. You must deliberately choose to inflect your words with emotion — even if you're not initially feeling that emotion. Once again, this is what actors do. Remember, acting in this context is simply learning to replicate reality. You want to do on the platform what you do so effortlessly in the coffee shop. Get into your description so your audience knows exactly how you feel about this person. Exaggerate if necessary so the character is larger than life.

How to Use Physical Characterizations for Dramatic Emphasis

Once you've selected words to introduce your character and added the vocal interpretation, the next step is to figure out how you can adopt the character's physical mannerisms and traits when you're portraying him or her. This can be accomplished with a simple shift of weight or a change in posture. It is not meant to be a broad characterization. You don't have to be Jim Carrey and do over-the-top impressions. This can be accomplished subtly, unless you are going for a laugh.

This on-your-feet exercise can give you an opportunity to "take-on" the physical traits of a character so you "become" him or her. Let's call this character Robin. Now, place this book down with its face open so you can read the following instructions and practice the footwork and movement. The idea is to shift your posture like the woman in Figure 1.

1. In Figure 1a., Robin is standing in a natural posture. Stand up now and observe the way you stand naturally. Look at your feet. How far apart are they? Is your weight equally balanced on both feet? Study everything about your body posture and memorize it. Hips forward or back? Shoulders back or slumped? Chin up or down?

2. Now shift your feet a few inches wider apart and angle your toes in or out so that they are markedly different than the way you stand. As Robin, take a few steps with this new stance.

3. Continuing in the same stance, change tempo slightly — think of a camel or a giraffe and amble as you walk.

4. Continuing as Robin in Figure 1b, shift your hips forward two inches and continue to walk with this new physicality. What did the shift in your hips do to the positioning of your head and shoulders?

5. Keeping your feet the same, shift your hips back four inches and continue to walk.

6. Change tempo again. Think of a squirrel. With the hips back, walk like a squirrel.

7. Resume your normal posture and walk as you do naturally. Shift back and forth from you to Robin.

8. Let's make another choice. Starting with your posture as our baseline — shift your shoulders forward and jut your chin forward as illustrated in Figure 1c. Walk around in this new version of Robin. What has happened to your arms?

9. Return to your posture. Pull your shoulders back and lift your head high. What does this do to your hips? Experiment with different tempos.

This is how actors build the physical personality of a new character. Think of Academy Award winning actor Dustin Hoffman as

Create a Cast of Characters Your Audience Will Care About

Figure 1a   Figure 1b   Figure 1c

Tom Cruise's autistic brother in the movie *Rain Man*, or as the bum Ratso Rizzo in *Midnight Cowboy*. Daniel Day-Lewis transformed himself into a deformed but articulate man in *My Left Foot*. Meryl Streep's conflicted performance in *The Hours* was vastly different from the bubbly free spirit she played in *Adaptation*. Jack Nicholson was an obsessive-compulsive neurotic in *As Good As It Gets* and a frumpy disgruntled loser in *About Schmidt*. The same person and body — vastly different characters.

Are you ready to further develop that character you'd like to introduce?

> **Note**: Your character may be a woman or a man, but I'm going to use the plural "they" in the questions below for simplicity.

Get that person in mind; picture them as if they're standing in the room with you. Now, stand up and mimic how they hold themselves. Ask yourself the following questions and then try to adopt that body language.

- How do they stand? Feet together or apart? Weight on toes or heels?
- Where do they carry their weight? Legs, stomach, chest?
- Do they stand erect or slouch?
- Is their head sitting low to their shoulders or high on their neck?
- Is their chin forward or back? Head tilted or straight?
- How do they move through space when they walk? Are they a duck or a swan?
- Is their rhythm slow, moderate or fast? Squirrel or panther — hippo or beagle?
- What do they do with their hands? Do they hang down or swing?

In finding their physicality, it's often best to go "broad" at first (actor's term for exaggerated) and then pull it back to something simple. Eventually, you want to be able to portray the difference between their physicality and yours in one or two moves. Perhaps you look up with a plaintive expression on your face and then down with a comforting expression. You get the idea.

Once you've got their distinctive body language down, practice moving from your posture to theirs. Do this without words. Simply stand as you normally would and then shift into their stance. Do this back and forth until you can easily transfer into their physical personality as you talk about them. This ability to portray your different characters will come in handy during two-person conversations. You'll learn more about that in Chapter 20.

CHAPTER 15

Incorporate Comedy so Listeners Laugh While They Learn

A favorite story passed around the speaking industry goes like this: "A beginning speaker approached an experienced pro and asked earnestly, 'Do you have to be funny to be a professional speaker?' The veteran paused for a second and then replied, 'Only if you want to get paid.'"

It's true for professionals and it's true for you as well. If you want to hold an audience's attention, ya gotta be funny. You don't have to be drop dead hilarious. But you do have to be humorous enough to get a few laughs every now and then. And smiles, lots of smiles.

It's also true that funny people are generally more popular than grumps. People like to be with people who are funny. Humorist Art Buchwald was quoted as saying, "I learned quickly that when I made others laugh, they liked me. This lesson I will never forget."

Drama is also important — the ability to hold people in suspense and cause them to feel true emotion. Both of these are accomplished first in the crafting of the story, in the writing. If you don't conceive of the comedic moments in advance — you're dancing on the slippery slope of hope. While you may get lucky and get a laugh every now and then, you won't know why. Getting lucky is not what this book is about. We're in search of the Holy Grail of speaking and storytelling success here — predictable and verifiable results.

One simple difference between comedy and drama is this: comedy is big — drama is small. While the delivery of both requires physical and emotional energy, comedy requires big extroverted energy while drama requires small intimate energy. Comedy is like rock-and-roll. It's big and wild and sometimes loud. Drama is like a Gregorian chant. It's small and intense and often very quiet.

Of the two, comedy is harder because it's bigger than life. It challenges you to get outside of your comfort zone and let 'er rip.

There is a psychological impediment that prevents some speakers from being funny. They equate comedy with being un-dignified or un-professional, however they want to be more animated and witty because they know that's what makes audiences laugh. This sets up a conflict.

Where did we learn that we have to be serious all the time to be taken seriously? In my experience, it's just not true. As a speaker and trainer, I know that when people laugh, they learn. Laughter has four very positive effects on learning:

- It enhances respiration pumping more blood to the brain.
- It increases the number of immune cells leading to optimum health.
- It increases the release of endorphins leading to a positive attitude.
- It increases receptivation to stimulosis leading to retentivitus!

After coaching thousands of business professionals from CEO's to Toastmasters, I have come to one simple conclusion: everybody is funny. So why do so many speakers seek comedy coaching? Because they have spent so many years trying to be taken seriously that they don't have a clue what their funny looks, sounds and feels like. My job is to reveal to you what is already there.

Find Your Funny

My challenge for you is to be as funny on the platform when people are watching as you are at work or in your kitchen when nobody is watching. That means you must witness your funny behavior away from the platform in order to bring your "organic funny" to the platform. You must objectify your neurosis, categorize your quirks, and capitalize on your insanity.

In other words, you must be able to see yourself as the world sees you. Get this — you are a joke! Everyday you make silly mistakes and do dumb things. In trying to get your act together — it occasionally falls apart. You stumble into tables and chairs and drop things. You miss freeway exits and drop your soda in your lap while talking on the cell phone. You run off to a meeting and forget the contract that you are going to the meeting to get signed. It's true. You are completely fallible and human. It's what makes you real and adorable to those who love you. Embrace it. Learn to love it. It's your funny and nobody can do it quite like you can.

In this chapter we'll focus on eight elements that can make you a funnier speaker and storyteller:

Funny Element #1: The Element of Surprise

Laughter is the result of comedic structure combined with delivery. While delivery is essential, comedic structure is equally important. In fact, when the structure is excellent, almost anyone can deliver that material and get a laugh. The chances are — if you get a laugh when you aren't expecting it, you had naturally good structure and delivery working for you.

Comedy, whether spoken or visual, is usually predicated on the element of surprise. You create patterns in the audience's mind and then trick them. (Don't worry — it's a nice trick!) Crafting logical patterns that have an illogical element — usually at the end, creates surprise. The laugh occurs when the pattern is broken and the audience is surprised. Multiple patterns with multiple surprises linked together can lead to side-slapping humor.

I call laughs "brain farts." A laugh is an unconscious physical impulse that's the result of a surprise. Just as you jump and emit an involuntary sound when you are startled by an unexpected scene in a scary movie, you emit an involuntary sound when you are surprised by an unexpectedly funny line told by a speaker. That sound is the most wonderful noise ever to grace the ears of a speaker or storyteller. It is the celestial sound of laughter.

Go back to the beginning of this chapter where I listed four positive effects that laughter has on learning. Did you laugh or smile when you read the fourth one, "receptivation to stimulosis"? If you did, it was the result of comedy structure. Analyze the sequence of the four bullet points and you will find that the first three all fit together and made logical sense. They were all medically based benefits. At first blush the fourth bullet point sounded like medical terminology as well, until you got to the word retentivitus. At that point, you probably laughed, tittered or at least smiled as you realized you were tricked. By crafting a logical pattern and then inserting an illogical element, I made your brain fart.

So, the first funny element is to surprise your listeners by saying something they don't expect. A great example of this "gotcha" type of humor is this line from comedian Elayne Boosler, "My mother used to say, 'You can eat off my floor.' You can eat off my floor, too. There's thousands of things there." Gotcha.

Funny Element #2: Zinging

You may be wondering, "How do I find these surprising things to say?" I've been studying this process for over thirty years. Do you want to know what I've discovered? It's actually a very logical process.

I call it zinging. To zing is to make a creative leap from one place to another by combining things that don't normally fit together.

Start by looking around you. Look at everything in the room in which you are sitting. If you are in your living room, most of what's in that room belongs there. But what if there was a kangaroo sitting on the couch wearing boxer shorts watching TV with a remote in his hand? The kangaroo wouldn't fit — it doesn't belong. Now, use your imagination. What *could* be in that room that wouldn't belong? What could you do in that room that wouldn't normally be done in that room? Get the idea?

Here is a good analogy for zinging. Let's say you are sitting at a huge kitchen table working on one picture puzzle and your friend is sitting next to you at the same table working on another one. Your puzzle is of an English flower garden and his is of a stealth bomber. You put a number of pieces of your puzzle together and without being aware of it pick up one of the pieces from his puzzle — and it fits together perfectly with your pieces. The puzzle pieces mesh but they don't make any sense together.

I'll never forget the first Woody Allen movie I ever saw. It was back in the late sixties and the movie was *Bananas*. You know how there is always music in the background of a scene? Well Woody Allen is looking for something in the bedroom of a ramshackle house and you hear Mariachi music in the background. He goes over to the closet, as if he's still looking, and when he opens the closet doors the Mariachi trio is sitting in there, playing the background music. It was a visual zinger!

That's zinging. To find your zinger — leap from one logical place to another. Change categories. Go from cars to vegetables — from weather to lumber — from Ritz crackers to Vicks Vapor Rub. Keep your humor antennae up for mismatch possibilities. I'm not suggesting you could become or need to become a stand-up comedian like George Carlin or Ellen Degeneres. I am suggesting you can increase your humor potential and get more laughs in your presentations by including amusing, observational one-liners.

Comedians develop this ability to look for anomalies (defined as a "deviation from the common rule") until it's almost second nature. They are constantly alert to what's inconsistent — what could be a potentially funny mismatch. Here's a perfect example:

> *"At my gym they have free weights, so I took them."*
> — Comedian STEVE Smith

Now, I don't know Steve Smith, but I imagine he was in the gym and either there was a sign that said "Free weights" or one of his buddies said something like, "Let's work out with the free weights." Having a comedic mind, he immediately riffed off the true definition of the word "free" and quipped, "If they're free, let's take 'em." He then crafted that line so he could use it in his act.

Comedian Steven Wright — he of the droll humor and the hair out-to-here — is a master at zingers. His whole act consists of one zinger after another. He'll say something like, "I went by a shop with two signs in the window that said 'Self-Service' and 'Positions Open' — so I went in and hired myself." Another of his classic lines is, "Why are ballerinas on their tippy-toes all the time. Why don't they just hire taller girls?"

Funny Element #3: The Triple

Let's look at a comedy technique called the "triple." In this example, I use a triple to illustrate the difference in personality styles between myself and my stepson Bennett.

> My stepson Bennett and I couldn't be more different. I'm an extrovert — he's an introvert. I'm creative — he's linear. I'm verbal — he's ... an engineer.

Here's another one:

> It's like a cake without frosting. It's like a car without wheels. It's like Bud without — weiser.

In a triple, you use three examples. The first two set a pattern and the third breaks the pattern with a humorous twist. Triples get a laugh because of structure. In the future, regardless of whether you're telling a story or not, when you plan to give one "for instance" to illustrate a point, use three instead. In the first example used above, I always get a good laugh on the word "engineer." Why? Let's break it down.

First, I'm playing off our common knowledge of the personality differences between introverts and extroverts. That example lays the foundation for the whole bit. You have to start with something obvious and easy to grasp. Introverts and extroverts set up the pattern of opposites. "Creative" and "linear" continues the pattern because creative people are known to be non-linear thinkers. Creative and linear are opposites.

Make Your Business Presentations Capture Attention, Inspire Action, and Produce Results

When I say the word "verbal", the logical progression of opposites would be "non-verbal." That is where you break the pattern and get the laugh. By substituting the word "engineer" I have used the ultimate weapon of comedy structure, surprise. It is an illogical, logical substitution. Engineers are usually considered to be non-verbal. Since there are engineers in most business audiences, and since engineers are known to be less vocal and more cerebral than most people, the device works.

> **Note**: Is it politically incorrect to poke fun at engineers? Perhaps. But notice, I'm not saying engineers are bad people. I'm simply playing off the stereotypical concept of an engineer to get a laugh. I've never yet had an engineer come up to me to protest. If you steer clear of everything that may be potentially offensive to people — you'll handcuff your humor. I think it is okay to "spoof" on people once the audience gets to know you. Please re-read what I just said — *once the audience gets to know you.* I wouldn't suggest using a spoof in the first few minutes of your presentation. The jury would still be out — so to speak. The audience may not have warmed to you yet — they might still be trying to decide if they like, trust, and respect you. Later on in your talk, after they've concluded you're a compassionate person who is *not* bashing people, they could take this remark on balance and know it's meant to be humorous, not mean-spirited.

To insure I get the laugh in my Bennett Story I gesture with my hands to indicate the difference between our opposite personalities. On the word "extrovert" I spread my hands wide and on "introvert" I bring them together. On the word "creative" my hands fly all over the place in a random pattern and on the word "linear" I hold my hands in front of me with the palms facing each other about three inches apart. I then move them from right to left as if organizing my socks into neat little columns by the day of the

Incorporate Comedy so Listeners Will Laugh While They Learn

week. On the word "verbal" I bring my fingers close to my mouth and then move them away from my mouth as if to show words flying out. When I pause and then say the word "engineer," I simply drop my hands to my sides.

In the second example — cake without frosting and car without wheels — I once again create a pattern and then break it at the very end. When I say the word "Bud" you're not expecting "weiser." As a matter of fact it takes a moment for your brain to figure out what the heck I'm talking about. Since it's just plain silly — you laugh (or at least I hope you do.)

There are two patterns to be aware of when we're setting up a triple. The first is conceptual and the second is rhythmic. Cake without frosting and car without wheels are both conceptually the same — they're something that doesn't make sense *without* something else. A cake without frosting is only half a cake. A car without wheels is useless. That's the conceptual pattern that sets up the joke.

The rhythmic or musical pattern is equally important. Each triple has its own rhythmic or musical pattern. If you say "cake without frosting" out loud and listen for the rhythm you will hear — bump, bum pum, bum pum. One syllable, two syllables, two syllables. Car without wheels ... bump, bum pum, bum pum. One syllable, two syllables, (sounds like) two syllables. They're rhythmically identical. So the third piece of the triple has to fit in with the music or it won't work.

> Cake without frosting — one syllable, two syllables,
> two syllables
> Car without wheels — one syllable, two syllables, (sounds like)
> two syllables
> Bud without weiser — one syllable, two syllables, two syllables

Work your triples out loud as you're writing them and you'll eventually find the triple that has the right rhythm. You may need to write ten or fifteen combinations until you have your first two ready to go, and then it's time to get creative to find the third one that zings.

Remember, from now on, whenever you say the words "for instance," or "it's like" to use an example to make your point — use three examples instead of one. You'll generate an even bigger laugh because you've just hit a triple.

Funny Element #4: Self-Deprecating Humor

Why not learn now how to become amused with our human foibles? Poking fun at ourselves is called self-deprecating humor. For instance — I'm a pretty average looking guy, 5' 9" and 140 pounds. I can get a laugh by comparing my good looks to Harrison Ford or Tom Cruise when I really remind people of George Carlin or Steve Martin. I also get laughs by comparing my massive (not!) physique to Arnold Schwarzenneger.

This form of humor requires a healthy dose of objective self-esteem. Insecure people can't get away with it because they're too sensitive about themselves. All you have to do is take a look in the mirror and you have material for self-deprecating humor. If you're bald — play off it. If you're tall — make fun of your height. If you're not, well, follow Karl Haas' example.

Have you ever listened to Karl Haas' program on National Public Radio titled *Adventures in Good Music*? Karl plays classical music and gives "behind-the-scenes" information about how our most beloved symphonies were made and why they work. He's renowned for his resonant baritone voice — which in itself is a

Incorporate Comedy so Listeners Will Laugh While They Learn

musical instrument. He was scheduled to speak in Hawaii and a friend of mine who's a big fan of his went to his program. She said the audience was eagerly awaiting this rare opportunity to see their radio hero in person. The emcee gave an impressive introduction and out walked Karl Haas.

The audience gasped out loud. Karl Haas, he of the big deep bass voice, was about five feet tall. He had obviously anticipated this reaction because he leaned out towards the audience with a twinkle in his eye and said, "I didn't know what *you* looked like either." Bravo. My friend had an opportunity to talk with Karl Haas after the program while he was autographing his books. She complimented him on his quip and he said, "Everywhere I go people are startled by my size. I figured I could either be frustrated by it or have fun with it."

Double bravo. That is the essence of self-deprecating humor. If there is something we're sensitive about, it behooves us to lighten up instead of tighten up. By modeling the ability to laugh at ourselves, we give our audience permission to laugh with us (rather than at us).

- Are you a neat freak? Make fun of your tendency to organize.
- Dependably tardy? Make a joke about the one time you were on time.
- A control freak? Have fun with your fondness for delegating.
- A punster? Make a pun about your need to make puns.
- Nine months pregnant? Inquire if anyone has a pickle to go with the ice cream they're serving with dessert.

In the midst of a good story — particularly an edgy, dramatic moment — insert a self-deprecating comment to get a laugh and relieve the tension — then move on. By admitting human error or by allowing yourself to appear faintly ridiculous, you become endearing. What is your particular foible? Exploit it for laughs and your audience will not only laugh with you — they may even learn to laugh at themselves as well.

Funny Element #5: Exaggeration

I have yet to work with a student who wasn't able to get a laugh simply by exaggerating a reaction to something someone else said. In comedic terms, exaggeration simply means you go farther. Take a normal idea, gesture or example and keep going, broaden it, blow it all out of proportion to what is expected.

One of the reasons exaggeration works is because we know the person doesn't really mean what s/he's saying — and therein lies the humor (hah!) For example, Drew Carey says, "I admit it. I'm chunky. In a bathing suit, I look like a Bartlett pear with a rubber band around it." How can that not bring a smile to your face? It's exaggerated, self-deprecating humor — all wrapped up in one. We know he doesn't really look like a Bartlett pear but there's enough truth in his statement to make us chuckle.

To add humor to your humor (yes, that's what I meant to say) you can also use exaggerated gestures. When you tell a joke on yourself, punctuate it by "mugging" to the audience. Roll your eyes. Scrunch up your mouth. Shrug your shoulders. Raise your hands, palms upward and out in the universally recognized gesture of "Why me?" This physical comedy adds to your verbal comedy to make it even funnier.

There are several specific ways you can get laughs with exaggeration. Here are three:

- **Exaggerate by Re-writing History:** I have a saying. "Never let the facts stand in the way of a good story." In other words,

Incorporate Comedy so Listeners Will Laugh While They Learn

there are some facts that are so irrelevant to the reality of the story that if they were changed and the story became funnier — no one would complain. After all, this is storytelling. We're not reporting news from the scene of a crime. If you want laughs, you may need to take some liberties with the truth — what we in show biz call creative license. Remember — we're talking about exaggerating the facts for comedic effect, not changing them completely.

Example: In one of my stories, I talk about the rainy season in Los Angeles and refer to it as Monsoon season. I go into great detail about how when it rains during Monsoon season, the streets become raging rivers. An exaggeration? Yes. But an exaggeration on the truth. Ask anyone who's lived in L.A. for awhile and they'll tell you that they do occasionally get torrential rains that cause the streets to flood. Monsoon season? Not really. But it's a more interesting description and it's close enough to the truth to work.

• **Exaggerate with Bold-Faced Lies and Retractions:** Another form of exaggeration is to tell a bold-faced lie and then scale it back.

Example 1: So I went up to the 12th floor and had a talk with the CEO about my idea for streamlining the production process. (Stammer a bit) Okay well ... the CEO wasn't available so I set an appointment for first thing tomorrow morning. (Stammer some more) Okay well ... first thing tomorrow I'm going to send him an email. If they hire me that is. If I get an interview.

Example 2: I made a million dollars in my first year in real estate. Well I didn't really make that much — I sold that much. Well not quite a million, more like $400,000. And one of those deals was split with two other Realtors. I think I made just under $100,000. I think the exact number was 38, 28, $21,000 . . . something like that. Maybe I'm not cut out for sales.

See what's happening here? The claims are so outrageous that people know you're exaggerating the truth — however this is revealed slowly over the course of the joke so it "dawns" on people as they hear the joke unfold.

- **Exaggerate by "Catastrophizing":** The process of making molehills into mountains is called the art of "catastrophizing" (my word). It is a neurotic backward spiral of exaggerated negativity.

  Jason Alexander's character, George, on the TV program *Seinfeld* is a perfect example of "catastrophizing". He can start with a small problem and turn it into an enormous problem with dire consequences — all in a few sentences. A few sniffles turns into a full-blown cold which morphs into pneumonia — all within seconds and all inside George's obsessive-compulsive mind. A woman casually remarks that she thinks he's funny and he twists it into meaning she thinks he's a clown — not to be taken seriously — an imbecile.

  Woody Allen is another master of exaggerated neurosis. He makes a hypochondriac seem like a positive thinker. As he ponders a problem, he implodes in on himself with self-doubt and insecurity.

  If your story plays on any form of insecurity or self-doubt — exaggerate that insecurity by catastrophizing it. Magnify it all out of proportion. If you get a phone call and your boss wants to see you — make a list of all the reasons it could be bad. After you've complied your list — sequence the reasons from the least bad to the worst and let the intensity build as you get to the end of the list.

Funny Element #6: Irreverence

Comedy often teeters on the precipice of bad taste. Irreverent humor is only for the daring. It may contain slightly off-color language without being vulgar. It is not dirty nightclub humor. It is however, humor that pushes the boundaries.

As you develop your speaking skills and become more comfortable on the platform, you'll feel freer to become irreverent — especially if this is a natural part of your personality, as it is with mine. I think of irreverence as the courage to tell the truth in a funny manner.

Some of you may have been questioning the wisdom of my use of the Streaking Story with business audiences. You may believe it's not appropriate to use in corporate settings. Well, it works for me. Having read this far in the book, you know me well enough by now to know I'm a little bit "out there." That's one of the things that defines me, that's part of my personality. Instead of worrying about whether that story is politically correct, I trust that audiences appreciate someone who's "real" — someone who is himself on stage instead of someone who plays it safe by adopting a beyond-reproach "professional persona." With me, what you see is what you get.

Many presentation coaches and books give a list of subjects to "stay away from" that include everything from politics to blonde jokes to ethnic humor. I understand that. I really do. I also think sometimes we need some shaking up. This joke by Rita Rudner addresses one of the often "forbidden" topics — religion. See for yourself whether this offends you. "The Vatican came down with a new ruling: no surrogate mothers. Good thing they didn't make this rule before Jesus was born."

That observation could rub some people the wrong way. However I think it has the potential to lead to a thought-provoking discussion. You could "riff" off Rudner's joke and then segue into an exchange of ideas on how important it is to consider long-term consequences before making decisions. I think, when used properly, irreverent humor can challenge normal ways of thinking and lead to stimulating, provocative interaction with your audience.

Don't be afraid to be a little irreverent. You'll have to trust me on this. That old expression, "Better safe than sorry," is a death knell for speakers who want to get laughs. In comedy, safe often results in silence — the absence of laughter.

Funny Element #7: Danger

The same people who are sitting in your audience are going to action and horror movies to be scared out of their wits. People like danger — when someone else is doing it. Why do you think all the reality TV shows like *Survivor, American Idol,* and *Fear Factor* are so popular? Audiences love watching other people take chances and put themselves in dangerous situations. They get to feel the fear and elation that the characters experience without any personal jeopardy. It's a vicarious thrill.

These same people love it when you self-reveal with an imbroglio or crucible story. They get to watch as you encounter an embarrassing or painful obstacle and overcome it. It's live theater — Story Theater. The riskier, the better. As you go off on your journey, their adrenalin starts pumping, just like it does in the movies or when their favorite character on *Survivor* is fighting for their figurative life — to not get kicked off the show. That's one of the reasons I feel it's more than okay for you to share the material you initially think you shouldn't. Go out on a limb — that's where the laughs are.

Funny Element #8: Idioms

"Don't make me stop this car." When you hear that phrase, can't you just see your mom or dad sitting in the driver's seat of your old station wagon, yelling at you and your brothers and sisters in the back seat? I can. It's a phrase that has become an idiom in our cultural dialogue. Another one is, "I'll give you something to cry about," which ranks right behind, "You just wait until your father gets home."

Idioms are a great way to connect with your audience. Because of my playful personality, I like to use them as spontaneous ad-libs when joking with my audience. If I have a wise guy in the audience who is having fun bantering back and forth with me, I'll often turn to him and say, "That's it. You're grounded." If two people are talking back and forth when they're supposed to be listening to me, I'll say, "Do I need to separate the two of you?"

In the case of "Don't make me stop this car," you can use it to make a point about the need for people to resolve conflict quickly in the workplace. I imagine a story about two people who have different learning styles or different personality profiles who must work together, but who don't see eye-to-eye. A project is suffering because the two of them spend more time bickering than moving forward. The image of a supervisor saying to them, "Don't make me stop this car," amplifies how childish their behavior is and how they need to grow up and get along. If presented with a nod and a wink, it will garner a laugh while it skewers bad behavior.

Idioms are effective because they are part of the universal psyche.

In order to use them in a story, you must understand your audience. An idiom that works in the United States probably won't work overseas. Some idioms that work in Tennessee and Kentucky may not work elsewhere in the country because they are regional idioms. I know this because I've done Story Theater Retreats and seminars all over the world and I've heard some "doozies."

To make use of idioms in your stories, probe your childhood memory for the phrases you heard again and again. There are also resource books at your library or favorite bookstore in the reference section on idioms and common phrases. A couple of my favorites are *2715 One-Line Quotations for Speakers, Writers, & Raconteurs* by Edward Murphy and *Peter's Quotations: Ideas For Our Time* by Laurence J. Peter. Check them out.

There are a number of ways to insert idioms into your story. Here are a few to get you started:
- Have another character say an idiom to you in conversation. Re-write history if necessary.
  - You know Jenna; you can't turn back the clock.
- Use one as an example to explain your behavior
  - I finally figured out what my problem was. I'd always heard that "Practice makes perfect"— but it's not true. Not if you don't know how to practice. Then a coach said to me — "Perfect practice makes for perfect performance." He taught me how to practice the right way so I could perform the right way.
- Remember one from childhood in the midst of trying to solve an adult problem
  - Remember that old saying, "It's not whether you win or lose, it's how you play the game?" I think the reason I'm so unhappy is it's become all about winning or losing for me. As a salesman, all I think about is the next contract. I'm not even happy when I win anymore because I hate what I do. That old saying is true. It *is* how you play the

game. I'm either going to get a new job or figure out how I can start enjoying this one.

One Final Thought About Humor

Remember, you don't have to go for guffaws. Gentle humor works too. People love Bill Cosby because he tells what I call "story humor." He doesn't throw out one-liners — he simply describes and relives the warm, funny moments we all experience in life. If you have kids, I guarantee you, you have material. When they say something funny, write it down! My friend was sharing dinner with her two sons and they were discussing weekend plans. Her teenager looked a little distracted so she asked, "Tom, are you listening to me?" "Sure Mom," he replied. "You have my undevoted attention." Now, that's not a side-splitter. However, if you're giving a presentation on customer service, you could share that with your audience and then segue right into the point that we're often so busy we give customers our undevoted attention — instead of our undivided attention.

Next time you and your co-workers share a laugh about something that goes wrong, write it down, and then immediately start thinking how you could weave that into your next presentation. If you "mine" the amusing situations that happen to and around you on and off the job, you'll have enough funny material to get laughs every time you speak.

Build Drama to Keep Your Audience on the Edge of Their Seats

C omedy is big — drama is small. Remember that statement? Think about Jim Carrey for a moment. He became the highest paid actor in movies on the strength of his outrageous performances in the two *Ace Ventura* movies. *Dumb and Dumber* was more of the same. His physical schtick is so over the top it constantly surprises and delights. It's the same kind of slapstick comedy many of us grew up watching. He is a brilliant physical comedian in the mold of The Three Stooges, Abbott and Costello, Lucille Ball, Red Skelton, Jerry Lewis, and Carol Burnett.

Now think of Jim Carrey in *The Truman Show* and *The Majestic*. While that big goofy smile of his was still in evidence, he toned down the energy level of his performance for dramatic effect. He shifted his energy from outward to inward. The gross physical elements faded away so as not to distract from the inner process. His ability to go big for comedy and small for drama illustrates the juxtaposition between comedy and drama.

Drama is about telling the truth. It requires that we remove the mask of superficiality and appropriately reserved social behavior and let people see and feel our most intimate private behavior. It is about giving voice to the inner world of thoughts and feelings.

Make Your Business Presentations Capture Attention, Inspire Action, and Produce Results

Go Deep

The drama in your stories is drawn from when you encounter an obstacle. In performance it is often portrayed in stillness — with little or no movement. The language you use when crafting this moment in your script is critical. You must go back in time to the exact moment you encountered the crisis and "go deep." Ask yourself, "What was the truth of that moment? What thoughts ran through my head? What emotions did I encounter? What fears did I face?"

Write out your answers to these questions and anything else you can remember. Record every sensation, feeling, fear, concern. Worry about what to do with them later. The goal at this point is just to remember as much as you can. Leave nothing out. Plumb the depths of that experience for possible meaning. What did you learn? Was this moment a repeat of similar crises in the past — the culmination of a pattern of behavior that always resulted in the same situation?

Once you have purged your mind of every emotion surrounding that event, choose the most profound meaning and decide upon the lesson you wish to share. Once you've identified the dramatic moment you want to feature — your goal is to reenact it in a way the audience sees, feels, and experiences that moment with you.

A coaching client, Marcia Steele, told the story of going for her annual physical. While doing a routine examination of her breasts, her doctor noticed something. Marcia described how the doctor, without saying anything, moved her hands from her breast up to her armpit. At that moment in the story, Marcia froze and stopped speaking. After a few moments of silence, she lifted her head and said simply, "My entire body went limp. I realized they don't check your lymph nodes unless they suspect — cancer. This was not good. This was not — good."

Build Drama to Keep Your Audience on the Edge of Their Seats

It was a brutally honest moment of truth. Notice that when Marcia described the doctor shifting her hands up to her armpit, she froze and stopped speaking. Moments of truth like that provide the perfect opportunity for a technique called Hold The Moment. By not talking for those few seconds, she built the tension and anxiety in us just as it must have built in her as she waited for the doctor to deliver her diagnosis. In a way, we were waiting for the diagnosis along with Marcia.

From there, Marcia went on to recount how she had battled the cancer and won. She talked us through each setback, each challenge. We were there when she endured weeks of radiation. We were there when she went through chemotherapy. And we were there when she described how the chemotherapy had caused her to lose her hair and, in a magnificently bold gesture that was met with thunderous applause, she swept off her wig and revealed her bald head!

Marcia dared to reveal her innermost private thoughts during a dramatic event in her life. She dared to go deep, and in doing so, took all of us with her. We felt the anguish of her pain and the exhilaration of her victory. There was no one in that audience who was not moved by her brave story and performance. It was a masterful example of how a willingness to explore the depths of human drama can pay off for the speaker and the audience.

Learn from her example. Don't be afraid of the pathos in your story. Portray it with humility and dignity. To do so requires that you go deep when recalling and writing the story, so you bring back the colorful language that will do justice to what you experienced. That language will ground you in the experience and remind you of what you were feeling so you can re-enact the emotion of the moment for the audience. Remember, acting is simply replicating reality. The beauty of storytelling is that your audience can extract the lesson vicariously from your painful experience.

They don't have to go through it themselves — they can learn from your dramatic example.

Turn Your Dramatic Story Into A Set Piece

Once you develop your dramatic story, you'll want to practice it until it becomes a "set piece." By that I mean it will be scripted, memorized, and performed almost identically every time you tell it. Trust me. This doesn't mean you go on automatic pilot and tell it robotically or mechanically. Just the opposite. The purpose of spending so much time crafting it until it's "just right" is to guarantee you can deliver it with maximum impact every time you speak.

You see — I come from a theater background. I had the privilege to perform Shakespearean plays where the language was dazzling, the characters were intricate, and the plot development was brilliant. Each actor had the same lines and actions every night and it never got boring.

Some speakers tell me, "I'm at my best when I'm winging it." I agree that spontaneity can be a good thing. Responding in the moment to audience feedback and events in the room is an essential part of speaking. However, an entire speech based on impromptu extemporization won't reach the dramatic heights of an intricately crafted and performed set piece. I think it's best to balance spontaneity with stories that have been crafted and scripted for maximum impact.

If you want to attain a level of "consistent brilliance" (those are the operative words), it's in your best interest to develop your material and practice it again and again until you master it. The more you rehearse your dramatic stories, the better they get, not the other way around. The tenth time you tell a story, you start noticing the

Build Drama to Keep Your Audience on the Edge of Their Seats

little things that make it more effective. You discover that by pausing before a punch line, you get a bigger laugh. You discover that drawing out a particular word lends it more impact. You find that changing a phrase so it rhymes with a phrase in the previous sentence sets up a resonating rhythm that produces a more powerful Phrase That Pays.

Telling a dramatic story the same way every time doesn't make it boring — it makes it better. Instead of being anxious because you don't know if the story will work, you can relax because you know it's going to work. You can be confident because you've "been here, told this."

Take Time To Shine

Some speakers tell me they don't have the time to work on their stories. Others tell me, "I'm doing fine with my stories the way they are." Well, that's okay — but are you content to stay okay? Why not be the best you can be instead of just being okay? It's time to invest the time to shine when:

- Being okay is no longer okay
- The regret of falling short of excellence becomes too painful
- Winging it gets you lost in the woods — again
- You witness brilliance in another storyteller and want it for yourself

At a National Speakers Association convention, a tall southern belle (former third runner-up in the Miss America contest) took the stage. She proceeded to do what she does best, tell stories. At least that's what we call it when a speaker spins yarns. We call it "telling a story." But to say that Jeanne Robertson simply tells stories would be a disservice to her skill and talent. She is a master of timing, inflection, body language, voice, structure, and delivery.

She is an actress, comedienne, and brilliant storyteller all rolled into one. She doesn't just tell a story, she re-lives a story.

Jeanne had us on the floor with her signature "baton" story. You didn't just hear and see her story, you participated in it. We were right there when, in the talent part of the contest, she threw up her baton — and it didn't come down. We were howling and holding our sides as Jeanne decided to continue her baton routine — without the baton. Jeanne is so good at what she does, she makes it seem effortless. Those who know her though will tell you that producing such mastery is far from effortless. Jeanne has a reputation for spending hours, weeks, sometimes months preparing a single keynote. She rehearses every move, memorizes every line, and perfects every nuance. Why? Jeanne wouldn't think of being less than her best. She takes her craft seriously and won't settle for anything but excellence. As a result, Jeanne is one of the most successful motivational humorists in the United States. She deserves to be.

Watching Jeanne tell a story is like listening to Celine Dion sing a ballad, like watching Kobe Bryant drive to the basket, like watching Dustin Hoffman disappear into a character. You are simultaneously aware of two things. Number one: the performer is loaded with talent. Number two: they've worked very hard to be that good. Celine Dion practices singing every day of her life. Kobe Bryant has taken thousands of shots with a basketball. Dustin Hoffman has studied acting for years and has immersed himself in his craft. Their talent may seems effortless. Their technique may be invisible. But that's because they've worked hard and committed themselves to being the best they could be.

Here are four things you can do to be the best speaker you can be:

1. Schedule at least 10 hours over the next 30 days to work on your story.
2. Work in 30 to 60 minute chunks of time.

Build Drama to Keep Your Audience on the Edge of Their Seats

3. Write your story, word for word, and rehearse it out loud at least ten times.
4. Conduct at least ten "walk and talk" rehearsals at home before you get up in front of your audience.

> *"One important key to success is self-confidence. An important key to self-confidence is preparation."*
>
> — tennis player ARTHUR ASHE, JR.

Excellence does not come without a price. That price is setting aside time to perfect your craft. The good news is, if you dedicate yourself to developing your dramatic story, if you invest time to shine, your light can illuminate your audience. You will exponentially increase your ability to positively influence your listeners. It's worth it.

PART FIVE

Put Your Story
On Its Feet

CHAPTER 17

Move It or Lose 'Em with Show and Tell

The form of storytelling I believe works best in live performance is a combination of SHOW (act) and TELL (content).
Instead of just narrating stories as past events, you will re-enact
parts of them so they come alive. You'll SHOW the action and
interaction parts of the story and TELL the narrative parts. The
SHOW part is the "theater" in The Story Theater Method.
Speakers who SHOW and TELL are more effective than those who
just narrate.

My challenge with the way most speakers approach storytelling is
that they just talk. They stand still, and with very little movement,
explain what happened. They rely on the words to do all the work.

As explained earlier in this book, we need to provide audio, visual,
and kinesthetic stimulation for our audience. These Story Theater
techniques are designed to accomplish just that. When you SHOW
and TELL, you bring in all the preferred learning styles and tap
into something primal that goes back to early childhood.

Imagine it's bedtime and you are five years old. Did your parents
bribe you with the promise to read a story if you brushed your
teeth and got in bed? Do you remember snuggling up close to your
mom or dad, listening to the lulling cadence of their voice, and
falling asleep to the sound of "Once Upon a Time"? Those were

charmed moments, and for most of us, they were how we acquired a life-long love of stories. Those stories of far-away places, long-long-ago, were where we first learned about the power of language to transport us.

You have the same power to transport your adult audiences. When you tell a story with the techniques we cover in this book, something magical happens. The people who are distracted start paying closer attention. The people with pens in their hand, furiously taking notes, look up from their workbooks (or laptops), set their pens down or take their fingers away from the keyboard, and lean back in their chairs. Their preoccupation becomes enchantment. They become like little children, open and receptive to listen and learn. It's an amazing phenomenon.

Get IN to Your Story

In the theater, the actors on stage create an imaginary reality. Their goal is to act as if everything they are doing is for the first time. Their goal is to re-create the reality of the moment. That is what you will do with specifically chosen moments in your story. Those moments are called IN moments. Rather than using past tense narrative language, you will step IN to a present tense re-creation of a moment in time.

Rather than talking about what you did — you do it. For example, if you just learned you were accepted to a Masters degree program, you react as if you just heard the news. You don't tell the audience what you did in response to that news — you *do* what you did when you received that news. You re-feel the emotion, which produces the thought, which produces the action. You pump your fist, jump for joy, or shout out loud. An action is better than a thousand words.

Move It or Lose 'Em with Show and Tell

If you're telling a story about standing in line at the grocery store at 5:45 p.m., you act out being in that grocery line. You crane your neck to see how long the line is. You feel the frustration of running late, knowing the lone checker is going to take forever. As you feel your frustration, your mouth probably turns up in a scowl. You may even let out an exasperated sigh without consciously thinking about it. As you get more and more anxious, your audience gets more and more anxious. As you start tapping your foot, looking at your watch, and doing a little "hurry up" shuffle, your audience gets antsy too. Finally, you lose all patience and yell out, *"My ice cream is melting. Can we get a checker on aisle three?!"* Your audience bursts out laughing.

Their laugh was not intellectual. You transported them right into that grocery store with you — and they loved it. You created dramatic tension and then released it and they had no choice but to laugh. Why? You took the time to craft and rehearse your story and then you performed it with energy and commitment. You created a moment of theater.

Use the Four Types of Language to Replicate Reality

Wouldn't you agree, the best actors don't look like they're acting? Their technique becomes invisible. We know intellectually that those are actors up on the screen or stage performing a script—but we "lose sight" of that and become immersed in the story. It's called the "suspension of disbelief." The audience chooses to suspend their reality in favor of the imaginary one being portrayed in front of them.

In order to make it easy for your audience to participate in this imaginary reality, employ the following four types of language.

1. Verbal Language

The foundation of your speech is your language — the vocabulary of your content. It is the pillar upon which your entire presentation rests. In Part Four we covered how you can use the thesaurus to generate original words that make your material come alive. We covered how you can create powerful Phrases That Pay so your message is more memorable. If however, the *delivery* of those colorful words is less than captivating, they alone will not hold your audience's attention or get your message across.

2. Vocal language

The emotional inflection your voice gives to your carefully selected words is your single most influential vehicle of communication. Your modulation, volume, tone, and tempo can either caress a word and make it full of compassion or force out a word and make it full of spite. Take the word "Mother." If you were lucky enough to have a good relationship with your mother, you probably say that word in a round, rich tone that connotes affection. On the other hand, if you had a less than favorable experience with your mother, you may say that word so it comes out sounding like a curse. How many times have we heard, "It's not what we say, it's how we say it." Actually, it's *both* what we say and how we say it that determines whether audiences choose to tune us in or tune us out.

3. Physical language

This includes everything you do with your body — from the way you stand to the way you walk. It encompasses gestures, eye contact, facial expressions, posture, and movement. Your body language needs to be congruent with your content to count. If there is a mismatch between your words and your actions, people will believe your actions. Remember the expression "Actions don't lie?" If you say, "I'm glad to be here today" but you are standing stiffly at the lectern clenching it with both hands — those words will be disbelieved. Body is language. Use it.

The good news is, if you commit to "throwing yourself" into your presentation with energy and enthusiasm, your body language will take care of itself. If you choose to tower instead of cower; if you hold your head up and vow to yourself that you will exude confidence, your body language will follow your command. If however, you disconnect from your body and lock down on your emotions in an effort not to feel fear, you will feel numb, awkward and unnatural. Your audience will have a hard time relating to you because you're so obviously uncomfortable with your body.

4. Emotional language

This is simply the ability to access and express how you felt at the time — and how you feel now. As said before, if instead of just *talking* about what happened (which keeps you distant and removed from the event) — you actually go back to that event in your mind and re-experience it — you won't be able to help yourself from re-feeling the emotions of that moment. And, as you tap into how you felt, whether it was anger or elation, that emotional energy will permeate the room. Immersing yourself in the emotion of the event you are describing is contagious. Emotional language, combined with the other three languages, is what brings you and the audience together as one.

Bring Yourself to the Platform

The four types of language I've just outlined are all organic forms of expression. So why is it necessary for me to emphasize (and re-emphasize) their use during a speech or presentation? Because many speakers are like my coaching client Leslie, who didn't know how to be herself while giving a presentation. Many novice speakers try to become somebody else — or they try to disappear and become nobody.

Leslie began her story with her arms hanging limply by her sides, speaking in a timid, listless voice. When she came to a point in the story where her supervisor had complimented her in front of her peers on a job well done, she told us she had been ecstatic. Her body however displayed no emotion. I asked Leslie to repeat the line again, and this time to act out what it means to feel ecstatic. This time when she talked about how delighted she was to receive this public praise, she gave a little wriggle with her shoulders and her arms and fingers flew up in excitement. Her whole face became animated and lit up. She even took in a deep breath through her nose that signified joyous excitement. She looked and sounded ecstatic.

Afterward, I asked how that felt. "It felt natural," she replied. "That's what I'm usually like. I'm not a stiff person at all," she continued. "I'm only stiff when I speak, and I hate being that way."

I contend that the journey to becoming a confident speaker is nothing less than a journey back to self. If you have an irrational fear of public speaking, it is important to realize that what you fear is inside, not outside. What is needed is to get out of your own way, and be yourself.

I told Leslie, "You don't need to learn how to gesture — you gesture just fine already. You don't need to learn how to modulate your voice — you modulate just fine already. You don't need to learn how to speak more eloquently — you speak just fine already. If during the course of a normal day, you speak with natural vocal inflection and use gestures, you can do it when you're giving a presentation. You have everything you need to be the speaker you want to be — right there, right now," — and I pointed to her head and heart.

Move It or Lose 'Em with Show and Tell

It was an epiphany for Leslie that she didn't have to do anything "special" — she just had to bring herself to the platform. Who you are in "real-life" is who you ought to be "up there."

Get Out of Your Own Way

Bill Cosby said, "People say, 'God will find a way.' God can't find a way if you're in the way." Here are some things to STOP doing so you too can get out of your own way and start speaking naturally, using all four types of language.

- STOP trying to speak like a university professor. Write a speech that sounds like you.
- STOP thinking about your hands. Let your gestures reflect what you're saying.
- STOP worrying about your voice. Inflection is connected to emotion. Feel something.
- STOP standing still like a lifeless mummy. Walk and talk like you normally do. Use your body to communicate how you feel.

The rest of the book details how you can put your story on its feet, integrate your "organic" vocal, verbal, physical, and emotional forms of expression, and release the actor inside you. You will learn a variety of ways to be the confident, convincing speaker you've always yearned to be.

Who is the best speaker you've ever seen in action? What was it specifically about that person that caused you to respect him or her so much? Remember exactly where you were, what s/he talked about, the details of the stories, the reason s/he had such an impact on you. Without even knowing who that person is, I can almost guarantee that whatever they did that was so powerful will be covered in these next few chapters. Read 'em and reap.

CHAPTER 18

Use Physical Language so Participants See What You're Saying

Every story has action, reaction and interaction. Stuff happens. You pick up the phone and learn that your father is in the hospital. Your computer goes down in the middle of a PowerPoint presentation. The zipper on your skintight leather pants breaks just as you're about to step on the dance floor during your high school reunion.

Those are the obstacles — the challenges. Without them, there's no story. As you vividly describe encountering and overcoming the obstacle, it is natural for your audience to see you doing it in their mind's eye. They feel your distress at hearing that your dad is sick (and maybe think about a time they got a similar call with bad news.) They see your computer going down during the presentation and feel the same sense of frustration you felt. They empathize with your embarrassment about being "too big for your britches." That's the inherent power of story — it's interactive.

In The Story Theater Method, when there is an important action, reaction or interaction, you will Step IN and SHOW that moment instead of describing it.

The Difference Between an IN and an OUT Moment

An OUT moment is any time during the telling of a story when you are speaking to the audience.

During an OUT Moment:

- You are addressing the audience
- You are making eye contact with the audience
- You are speaking in a past tense narrative voice

An IN moment is an acting moment. During an IN moment you portray an action, reaction or interaction from your story as it happened. In an imaginary sense, you are no longer a speaker in a room with an audience.

During an IN Moment:

- You are not addressing the audience directly
- You are not making eye contact with the audience
- You are in an imaginary reality in real time
- You are speaking in present tense language, or
- Your eyes focus IN while your language remains past tense narrative
- You are showing private behavior
- You are revealing private thoughts
- You are feeling real or approximately real emotion
- You are re-enacting a moment from your story

Actors in a play are constantly IN. Except in rare cases where the script calls for an actor to address the audience, the actors are IN an imaginary reality. The audience watches them through the "fourth wall." If for instance, a scene from the play takes place in a living room, the actor's reality is that they are in a room with four walls. The set is made up of three of those walls, the back and two sides. The "fourth wall" is invisible. It is the one in between the audience and the actors. The audience peers through the imaginary fourth wall.

During an IN moment in your story, you become like an actor in a play. The audience becomes like a silent partner for the duration of the IN moment. You SHOW as well as TELL what happened.

Remember Leslie and her reaction to being complimented by her supervisor? Her IN moment simply consisted of SHOWING her real reaction. It lasted all of three or four seconds. But that simple moment of humanity and reality made all the difference. That simple autobiographical moment, coupled with her re-imagining what it was like to receive that praise, is what Story Theater is all about. Moments.

Show Private Behavior — Reveal Private Thoughts

Think of an IN moment this way. All day long, in everything that you do, you are living a constant IN moment. The actions, reactions and interactions you have are the stuff of IN moments. They consist of your thoughts, feelings, and behavior. They reveal you when you are not in front of an audience — the real you, ordinary you, extraordinary you.

Some of the behavior you show during an IN moment is private behavior. It's how you act when no one is watching. It occurs most naturally in your story when you encounter and overcome the obstacle. As you confront the problem and react to its severity, you show private behavior.

As you ponder your next move in how to overcome the obstacle, you talk out loud — expressing the thoughts that are going through your head. You may be thinking (and thus saying):

- "I never should have done that."
- "Why does this always happen to me?"
- "I wish I could take that back."
- "What the heck am I going to do now?"
- "I can't believe this is happening."
- "I don't know what to do."

These are the kind of "self-talk" responses we commonly have when something happens to us in real life. And these are exactly the private thoughts we're going to articulate in our speech so our audience can see into our minds and know what we were thinking when this event happened. Reproducing these inner thoughts and private behaviors for an audience is called acting. In Story Theater, it's called an IN moment. When you Step IN, your audience goes IN to your imaginary reality with you.

Example

Stacy James was telling the story of her experience competing in the New York City marathon. She is a wheelchair racer and this was her first marathon. Although she'd competed in wheelchair races before, none of them had been as long as this.

Her first IN moment was at the beginning of the race when she lined up on the starting line with 30 other wheelchair racers. She looked around and described the scene. Her language was present tense "self talk." It was as if she were verbalizing out loud what she was thinking.

> "Look at all these wheelchairs. Some of the chairs are deco-rated with balloons and banners. This is wild. I've never seen so many people. Look at that guy in a Superman outfit. And there's Spiderman. This is insane. Now I know why this marathon is so popular, it's a party."

Use Physical Language so Participants See What You're Saying

Her next IN moment was when the gun went off to start the race. As she acted out pushing the wheels of her wheelchair forward, she looked out in front of her at the Verrazano Bridge.

"Oh my gosh. Mary didn't tell me that the race starts out uphill on a bridge that's over a mile long. Oh well, I can do it. I've been training for months."

Later in the story came the most powerful IN moment of the story. In The Nine Steps of Story Structure this is step four where you encounter the obstacle. Stacy's obstacle was "hitting the wall" at 22 miles, which for runners means your body has run out of energy and you are completely exhausted. This happened to Stacy in the late afternoon in Harlem. The wind was picking up, it was getting cold, and the thousands of cheering onlookers had discarded their posters and gone home. She was in the back of the pack and most of the competitors had passed by hours ago. Stacy was in terrible pain, wheeling down a street filled with trash, in a rather isolated and scary neighborhood. She felt alone, depressed, and afraid. Her IN moment consisted of re-enacting that moment of despair.

"Where am I? Look at all this trash. I'm rolling over drink cups and food and getting it all over my hands ... Eucch ... it's sticky ... I'm so tired ... I don't know if I can do this. It's cold; the leaves are blowing all over the place. Where did everybody go? Look at this mess. Everyone just threw their support signs on the ground and went home. Now I'm rolling over them."

(As Stacy said this she stopped — and looked down on the ground to the right) "Look at this one, 'Go Larry.' There's another one, 'Go Harry.' I guess Larry and Harry must have run by already. (Stacy wheels forward — looking down to left) There's one I can use. 'Never give up.' Hah! That's a good one. Easy for people to say standing on the side — you gave up and went home. (She slumps in her chair — depressed and alone) I've can't believe I have four more miles. At this rate, it will take me two more hours. (Hold the Moment transition) Wait a minute. I've already come 22 miles. I didn't come this far not to finish and get a medal. (With that, Stacy sits up — positions her hands on the wheels) One more push. (She does so) One more push. Never give up. Never give up."

Eleven hours after she began the New York Marathon, Stacy crossed the finish line. She was almost two weary to lift her arms in celebration. Her last IN moment was crossing the finish line, slumping over in exhaustion, a weary but supremely triumphant smile on her tired face.

Because of the IN moments in her story, Stacy took us with her into the experience. It was always a powerful story, and with these Story Theater techniques, it was even more so. The key difference is that she didn't just talk about her obstacle — she encountered it again. As she hit the wall, we did too. As she proudly crossed the finish line, we were right there with her. By stepping IN, she allowed us to see, feel and experience that marathon as if we were striding alongside her. To read Stacy's inspirational story, please visit her website, www.WalkingVictorious.com.

Stacy's IN moments contained:
- Action and activity — rolling her wheelchair, looking down at the signs
- Emotion — "Oh my gosh, it's sticky, I'm tired"
- Verbalized self-talk — "I don't know if I can do this"
- Multiple imagined realities — looking at the bridge, rolling along the littered street
- Private behavior — feeling exhausted, fatigue, willpower
- Emotion — determination "I didn't come this far to not finish"
- Her Phrase That Pays — "Never Give Up"

Use Physical Language so Participants See What You're Saying

Make Motion Pictures

If you had been in Stacy's audience, witnessing her behavior, listening to the despair in her voice, and feeling her frustration, you might have experienced one or more of the following sympathetic responses:

- You became her in the wheelchair
- You felt pain, fear and frustration
- You became another wheelchair racer in the marathon
- You stood on the sidelines cheering her on
- You were Harry or Larry
- You tossed down your sign and went home when it got cold
- You were Spiderman

Whatever you felt, the amazing thing is that you became part of the action. Your challenge, as a speaker, is to keep your audience involved when all they are really doing is sitting there, watching and listening to you. When you tell a story as comprehensively as Stacy did, using all four types of language, your audience will feel as if they are inside the story.

Consider your experience in the movie theater. It's a dramatic moment in an *Indiana Jones* film. Harrison Ford is about to go into an underground cave where the bad guys are. His gun is drawn. Sweat drips down his face. The cave is dark. Water is dripping from some unknown source. As he moves cautiously around a corner, a rat scurries past, inches from his face. You jump in your seat. As the suspense builds, you move and fidget in your chair. You tighten your fists and lick your lips. Your mouth is parched. You reach for your drink.

Hey! What's with you? What in the heck is going on? You're sitting in an air-conditioned movie theater in Columbus, Ohio, for crying out loud. It's not real. It's a movie. Why the parched lips?

Try this one — Julia Roberts in *Erin Brockovich*. She's in the car driving home in the dark of the night from a long day taking depositions from plaintiffs. She's on the cell phone with her boyfriend who is taking care of her kids while she works. She asks him how his day went. He tells her that her youngest daughter spoke her first words today. Tears stream down Julia's face as she feels the remorse and emptiness of missing her daughter's first words. Unless you're a heartless slab of granite, tears stream down your face too.

Once again I ask, "What's going on? Why the tears, big fella?" I'll tell you why — because you felt your own remorse and emptiness. You're not crying for Julia — you're crying for yourself. Every emotion you're feeling is yours, not the actor's. It's called transference or — as I called it way back in Part One — a sympathetic experience.

This experience happens most powerfully to audience members during the IN moment. The storyteller paints the picture with well-chosen words and then transforms the picture into a motion picture by replicating the actions, reactions and interactions inherent to the story. The result? You've got a hit in which everyone gets his or her emotional money's worth.

Percentage of IN to OUT Moments in a Story

In the past, your entire story was most likely spoken OUT as a past tense narrative. From this day forward, most of your story will still be OUT to the audience. The IN moments are spice. They are not to be overdone. Think of IN moments as cayenne pepper. Too much is too much.

At first as you are getting used to this new concept of IN moments,

Use Physical Language so Participants See What You're Saying

strive for 20% IN and 80% OUT. Depending on the story, the most you want is 40% IN and 60% OUT.

You don't have to follow these percentages exactly. It's just that coaching clients often ask me what proportion of their talks should be IN and OUT, and I thought you might appreciate having a formula as a guideline. With the right balance, you can move your audience, if not the world.

Criteria for an IN Moment

An IN moment will always be an action, reaction or interaction between you and someone else. These are the moments you disappear into the voice of your head and talk out loud what was happening internally during the scene. Not all actions, reactions and interaction should become IN moments however. Use the following guidelines to choose your IN moments carefully.

Guidelines for an IN moment:

- The main action or activity of your story
- An important conversation between two people
- A critical telephone conversation
- A reaction to something you heard or saw
- A transition moment when you are alone making a decision
- When you encounter the obstacle
- Moments of tension, anxiety or fear
- Moments of elation, celebration and victory
- Moments of anger, frustration or resolve
- Embarrassing moments
- Tender private moments
- Any moment that has dramatic or comedic potential

The Exception to the Rule

When you are OUT, you will always be speaking about what happened in the past tense narrative voice.

> "Back in 1998, I *was* attending a graduate program. The teacher *was* a woman who really worked us hard. Her classes *were* intense and her expectations *were* very high"

When you are IN, you will *most often* be speaking about what is happening in present tense language.

> "This *is* ridiculous. How can they expect me to get this done by end of day? I *am* running late as it is. *I'm* going to miss the party at Steve's for Emily. That's okay. Emily will understand."

Occasionally, during an IN moment, you will use past tense narrative to describe what you are seeing or experiencing. Your body language and eyes however, clearly communicate that you are IN. For instance, let's say you walk into a huge home improvement warehouse store. You're shopping for a sink for your kitchen.

As you act out walking down the main aisle, your eyes are scanning the signs up above for the plumbing department. Your body language communicates to the audience that you are IN the imaginary reality of the home improvement store. It is clear that you are not a speaker in a conference room, but are acting out the moment. Your language however is past tense.

> "I *was* walking around in this mammoth warehouse with 90 foot high ceilings looking for the plumbing department. (Scan the aisles for signs) High overhead, at the end of each aisle *were* signs. (Move head from sign to sign) Electrical, lawn and garden, paint, plumbing. Then I *saw* it — clear on the other end of the store. Figures. So I *went* out to the

parking lot, (Take a few steps and then stop) got back in my car and *drove* down a block or two to the other entrance — just kidding. Might as well though. Later that day I *arrived* at my destination and there they *were*, halfway down the plumbing aisle — kitchen sinks."

This is the exception to the rule. Some IN moments simply don't work as well with present tense language as they do with narrative past tense language. Use your best judgment.

Transitions

The transitions from OUT to IN — from narration to action — can be tricky. If stepping IN and stepping OUT is going to work you have to be completely comfortable with your material — to know it inside and out. The more you practice, the more natural it will become. Think of these as dance steps — like the Rumba. At first they will be robotic, but with practice, over time, you'll be able to dance fluidly and with style.

Practice by rehearsing on your feet. Run the IN and OUT sequence five times in a row. It's hard to ad-lib stepping IN and stepping OUT. In time however, it will become effortless. You'll get so comfortable acting out little moments you'll instinctively know when to SHOW — to step IN — and when to TELL — to step OUT.

One Moment at a Time

Caution: We have been talking about how to craft and deliver a powerful story. Here's a challenge for you. Since you know what's coming in your story, it can be tempting to foreshadow your ending. If you know bad news is coming, it's easy for your anticipation of that to creep into

> your voice and the audience will sense something awful is
> about to happen. Don't give in to this temptation.

Remember what we said earlier about the power of surprise? It's
the key to comedy and drama. You don't want to go to a movie
when you already know the ending. It takes all the fun out of it.

The challenge is to play one moment at a time. In an IN moment,
you're not supposed to know the next line until you arrive at it.
You are always in the present, never knowing what lies ahead (kind
of like life!) That's why, when delivering your stories, it's important
to slow down. Instead of rushing ahead to a foregone conclusion,
take it one … moment … at … a … time.

Body Language, Movement and Gestures

In theater, movement around the stage is called blocking or staging. The director tells the actors when to move from place to place
and where to stand or sit. In dance, prescribed movement is called
choreography. As a speaker, you need to be your own director and
choreographer and stage your movement so it reflects your narrative at that point.

If you say:

- I bent down to pick up my bag — bend down and pick up an
  imaginary bag
- I stubbed my toe on the corner of the desk — stub your toe
  and feel the pain
- I walked over and opened the door — walk a few steps and
  pantomime opening a door

Want to know how big or small to make your actions — how
grandiose or demure you should act? Follow this maxim: comedy

Use Physical Language so Participants See What You're Saying

is big — drama is small. Yes, this is a generalization, and yes there are exceptions, but this rule of thumb works most of the time.

COMEDY: The bigger your movements and gestures are, the bigger the laughs will be. I've found that audiences respond in direct proportion to the scope of the exaggeration, volume, and intensity in which the comedy is delivered. Wild and crazy comedy gets wild and crazy laughs. Think Robin Williams. Small and subtle comedy gets small and subtle laughs. Think Bob Newhart.

DRAMA: For serious moments — confine your movements and gestures to what is realistic. One of my students created an IN moment where she went online and performed a Google search. Her initial performance was implausible because she mimicked typing with her fingers pounding away on a gigantic keyboard with a pretend computer screen that must have been three-feet across. She was over-acting. I suggested she type as if her hands were on a real keyboard and to shrink the screen down to real size. After she did it the second time, she was amazed that her toned-down movements were easily discernable from the audience's perspective.

I once read an interview with the actor Ed Harris about what it was like acting in movies. His comment, and I'm paraphrasing, is that acting for the camera is fun because all you have to do is think and feel and the camera picks it up. Smart man.

The next time you watch a serious movie or TV program, observe how small the gestures and facial expressions are at dramatic moments. Notice how the vocal language, facial expressions and gestures flow from intention — from a sense of purpose. When you feel the emotions and think the thoughts appropriate to what is going on in the moment, your performance will flow from you as a natural extension of what's going on *in* you in that moment.

Try the following exercise to practice what it's like to have your emotions flow from the inside out. When done right, this produces an outward physical expression that telegraphs to others what's going on in you.

Imagine someone in public has just embarrassed you. Perhaps you're overweight and someone made a cruel remark about your size. Maybe you don't have a degree from college and a fellow manager made fun of this fact in front of your staff. Perhaps your children were misbehaving in a grocery store, and the store manager came up, told you to leave, and said you obviously needed parenting classes because your kids were out of control. Imagine that this situation was extremely awkward for you and everyone else. You walked out in a huff and got into your car. Before driving away, you sat there for a moment and reacted.

What emotions did you feel? What thoughts ran through your head? What movements, gestures and body language resulted from feeling those feelings and thinking those thoughts?

Now, stand up and act out exactly how you felt in that situation. Remember — if you do the inner work correctly, the outer work of gestures and movement will flow naturally.

CHAPTER 19

Use Vocal Language so Your Audience Feels What You're Saying

D o you play or sing music? Imagine you're going to be playing a concert and you've just received the sheet music for the opening number. As you read over the sheet music for the first time, you're not just looking for the notes to be played. You're also looking for the rests, the pianissimos (to be played gently and softly), the fortes (to be played powerfully and loudly), and the pace of the notes so you know when to speed up to connote fury and when to slow down to connote tenderness.

Can you imagine what music would sound like without this vocal variety? It'd be a one-note performance.

Now imagine you're going to present the opening speech for your local professional association's annual conference. You've written out the words for your presentation, and you're now looking over your script to start preparing for your performance. Realize you are composing word music. You have created a piece of original work that will be heard just as a song is heard.

You need to put in rests (pauses), pianissimos (where you speak gently and softly), fortes (where you raise your volume and speak forcefully), and pace so you know when to speed up and express excitement and when to slow down to show peacefulness.

Once you have scripted in the vocal variety just as a musician would, you need to practice just as musicians do — out loud. They wouldn't think of performing a concert without first practicing and playing their instrument (whether it's a piano, clarinet, or saxophone) out loud. You shouldn't think of presenting a speech without first practicing and playing your instrument (your voice) out loud.

Your voice really is a marvelous musical instrument. It can warm your audience to you or it can drive them away. This chapter's purpose is to give you five specific ways you can make the most of your vocal instrument so it helps you, rather than hurts you.

Vocal Tip #1: Use Sprints and Drags

When people are stressed out they tend to talk really fast. I call this rapid verbal assault "The Sprint." Makes sense, doesn't it? When you sprint, it adds intensity to your story and keeps the audience on their mental toes. It is also a common vocal pattern that people recognize and relate to because they've either done it, heard it, or both. If you grew up in a large, talkative family, you probably heard lots of sprints growing up — probably around the crowded dinner table as everyone fought to get a word in edgewise.

Use The Sprint to illustrate:

- Stress or anxiety
- You're at the end of your rope
- Frustration or exasperation
- Impatience or being in a hurry
- Anger or rage

Use Vocal Language so Your Audience Feels What You're Saying

- Annoyance or irritation
- Desperation
- Freaking out and losing your temper

When you talk really slow, you're using a technique called The Drag. People in shock or disbelief tend to draw out their words and speak haltingly. They may over-enunciate each word or give each word equal, pronounced emphasis. They may be dragging out their words because they're thinking on their feet or forcing themselves to say something they'd rather not. One of the purposes of a drag is to express a heightened emotional state.

Use The Drag to illustrate:

- Shock or disbelief
- Boredom or lethargy
- Dread or apprehension
- Controlled anger
- Exhaustion or fatigue
- Giving up or defeat
- Resolve or determination
- Condescension or being patronizing

An example of something people say that could either be a sprint or a drag depending on the situation is, "You've got to be kidding." If you've just heard traumatic news and you're in shock you might say it slowly as a drag, "You've .... got .... to .... be kidding." If, however you're in the middle of an argument and someone says something preposterous, you might spit it out as a sprint.

Notice that the words themselves don't determine whether they should be said in a sprint or a drag, your motivation and intent does.

Vocal Tip #2: Use Whoops and Whines

Everyone I know makes involuntary sounds when they react. Extremely good news causes them to whoop and holler — bad news makes them whine or heave a deep sigh. Think of a whoop as any sound you might make to signal joy or celebration, and a whine as any sound you make to signal disappointment or displeasure.

Vocal language is often not a word at all, but a sound. I suggest you write in "Loving sigh" on your script when you talk about seeing your grandchild for the first time. If you are telling a story about the time you went hiking near the Banff Wilderness in Canada and encountered a bear, write in the word "AACCHHHHH!" or whatever noise you made when you came around the corner and saw that 300 pound black bear standing in the middle of the trail.

In the beginning, you won't make these natural sounds unless you remind yourself to do so. When Stacy was describing how tired she was at mile 22 of the New York Marathon, she didn't just look dejected, she didn't just say the words "I don't know if I can go on," she made a sound in her throat that let us know she was at the end of her rope. THAT was Story Theater!

Writing this reminds me of how much our personality is revealed by our reactions. The specific way we react vocally and physically to the people and events around us is one of the things that make up our individuality. Yet those unique vocal patterns are one of the first things to go when we step up on the podium to speak.

Here's an assignment for you. As you go about your business today, observe your vocal behavior. What kind of sounds do you make when you're sad, mad, or glad? Keep your notebook handy and write down what you typically say and do when you're caught off guard. Do you stutter or stammer? Write that down. What sound

Use Vocal Language so Your Audience Feels What You're Saying

do you make when you see a friend you haven't seen for a long time? Do you let out a little squeal? Write that down. Catalog these vocal traits for future reference and make sure you script them into your future presentations. Let those rich and expressive sounds be a part of your storytelling persona — just as they are part of your everyday persona. Take your language by the lapel so it's robust instead of lifeless.

Vocal Tip #3: Use Sound Patterns — Warping — for Effect

Now, on to Warping. Warping is a technique that relies on a sound pattern that is based on the repetition of a specific word or phrase. As the word or phrase is repeated, the sound pattern and inflection changes to reflect changes in meaning.

Let's take the word "No." Imagine you've just read a memo informing you that funding for your project has been cancelled. You've been working on the project for nine months and you're coming down the home stretch. Not only that, you've made many personal sacrifices for the project. You've missed your daughter's ballet recitals while sleeping in anonymous hotel rooms in far-away cities. You've worked late and laid awake at night, staring at the ceiling, worrying about cost overruns. On top of that, canceling the project means you may lose your job. Let's use the warping technique to create some "vocal language" in your story.

Your first reaction to the news is anger. You explode with a loud and emphatic, "NO!"
After a pause, you sprint nine consecutive "no's" in a row. "No, no, no, no, no, no, no, no."
Now you're determined not to let this happen. "No. Uh uh. No way. No."
You realize your idea is pure folly. It won't work. "No . . . . . . no."

You let off steam by whining another series of "no's." "No, no, no, no, no, no, no, no."

It dawns on you what this means — you're going to be fired. "Oh no. No."

Finally, it dawns upon that this could be a good thing. You're relieved because you realize you actually have a fairly sizable severance package. Perhaps now you can buy that franchise you've been wanting for years. "Yes!"

By giving each section of the sound pattern different meanings, the line delivery and inflection changes. Have you ever done something like this in real life? We all have. Review your story script to find a place where you could include warping to add vocal flavor to your presentation.

Vocal Tip #4: Use Comedic Timing and Word Jazz

For natural comedians, timing is an instinctive ability to know when to pause and for exactly how long. For them, timing is like the syncopation of music. At its best, comedic timing is the interplay of tone, pacing, style, and rhythm. It's like jazz with words.

When I am working with a client, we may spend five minutes on the timing of a specific phrase or sequence. You have to hear the rhythm of the words. This isn't something you can teach on paper (although I'm doing my best!) You have to spend enough time playing with your words until they "feel" right. All of the sudden, the light bulb goes on and you know the language swings. You may not be able to articulate why — you just know this timing or phrasing sounds better.

The good news is — there is a way to learn how to improve your comedic timing and ability to create and perform "word jazz."

Use Vocal Language so Your Audience Feels What You're Saying

Rent comedy concert videos. Here are a few of my favorites and then I'll tell you what to look for when you're watching them.

- BILL COSBY is one of the best storytelling comics around. Study his style for writing, exaggeration, character development, and a warm rapport with his audience. He is a big, cuddly, teddy bear (kind of like Rueben Studdard — the winner of the *2003 American Idol* program). His humor is also clean.

- LILY TOMLIN's concert video of *The Search for Intelligent Life in the Universe* is great to watch for writing, timing and character development. Remember her little girl in the big rocking chair and her classic telephone operator "Is this the party to whom I'm speaking?"

- ROSEANNE BARR is good to study for sarcastic humor. If there are any PHYLLIS DILLER video-tapes available, she's good for sarcastic humor as well.

- DENNIS MILLER has a brilliant wit and a wisecracking style. Study him for intelligent humor, style and timing.

- JERRY SEINFELD provides a wonderful perspective into the mind of someone who sees ordinary things in an extraordinary way. An example of his observational humor is his line, "There's no such thing as fun for the whole family." See? That one line can make you chuckle for days after you read it. Study his style and thought process.

Use the following suggestions to get maximum value while watching your comedy videos.

1. First, watch the video all the way through just for fun. Don't study, just enjoy.

2. On the second viewing, close your eyes and listen. Listen for the timing, the pauses, vocal attitudes and inflections. When you hear something really funny, rewind and listen again. With your eyes closed you will hear the rhythm and tempo, the music of timing.

3. On the third viewing, turn down the sound and watch the comic's physical expression and use of body language and gesture.

This exercise is particularly helpful if you can find a video of someone who has a similar presentation style to your own. Watching a pro who has made it big with your style of comedy helps validate that you can do it too. So, the next time you rent a video that makes you laugh, don't just leave it at that. Go back and re-watch it to figure out how and why it made you laugh — and then start practicing those techniques so you can use them with your next audience.

Vocal Tip #5: Develop a Quality Voice

Some people are blessed with quality voices. They've got good, strong vocal chords. They are pleasant to listen to because their tone is in the mid-to-low register and it has resonance. For them, vocal nuance and inflection is easier to accomplish because of their "pipes." Think of your favorite radio disc jockey. Chances are you enjoy listening to this person because he or she has a rich, melodious voice that makes for easy listening.

Some people have weak voices. They may have a habit of speaking timidly or they may have a high-pitched, scratchy voice that is hard on the ears. Have you ever taped yourself? Do you like the sound of your voice? Would you like to listen to your voice for hours on end?

Use Vocal Language so Your Audience Feels What You're Saying

The good news is, you can develop a voice that serves rather than sabotages you. This is an important issue. A strong voice signifies power and commands respect. A tremulous or tentative voice signals a lack of confidence and competence. I know. It's not fair. You may be the expert on your topic, but if you start off with a soft voice, the audience may conclude you don't know what you're talking about. If your voice lacks authority, they may not give you the respect you deserve. Just because you have a timid voice, shouldn't mean you will be taken lightly, but it often does.

One way to strengthen your voice is to sing. It doesn't matter if you sing off key — sing! Sing in the car as loud as you can. Sing in the shower — the tiles make your voice resonate. Experiment with your voice. Run up and down the musical scales as if you were warming up to sing at a concert.

Singing forces you to learn how to breathe properly while strengthening your vocal chords. Consciously move your voice down to your diaphragm. Place your hand on your lower abdomen and belly-breathe so your voice is coming from your center. Huummmm and find out where the vibration is coming from. If it's in your nose or throat, try to consciously move it down into your chest so you have a fuller sound. Instead of sounding nasal, deepen your voice so it sounds like James Earl Jones with his full, round sound.

The bottom line is, you can learn to play your voice instrument just as you would learn to play a musical instrument. Determine that the next time you stand up to speak, the first words out of your mouth will pleasantly surprise your audience with their rich, warm, trustworthy tone.

Act Out Conversations Between Characters

M ost stories have more than one character — the storyteller and one or more other persons. At least one of those other characters is a main character — your boss, co-worker, doctor, child, parachute instructor, relative, or singing coach. This chapter tells you how to conduct conversations between yourself and the other characters as realistically as possible so the audience feels like they are the proverbial "fly on the wall."

If you do the entire conversation the old way, as an OUT, past-tense narrative, it will contain a ton of "I said to her," and "she said to me." That way works okay. But I think we've already established that you're not okay with just being okay, right? Here's how you can create your own fascinating version of *My Dinner with Andre*, a two-hour movie about two guys having a far-ranging conversation in a restaurant. It has become somewhat of a cult classic!

The Two-Character Two-Step — (Formerly The Two-Character Shuffle)

The technique for having a two-character conversation is called The Two-Character Two-Step. It is considered an IN moment. This technique will allow you to have more fun with the other character, create a more vibrant relationship, and make the conversation more realistic.

The premise behind The Two-Character Two-Step is that you re-create the interplay between your personality and theirs. The two-step part takes place with some fancy footwork. It requires that you turn your body 90 degrees in between each character speaking. You can turn 90 degrees, can't you? Thought so. You can do this.

Before we go any further, choose a conversation you'd like to work on. Make it a short interchange — perhaps you each say four lines — each one or two short sentences or less in length. Sometimes in a conversation you reply with three or four words rather than an entire sentence. Here's a short example:

> Doug: I heard that you're being laid off. What's going on?
> Charlie: My project got cancelled. We lost our funding.
> Doug: What are you going to do now?
> Charlie: I'm going to take the severance package, take a month off and then I'm not sure. I've always wanted to work for myself — maybe buy a franchise.
> Doug: I wish they'd lay me off and give me a severance package.
> Charlie: What would you do?
> Doug: Go to Aruba for a couple of weeks and see how tan I can get.
> Charlie: You know what? I always dreaded this moment and now that it's here, I'm relieved.

Now, following the structure above, write out a conversation you'd like to develop using the ideas in this chapter. Go ahead, get a piece of paper and do it now. You're going to need it in a minute.

Note: The Exception to the Rule: Remember when I said your eyes are OUT to the audience for an OUT moment

Act Out Conversations Between Characters

and IN your imaginary space for an IN moment? You're not supposed to make eye contact with the audience in an IN moment, *except* in a Two-Character Two-Step. Here, you actually choose one audience member on the left side of the audience to be the other character and one audience member on the right side to be you. That way each of you has someone specific to talk to.

Let's say you're talking to your friend Solomon. As you turn 45 degrees to the left — you make eye contact with and talk to an audience member as if he were Solomon. When you're finished and it's Solomon's turn to talk, two-step 90 degrees to the right, pretend you're Solomon and talk to an audience member as if she were you. You never want to turn completely sideways — a full 180 degrees — because that means half of your audience is looking at the back of your head.

There are three stages to learning The Two-Character Two-Step. Let's take them one at a time.

Stage #1 of The Two-Character Two-Step: Put the Dialogue and Footwork Together

We'll refer to the two audience members as Stand In #1 and Stand In #2. Imagine you start your presentation and you get to the part where you're going to introduce the conversation. Your last OUT words before you turn to begin the two-step will be, "and Solomon said..."

Refer to Figure 2:

1. STEP ONE. After the words, "and Solomon said," turn both your feet 45 degrees to the right as in Figure 2a. Make eye

contact with Stand In #1. Say Solomon's first sentence as Solomon would say it to Stand In #1. The audience member that you're talking to is standing in for *you.*

2. STEP TWO. Bring your left heel behind your right heel and turn your body, as in Figure 2b. Your feet now form a 90-degree angle with one heel behind the other.

3. STEP THREE. Pick up your right foot and rotate it 90 degrees to the left so that both feet are parallel facing left as in Figure 2c. Make eye contact with Stand In #2 and say your response to Solomon, to them. That audience member is standing in for *Solomon.*

4. When you're finished talking, reverse the footwork so that you turn to the right again. You are now pretending to be Solomon responding to you.

5. When you're finished talking, reverse the footwork turning left again. You are now *you* talking to Solomon.

You may have seen someone do a two-character conversation poorly. They usually face 180 degrees sideways for one character and then take two or three steps forward, turn 180 degrees the other way and say the next line as the second character. It's awkward, isn't it?

With The Two-Character Two-Step — there is no walking in-between characters. There is no gap — you simply shift your feet in place — like you're dancing the two-step.

Stage #2 of The Two-Character Two-Step: Add Physical Characterizations

Now that you've combined the lines and the footwork — let's add the physical characterizations. You may not be able to do it as well as Fred Astaire or Mikhail Baryshnikov, but you can still bring your conversations and characters to life.

Act Out Conversations Between Characters

The physical transition from one character to another — from you to Solomon for instance — happens before
you turn. Stand up to practice this next
part. You have to do it on your feet.

Figure 2a

- Get the conversation you wrote
  earlier for this exercise.
- Change your body posture to
  mimic Solomon. Turn 45 degrees
  to the right. Say his first line.
- Transition. Return to your normal
  body posture.
- Turn (two-step) 90 degrees to the
  left *as you.*
- Maintain your normal body posture as you deliver your line to
  Solomon.
- Transition to Solomon's body
  posture.
- Turn (two-step) 90 degrees to the
  right *as Solomon.*
- Maintain Solomon's body posture
  as you deliver his line to you.
- Transition to you. Turn left and
  deliver your line to him.
- Transition to Solomon. Turn right
  and deliver his line to you.
- Repeat the same procedure until
  the conversation is finished.

Figure 2b

Figure 2c

Because the transition from one character to another happens in the same
physical plane — before turning — it is
seamless. There is no clunky gap — no

awkward walking and turning. The last step in the physical characterization is to react physically as you would and then as the other person would. These reactions complete the physical aspect of the characterization.

Stage #3 of The Two-Character Two-Step: Add Vocal Characterizations

You may have found that when you added the physical characterization of the other character, his or her voice came along for the ride. That's good. If that didn't happen — ask yourself the following questions to discover their voice and then practice using it in your staged conversation.

- Tone: Is it high or low or ordinary?
- Speed: Do they talk slow or fast?
- Accent: Wisconsin? Texas? Calcutta? Liverpool?
- Volume: soft-pitched or breaks windows?
- Attitude: Snippy, dippy or laissez-faire?

If you struggle with putting these three elements together, you're not alone. This is the most complex technique I teach, so please be patient. I guarantee you this — the first time you do a two-character conversation using this technique, even in a rough draft stage, your audience will love it. My coaching clients all tell me this is one of the best techniques they have ever learned. Go for it.

Hold A Telephone Conversation — On Stage

Back in the 70's, a comic named Bob Newhart came along and did something no one had done before as a stand-up comic act, he talked on the telephone. At least I'd never seen it done before. The brilliance of his routine was that he only verbalized his side of the

Act Out Conversations Between Characters

conversation, allowing the audience to figure out what the person on the other end of the line was saying. He was and still is, the undisputed master of the telephone conversation.

In some stories, your featured conversation takes place on the telephone. Most people try to portray that call with a lot of "she said" and "I said" language. They're often confused about what to do with the hand that's supposed to be holding the phone. Are they supposed to switch from side to side as the person speaking changes? How do you hold the phone — thumb up and pinkie finger down? Sometimes, the whole pantomime is done so self-consciously it draws attention away from what's being said. The power of what could be a pivotal moment is often diminished.

Have you ever eavesdropped on someone speaking on the telephone? (That was a rhetorical question.) Listening in and making comments to the person on the phone while they're trying to have a conversation is not only natural — it's accepted and expected. In my fabulous marriage with Deborah — it's the eleventh commandment for crying out loud. *"Thou shalt be allowed to eavesdrop and butt in on each other's telephone conversations."*

The goal however, is to have such polished "phone" technique that it becomes invisible. It should appear as natural as possible. To figure out what natural looks like, I want you to observe five people on the phone in the next couple days. They can be on a cell, a public phone, or a cordless — however they must be standing because you will be standing when you perform.

Observe their body language and what they do with their free hand. Maybe they curl a strand of hair around their finger while they talk. Maybe they tuck the phone under their chin. Maybe their eyes go unfocused as they concentrate on the person on the other end of the line. Their unconscious behavior is what you want to become aware of. Then, witness yourself during a stand-up phone conversation. What are your habits? Note the specific personality-making details so you can duplicate them during your conversation on the stage.

There are three critical elements to a telephone conversation:

1. **It is an IN moment:** Telephone conversations are private affairs. They may not be intimate but they are meant to be private. That is why you portray them as IN moments. We want the audience to listen in and figure out what is being said on the other end of the line. We want them participating as if they were part of our conversation.

2. **You need to script both sides of the conversation:** Talk onto paper. As discussed earlier in this book, make the dialogue real — half sentences and fragments are fine. Second, memorize both sides of the conversation but only voice your side. That means you have to "say their lines" silently to yourself so that it appears as if you are listening to the other side of the conversation. Your emotional and non-verbal reactions to what "they" say are critical. Go back to your observation exercise and clarify how people behave while they are listening on the phone. They nod their head and cross and uncross their arms. They don't stand still. They're sometimes preoccupied, people watching, or doodling while half-listening to the other person.

   This is what a client's conversation sounded like after we finished crafting it. I'm purposely not setting this story up so you can see for yourself how you can still tell what's happening — even when the storyteller is verbalizing only her side of the conversation.

   Claire: Hello
   Sally: Mom?

Act Out Conversations Between Characters

Claire: Hey Hon, howya doin?

Sally: Mom, I'm so excited, I had to call you.

Claire: Whaa …?

Sally: I sold my first house today.

Claire: You did what!? You sold your first house?!

Sally: You know, I told you about that client who came back three times.

Claire: The couple with the young baby?

Sally: Yeah, them, anyway, they called and said they wanted to take it and...

Claire: How much did it sell for?

Sally: This is the really good part — remember the owner...

Claire: The owner who was really difficult to work with, right?

Sally: Yeah. He got fed up with the house being on the market so long, and he slashed the price by 10%

Claire: Ohmigosh — he took 10% off the price just like that?

Sally: Yea, so now the couple could afford it.

Claire: I'm so glad to hear that. So, tell me, what's your commission?

Sally: Mom, are you ready?

Claire: I'm sitting down, o.k. tell me…

Sally: I made $7,000 in one week!

Claire: $7000 for one week's work?! What great news. I'm so happy for you.

Do you hear how natural that sounds? Did you feel like you were there with Claire and Sally? Did you see how they often cut each other off, finished each other's sentences, and repeated what the other person said? That's what we do in real life — and that's what you should do when re-enacting phone conversations in your presentations.

Make Your Business Presentations Capture Attention, Inspire Action, and Produce Results

This is what your audience will hear without Sally's dialogue.

Claire:	Hello
Claire:	Hey Hon, howya doin?
Claire:	Whaa . . ?
Claire:	You did what!? You sold your first house?!
Claire:	Oh, the couple with the young baby?
Claire:	How much did it sell for?
Claire:	The owner who was really difficult to work with, right?
Claire:	Ohmigosh — he took 10% off the price just like that?
Claire:	I'm so glad to hear that. So, tell me, what's your commission?
Claire:	I'm sitting down, o.k. tell me...
Claire:	$7000 for one week's work?! What great news. I'm so happy for you.

3. **You need to choreograph the physical performance:** Now let's work on the physical aspects of the call. Refer to Figure 3a and 3b for hand placement.

   • Make a fist with the hand you want to hold the phone with.
   • Extend your thumb up as if giving the thumbs up sign.
   • It is optional to extend your pinkie finger out. I don't.
   • Place the flat part of your middle knuckles on your cheek with the thumb extending up to your ear.
   • As you speak on the imaginary phone, keep your knuckles on your cheek.

The most important part of this technique is to keep your knuckles on your cheek. This allows you to move around while maintaining a stable position for the imaginary phone. This also prevents "telephone drift." I remember one client

Act Out Conversations Between Characters

Figure 3a   **Figure 3b**

who got so caught up in the excitement of her news, her phone started by the ear and ended up near her waist. The audience was laughing and she didn't understand why. Learn from her example and keep that phone glued to your cheek.

Once the phone is in place, feel free to pace or walk around as you talk, just like you do when you're on the phone with your friends or family members.

To emphasize the dramatic impact of Sally's good news, Claire set the scene for us prior to the phone conversation by saying she was in the kitchen preparing dinner for her and her husband when the phone rang. When she first picked up the phone, she was distracted because she had several pots going on the stove. She cradled the phone between her shoulder and ear and kept stirring the two sauces that were boiling. When she recognized who it was, she pantomimed turning the stove burners off, putting the spoon down, and giving her full attention to Sally. When Claire said she was going to sit down to hear the good news, she actually sat down on a chair she'd placed on the platform. As she heard the good news, she leapt up from the chair, broke into a huge smile, and twirled around the kitchen in a little celebratory victory dance for Sally's success.

A telephone conversation, performed in this manner, can be a powerful tool for adding suspense and drama to your presentation. One of the reasons this worked so well is that Claire had also told us about Sally's problems finding a job. After four years at one of the best colleges in the country and a degree in English Literature, Sally had not been able to find work for almost a year. Finally, almost in desperation, she had gone for her real estate license. Having that background information as context made Claire's acted-out phone conversation even more delightful to behold. Claire then segued into a point about the need to change directions when things aren't working out. Sally was going nowhere fast until she changed directions and became a real-estate agent. Claire ended with the Phrase That Pays, "Change Directions."

The Transition Two-Step

The transition from an OUT moment where you are talking to the audience, to an IN moment, doesn't need to be awkward. Enter The Transition Two-Step. If you are facing straight out and looking down the middle of the audience, you can simply turn 45 degrees to the right or left and you are IN. To define the transition from OUT to IN even more clearly, consider using the entire 90-degree angle you just learned to use for The Two-Character Two-Step. This full 90-degree turn from one side to the other is referred to as The Transition Two-Step.

In the three or four sentences prior to the start of any IN moment, such as a Two-Character Two-Step — simply angle your body 45 degrees to either side of center. Let's say you turn to the right. This

Act Out Conversations Between Characters

means you are sharing the narrative leading into The Two-Character Two-Step with the audience on the right side of the room.

After the words, "And then she said to me," two-step a full 90-degrees to the left and you've made the transition from OUT to IN. Try setting-up the transition from OUT to IN this way, using the full 90-degree two-step. I call it physical punctuation. From the audience's point of view, it is a more defined move.

This technique will also assist you in comedy timing and delivery. Here's how it works. I like to use this Lily Tomlin/Jane Wagner quote because it has a nice set-up and pay-off.

> *"I always wanted to be somebody, but I should*
> *have been more specific."*

Using The Transition Two-Step, say the first half of the sentence facing 45 degrees to the right. Two-step 90-degrees to the left and deliver the second half of the sentence. The 90-degree turn between the two lines syncopates the line delivery and physically punctuates the difference between the set-up and the pay-off.

There are two ways to execute The Transition Two-Step:

- Execute the 90-degree turn with your entire body using the two-step footwork
- Execute the 90-degree turn just with your head

I hope you'll keep experimenting with and practicing the techniques in this chapter. They're more advanced storytelling techniques and take more time to perfect, however, there's a huge payoff for you and your audience if you keep at it.

CHAPTER 21

Use Emotional Language so Listeners Connect with What You're Saying

E motional language is a wordless form of communication that everyone, regardless of gender, race, or nationality, understands and responds to.

If a dear friend walked into your house upset, no words would be necessary. Their dejected body language and emotional state would tell the story. Without saying a word, you would know that something bad or sad had happened to your friend. You would see, hear and feel her emotional pain and your heart would go out to her.

Is it possible for the heart to see and hear? Does it speak a language like no other? I believe it does. In this chapter we'll explore seven forms of emotional language.

Emotional Language Form #1: Hold The Moment

When something powerful happens in a story — a moment of truth, a revelation, or a crisis — what do you do? In real life, you'd probably react in some non-verbal way. You might stop dead in your tracks and just stand there, stunned. Your eyes may grow wet

Make Your Business Presentations Capture Attention, Inspire Action, and Produce Results

with tears of joy or sorrow. Your mouth may drop open in shock. You must resist the instinct to rush past these "turning point" moments, even if they are uncomfortable. Stop and "Hold the Moment."

Hold the Moment is an IN moment in which you stop moving and stand still. Think your thoughts so they register on your face. Fill the silence with the feelings resulting from the epiphany. It is natural in a "hold" for the thoughts and emotions to then initiate movement. A "hold" begins with a freeze, but does not remain one for long, because the emotions "take over."

I was coaching an executive in his late forties who worked for an international conglomerate. His job took him all over Europe and to the United States once or twice a year. It was a high-powered job with a glamorous title — but he longed to spend more time at home with his young son. He knew he was missing too many birthdays and soccer games.

One day, in the midst of a massive corporate restructuring, he received a phone call from his secretary. It was bad news. His division was being shut down and he was out of his job as CEO. The company promised to find him something "comparable" and instructed him to take a month off with pay.

What would you do? Would it take a few seconds for your head to clear? Would you rush around like a chicken with your head cut off or stand still like a zombie? Would you panic with concern for your family or be excited about a month's paid vacation? Would you rush out the door and jump in your car? Take a minute to imagine how you would react if you just received that kind of news. Now, imagine re-enacting this moment for an audience. Would your "hold" begin with stunned immobility and then transition into confused movements and gestures as you tried to do ten things at once?

Use Emotional Language so Listeners Connect with What You're Saying

A "Hold the Moment" typically contains:

- An initial freeze in movement
- Inner monologue thoughts
- Sense memory feelings
- Movements and gestures that emanate from the inside out
- A filled silence

Emotional Language Form #2: Display Reactions

Most emotional language occurs during reactions. Throwing your hands up in the air in disgust can be more eloquent than describing your disgust at something going wrong, for the umpteenth time. Standing with your mouth hanging open, eyes-wide, in stunned silence as your boss announces you just made the top 1% of all national salesman and you get to go to Hawaii for a week-long, all-expenses paid incentive meeting — is better than saying "Yippee."

Where in your story do you receive a shocking memo that upsets you? Where in your presentation do you talk about an angry customer who is berating you for something that's gone wrong — and you don't dare interrupt? Where in your story do you talk about landing a promotion or being put in charge of a multi-million dollar project? Where in your talk do you show how you feel when your in-laws show up at your home unannounced — for a visit — for two weeks — with their five kids? Don't just stand there — react!

Emotional Language Form #3: Inner Monologue

Another acting technique you can use to fill silence is called inner monologue. An inner monologue is a dialogue you have — with yourself — in silence. 'Fess up; you talk to yourself on a daily basis. It's how we figure things out. When faced with a complex decision, daunting situation, or troublesome relationship, we internalize all the options in order to determine the best course of action. We replay what happened and have non-verbal conversations in our heads almost constantly.

Consider this inner monologue from our "in limbo" CEO:

> "I can't believe this. This is insane. Something 'comparable'? Like what? What are they going to offer me, Poland? I'm not moving my family again. (Mental transition) Wow. A whole month off! I can read a book, an entire book. Heck I can write a book."

This "hold" might only last five or ten seconds. It doesn't need to be long to be effective.

Your inner monologue must be scripted with specific sentences in a linear progression. You'll need to memorize your inner monologue just as you do your spoken lines. For this technique to be effective in performance, you actually take "real" time to recite your inner monologue in your head. Doing so will cause you to have the appropriate facial and physical reactions that arise from thinking and responding to those thoughts. If you do it right, and doing it right means being very clear about each of the thoughts you're thinking and not rushing through them, you won't be able to keep the associated expressions off your face.

Now, as Paul Harvey would say, "For the rest of the story..." The CEO never went back to being a CEO. He started his own consulting firm and now spends plenty of time at soccer games. The last time we spoke, he proudly announced that he no longer qualified for Platinum status on Lufthansa Airlines.

Use Emotional Language so Listeners Connect with What You're Saying

Emotional Language Form #4: Sense Memory

The ability to recall the emotion tied to an event is a technique called "sense memory." It is literally the process of recalling the memory of an emotion from the past to use in a present moment. In my opinion, the tears you cry at an emotional moment during a movie are a form of sense memory. Once again, you're not crying for the actor or actress in the movie, you are either crying for their character out of a sympathetic response or you are crying tears of joy or sorrow for yourself because what's happening reminds you of a similar event that's occurred in your life.

While in a theater, the movie stimulates the recall of your emotion. When telling your story, *you* must stimulate this recall by going back into that experience and mining your memory of the good old days and the not-so-good old days.

Inner monologue thoughts and sense memory feelings exist side-by-side during a "hold" moment. Just as you script inner monologue, you must make a conscious effort to script or choose the emotion you want to convey. For our CEO, the emotions ran the gamut from shock to relief.

Think of a story that you intend to tell. What is its "turning point — the moment of truth, revelation or crisis?" How are you going to "hold the moment" and make it come alive with the thoughts and feelings that were present at the actual moment it happened to you? Are you going to reveal your inner monologue? Are you going to freeze and then let the emotional reactions flow over your face? In the future, never let a dramatic moment like this slip through your fingers. Once and for all, understand that the best presentations are not the ones crammed with as much content as you can fit in the time allotted.

What makes for a great presentation is when the speaker luxuriates in the full emotions of the stories and combines it with substantive, thought-provoking insights and suggestions. Promise yourself that in your next presentation you will *slow down* and experience your turning points — so your audience will too. The change in the audience will be palpable when you do this. If you were wondering what the next level of storytelling requires and how to do it, now you know.

Emotional Language Form #5: Silence Speaks

Actors are not afraid of silence — the space between the words. An absence of sound does not create a void. Quite the contrary; silence lives and breathes. Silence creates a delicate and intricate womb where something magical and tangible grows. Embrace this eloquent space and understand it is the tool of a masterful speaker. Without it, our words rush together. With it, our audience has time to absorb, reflect, imprint.

In the silence, the actor / storyteller moves the story forward. She ruminates, cogitates and formulates. Information is processed. Options are considered. Decisions are made. It is not a pause! It is filled with thought and emotion.

During the silence, audience members observe the storyteller with empathetic eyes. They listen with a knowing heart. They've been there. They recognize the behavior. They are watching the storyteller, but as if in a mirror. They see their own reflection.

During the silence, audience members have work to do. They put the pieces of the story puzzle together and form their own opinion about where the storyteller is going. Silence provides an opportunity for a yin-yang relationship with the audience. Instead of the speaker being stuck on "transmit" and the audience stuck on "receive" — the silence draws in the audience and gives them

Use Emotional Language so Listeners Connect with What You're Saying

opportunities to draw their own conclusions instead of being spoon-fed all the information. Like the speaker, they ruminate, cogitate, extrapolate, and formulate. They're busy — they're not passively waiting for the next word. They're working. They are filled with thought and emotion.

Emotional Language Form #6: Serve the Message

If you have chosen a story that makes a powerful point, you have a responsibility to make sure that the audience "gets it." It is not enough for them to *intellectually* understand the point of your story — they must be moved to a place of deep understanding. That requires you to be brave and serve the message.

The more powerful and important the message, the more dedicated you must be to using all of the tools at your disposal. You must go out on a limb and take them with you. You must bring them into the experience rather than just talking about it. If they sense that you are a sure-footed guide, they will follow you and learn the lessons you have to teach.

The most precious commodity people have these days, is their time. It is imperative that we do not waste it by being slick, unprepared or boring. We must do our homework. We must give them our best effort. When we do, they reward us handsomely.

I believe speaking to a room full of people who have given me their undivided attention is a privilege. I am there to serve them by serving the message. I believe in what I have to say and know that people will benefit, if I can get out of my own way and let the magic happen. In order to experience that miracle, I can't be worried about how I look or what people will think of me. My purpose is much larger than that. I want to make a difference.

How about you? If you believe you have a message that will help people, then you must stretch to encompass new skills that will allow your message to be seen, felt and heard. Serve the message by becoming the best messenger you can be.

> **Note**: Another part of serving your message is understanding that speaking is not meant to be a form of therapy. To share painful memories for your benefit only violates the privilege and responsibility of the platform. If you tell a traumatic story and are overcome with raw emotion, you are not ready to tell that story.

The rule for telling emotional stories is this: you must have enough emotional distance from an event or story to be able to go into it without getting lost in it.

You must use your professional skills to re-enact the event in such a way that it is obvious that you are crafting an experience for the benefit of your audience. You must be in control even though it may seem that you are not. The audience must feel safe, even though what you are portraying may be scary.

Having said that — if sharing a dramatic turning point will enlighten, educate, and/or inspire others, by all means go there.

Emotional Language Form #7: Feel The Fear and Speak Up Anyway

I want to acknowledge some of the obstacles you may face to do this work. It's going to feel awkward at first. The silence that is actually only seven seconds long may feel like seven minutes. It may be difficult for you to stand there and let your audience watch you think your thoughts and feel your feelings. This is normal.

It may be that you're uncomfortable expressing emotion

Use Emotional Language so Listeners Connect with What You're Saying

anywhere, much less in front of a room of people. Many of my students have admitted that they've unintentionally been hiding behind their content for years as a way to shield themselves from having to get in touch with painful experiences.

I realize that teaching these kinds of skills from a book isn't nearly as effective as having the opportunity to work together in person, where we can practice and fine tune as we go. I'd love the opportunity to work with you, to nurture and guide you forward.

I learned these skills in acting class with other students. Many hours were spent practicing while they watched, gave me constructive feedback, and supplied plenty of encouragement. I couldn't have done it alone. I needed many skilled teachers to get where I am today. I willingly asked them to help me find things inside of myself that I did not have access to at the time. Now, these acting skills have informed my business storytelling skills in such a way that I'm able to make my living speaking and sharing what I've learned with others.

It may be that you want to explore this level of expression, but don't have access to a teacher to help you learn and practice. First, seek out acting and improvisation classes in your community or at your local community college. If you have time, you may even want to get involved in Community Theater and do some acting. Take dance classes. I've studied ballet, jazz, modern and tap. I'm no Baryshnikov, but I am in touch with my body. I'm comfortable with it and I know how to use it on the platform to make my programs come alive.

Singing lessons or joining a choir or barbershop quartet will help you become a better performer. Yoga, tai chi, or Tai Bo will help you stretch, (so to speak) which is what learning how to act is all about. Acting class helped me to break down my barriers and confront my fears. It challenged me to do things I wasn't comfortable doing. The more intimidating things I did, the more confident I became. Now I jump out of airplanes and climb mountains. As long as I have fear, I will confront it when I see it.

If there are no resources for acting or improvisation in your community, you can always go to the movies and study how the actors do what they do. You can buy comedy videos or watch Jay Leno, David Letterman and Conan O'Brien to observe their comedic timing and develop your own.

And lastly, work on your stuff. You can't portray emotions you're afraid to feel. You can't teach what you don't understand. As a speaker, you have the ability to change people's lives, not just with your words, but also with your being. In order to do that, it means your heart, soul and spirit must be free.

How do you work on your stuff? I did it by going to personal growth seminars — lots of them. I participated in inner child journeys and inner teen journeys. I went to guilt and shame workshops and learned about co-dependency and how it was affecting my relationships. I went to therapy and dealt with long-suppressed issues of inadequacy.

It was scary, but I'm a better person for it. When I stand in front of an audience, I am not burdened with the fear of rejection. I am free to be me. Our audiences learn from us on many levels, therefore we owe it to them to keep learning and growing ourselves.

I can tell you from experience that business audiences are like any other audiences. They are people just like you and me who want to learn and grow. They want to laugh and cry and be made to feel something, as long as there is a useful point to the exercise. Don't waste their time with a boring presentation devoid of human drama and meaning. Take responsibility for teaching them something they don't already know in a way they aren't expecting.

CHAPTER 22

Conduct
"Walk and Talk" Rehearsals

I'll never forget the look on his face. I was working with a real estate agent on a speech he was working on to promote his services. We had just finished a productive coaching session. We tweaked his script, practiced a few IN moments and settled on a great Phrase That Pays. As we were wrapping up I told him to go home and rehearse what we'd just worked on to lock it in.

He looked up from his day planner and said, "What exactly do you mean by rehearse, Doug? You know what it means because you're an actor and all, but I don't know what to do."

I could hear the frustration in his voice. At that moment, I wondered how many other people had wanted to ask the same question but never had. How many hundreds of times had I told people to go home and rehearse? Of course I knew what it meant, and I had assumed others did too.

I remember back in elementary school when I won my first audition in forth grade. I was going to be Christopher Columbus in the Columbus Day pageant. I ran home after school and worked on my lines for an hour until I had them down. There were three of them. Then I stood in front of the mirror and said them out loud.

Mirror, Mirror on the Wall

Whoever came up with the absurd notion of rehearsing in front of a mirror was a well-intentioned idiot! Unless your entire wall is covered with mirrors from head to toe, it is a completely ineffective way to rehearse. All it accomplishes is to make you more self-conscious. You get so distracted and obsessed about how big your nose is and how much weight you need to lose or gain that you can't concentrate on what you're saying. All you're concerned about is how you look — which is not congruent with being a spellbinding speaker.

The best way to rehearse is to walk and talk. Rise up out of that chair, push away from the computer, and get out from behind that desk. Take your notes with you. Stop and re-read them when you have to, until you memorize them and your content and ideas flow naturally out of your mouth and mind.

When you walk and talk, you integrate your movements and gestures with your material. Your body language will spontaneously evolve from the context of the story. As mentioned before, you won't be able to help it. If you stay seated and rehearse by staring at your script, this will remain an intellectual exercise. You will be practicing your words but not your presentation style.

Immerse Yourself in Your Mental and Physical Rehearsal

Think of it like this: All professional athletes use visualization. Ice skaters picture themselves launching themselves into their triple jumps and landing them clean. Divers imagine walking to the end of the board, bouncing up, and then twisting and somersaulting through the air with a splash-less entry. High jumpers run their

Conduct "Walk and Talk" Rehearsals

approach routine through their mind, the exact number of strides, catapulting themselves up, arching over the bar, and flipping their feet up and over.

These step-by-step mental rehearsals play a big role in imprinting and producing their desired performance. However, these athletes don't stop there. They get out onto the ice, up on the dive stand, and out on the track and actually practice what they're going to do in competition.

You need to do the same thing. Reading and mentally rehearsing your script until you have the words down is important. But it's not enough. You've got to get on your feet and feel it. Unless you plan on doing your presentation sitting down, move around.

Any room can serve as your rehearsal platform. It doesn't even have to have the same dimensions of the stage on which you're going to speak. You may be practicing in your living room, which is half the size of the platform in the auditorium where you'll be speaking. That's okay. Just practice your story, complete with Two-Character Two-Steps, telephone conversations, and comedic and dramatic moments, in a scaled-down version. Instead of walking twenty feet across the stage, walk ten feet across your living room.

Have the audience "sit" on one end of the room and speak to them. Picture them out there. How many are there? Fifty? One hundred? Five hundred? Practice looking at all four quadrants of the room. Don't just focus on the people in the front row or the back row. Don't look over their heads and don't stare them down. Imagine making eye contact with each person to make sure they feel included.

See? It doesn't matter if there's no one there — they're there in your mind and you can conduct full-out dress rehearsals in the privacy of your home. Think about it. Confidence is based on frequent, recent, successful practice. If you've done something a lot and you've done it well, you think, "I can." You can walk in with confidence instead of doubts and fears because you've done your "homework." You know you can pull this off because you've done it many times in rehearsal.

Rehearsing out loud on your feet also aids memory. Movement stimulates synaptic activity in your brain. The higher your synaptic and aerobic activity, the better your brain works. Why? You are oxygenating your mind, increasing blood flow, and accessing and aligning both sides of your brain. That's why it helps to pace when you're working out a problem. Pacing turns lethargy into energy and engages all your senses, which increases the likelihood you'll come up with a solution.

Walk This Way

Here are a few helpful hints to help you get maximum value out of your walk and talk rehearsals:

- Find an uncluttered space to rehearse in that will be your platform.
- Decide where you will place the imaginary audience.
- Walk and talk from the beginning of the creative process.
- Experiment — first rehearse to discover; then rehearse to polish.
- Visualize the scene for the IN moments.
- Set up your 90-degree angle for Two-Character Two-Steps.
- Decide who will be where and on what side.
- Block your movements and actions.
- Practice holding the moment — take your time.
- Place imaginary objects such as desks and chairs.
- Allow gestures to evolve naturally — let your hands talk.

Conduct "Walk and Talk" Rehearsals

- Visualize yourself presenting the story to an audience.
- Have fun with the creative process.
- Schedule time to rehearse in half-hour increments.
- The more you rehearse — the better you will be.

Remember, the more realistic you make your rehearsal, the more confident you'll be in the real situation. The goal is to immerse yourself in practicing your performance so it becomes an extension of who you are. Rehearse until you know your lines, know when and where you're going to step IN and OUT, and until you are so comfortable with your story and so excited about this opportunity to share your message, you can't wait to get up on that platform.

PART SIX

Present Stories that Capture and Keep Attention

CHAPTER 23

Stand in Your Power

The two jobs you have when you give a speech are to dissem-inate useful information and to do it in a way that is effec-tive. Both require skill and advanced preparation, which you now know how to do. The final element in the equation is the presen-tation itself. If the presentation falls flat, all of your preparation was for naught.

You are a powerful person. Whether you believe it or not, it's true. You have power — how you use it is up to you. You can use it to strengthen your message or to sabotage yourself with self-doubt. Whether you accept it or reject it will be evident to your audience. Louie Schwartz (or was it Shakespeare?) said, "Who you are speaks so loudly, I cannot hear what you say."

To be an effective speaker, trainer or presenter, you must learn to stand in your power. That means that any hint of insecurity or self-doubt must be purged from your consciousness. There can be no second-guessing, no apology, and no wishy-washy hesitancy. You have to stand confidently in the knowledge that you have some-thing to say and you're going to say it with passion and poise.

Once you embrace and capitalize on your power, your audience will say, "Who you are speaks so eloquently, I respect and listen to everything you say."

Love Yourself and Let Them Watch

I'll never forget a student in one of my Story Theater Retreats. She was not a speaker at the time. As a matter of fact, she held a fairly ordinary job that had nothing to do with performing, but her comedic wit and timing were impeccable. She'd tried her hand at stand-up comedy once or twice and had written several humorous articles for the local newspaper.

She was standing in front of the class telling her story. It was a decent story with many well-conceived comedic lines. What I remember most, however, was not her story — it was her body language. It screamed, "Don't look at me. I'm uncomfortable with my body and I'm not sure if I'm any good." The truth was, she was good. In fact, her comedic instincts were brilliant. But, she was standing in her own way. She had a unique talent, but was burying it.

You cannot stand in your power and embrace the gift that you are unless you love yourself. Self-acceptance is at the core of personal power. It is the knowledge that you are enough. It is an oasis in the ocean of self-doubt. To speak with true authority, you have to love yourself and let other people watch.

This fabulously talented woman was uncomfortable with herself. She told the class it was partly because of her hang-ups about her body. She felt she was overweight and needed to lose 20 pounds. It was partly that she had been ridiculed by loved ones and had little or no self-worth left. What else was going on, only she knew — but it all showed up in her "get me outta here" body language.

The real issue was not her weight — it was her lack of self-acceptance. Countless female comediennes are overweight. She could lose 20 pounds only to find that her low self-esteem still remained.

Stand in Your Power

Do you want to shine when you speak? Do you want to be perceived as confident and powerful? Do you want the people in your audience to like and accept you? If the answer is yes to these questions — then stop looking outside for validation and start healing the wounds that bind you. You must love yourself as you are. Are you perfect? The answer is YES. You are perfectly imperfect — just like me and everyone else.

Joan Mills said, "I'd gone through life believing in the strengths and competence of others; never in my own. Now, dazzled, I discovered that my own capacities were real. It was like finding a fortune in the lining of an old coat."

You have a fortune to be shared, if you'll just accept it.

Self-Love is Not Conceit

Self-love should not be confused with self-centeredness. There is no arrogance in self-love. It merely means you can stand in front of people confident you have something of value to offer.

There is a spiritual principle involved in what I'm suggesting. It is the principle of non-attachment to the goal. For many of us, it is nearly impossible to seek a goal with all of our heart, mind, and soul while remaining unattached to the attainment of that goal. It's a conundrum, to be sure. But, as a speaker, it is necessary that we do this for the following reason.

A goal is an end result. It is accomplished by doing hundreds of tasks correctly, one at a time. While performing each of those tasks correctly — one must be focused on the task at hand, not the ultimate goal.

For the business storyteller, the task at hand is the telling of the story. It is *not* how the story will be received or interpreted, which is the goal. To achieve the goal of a well-received story, you must immerse yourself in the telling of the story only. One thing at a time. First you tell the story brilliantly — then you get the results.

The audience has come to hear the presentation you have prepared, not for you to compromise it because you have allowed doubts and fears to preoccupy your mind. Fulfill your commitment. Perform the play you wrote with guts and gusto. You owe them nothing less.

To Thine Own Self Be True

> *"To be nobody but yourself — in a world*
> *which is doing its best, night and day, to*
> *make you everybody else — means to fight*
> *the hardest battle which any human being*
> *can fight, and never stop fighting."*
> — E. E. Cummings

I am a speaking and story coach who helps people master their message. They come to me because they hope I can help them achieve their goals. More often than not they've seen me give a speech and they're impressed. They see how I put these skills into practice and they want to learn how to do the same.

What they don't realize is that before I can help them master their message, they must be willing to remove their mask. They must stop hiding behind the safety of too much content and reveal themselves through their turning point stories. They must be willing to be seen and accepted for who they are, a perfectly imperfect human being.

Somewhere along the line, "mask speakers" assume a persona that

Stand in Your Power

is false. In an effort to be accepted, they take on a sanitized professional demeanor devoid of personality or humor — or they do just the opposite and adopt an over-the-top "people-pleasing" persona that demands they be "on" all the time.

This sets up dissonance in both the speaker and the audience. Dissonance is defined as "inconsistency between our beliefs and actions." It is exhausting for speakers to keep up a façade, and it drains energy that should be dedicated to delivering the presentation. Furthermore, when speakers pretend to be somebody or something they're not, the audience senses they are not who they seem to be and trust goes out the window.

Before I can really help clients become the speaker they're capable of becoming, I have to convince them to take off the mask — and it's not always easy. Some of them have been wearing the mask for so many years, it is now instinctive. The mask allows them to hide and feel safe. It is a dangerous safety, though, because it leads to failure.

Before we can do our work, we've got to get real. I'm talking about authenticity. All of the acting techniques in the world won't help someone who is hiding something from the audience. Acting is reality replicated. It is not falseness. It is the truth.

Go Deep to Be an Authentic Speaker

In my opinion, the speakers and storytellers who make the most enduring impact on their audiences have one thing in common: they possess insight — the ability to look inside and find a profound truth. They see what everyone sees and choose to go deeper. They ask "Why?" Not for themselves alone, for humanity. They are seekers of the profound truth that can only be found by looking within. I call them authentic speakers.

Mask speakers look outside and observe. Observation allows them to stand aloof, apart, and separate. From the observation tower, they can avoid pain. They read the works of *other* authors, experts, and philosophers who have gone deep and employ *their* insights.

Why do mask speakers spend so much time studying the works of others rather than going deep themselves? Is it to avoid the pain of the past? By avoiding the turmoil and trauma of their past, they ride on the surface. By not looking deep inside, they speak from a place of comfort. That's a perfectly natural instinct. They have worked hard for comfort, fought for their sanity, struggled to gain distance from their fears. So, their stories are good, but not great. They amuse and educate. And for mask speakers, that's enough. It's safe.

But if we don't look inside, we cannot teach the deep truth that is hidden there. If we won't go there, our audiences don't get to go there with us. Speakers — leaders — storytellers must be brave explorers who share their discoveries. We must strive to continually remove the mask, to peel off the layers of safety and in so doing, to become truly authentic human beings.

My Story

When I first started speaking, I wore a mask. It wasn't intentional. It just happened.

I remember my first speech at the Holiday Inn in front of a room full of real estate agents, lenders and title insurance people. I was petrified. My face felt like leather, my palms were sweaty and I could hardly breathe. I stood behind the lectern like a statue — gripping its sides for balance. I have no idea what I talked about. It was like an out-of-body experience.

Stand in Your Power

My fear didn't make any sense. For the past 20 years, I'd been acting onstage in comedies, dramas and musicals. I'd been in front of hundreds of audiences — heck — I was even the lead singer in a rock-and-roll band! Why was I so petrified?

It occurred to me that as an actor I was able to hide inside my characters. I was speaking someone else's lines. If the play didn't work, if the performance bombed, it wasn't my fault. As a speaker, I *was* the character. They were *my* lines — *my* thoughts — *my* revelations. If the speech bombed, it WAS my fault. They weren't rejecting the play — they were rejecting me.

To insulate myself from rejection, I took on a character. That's what I knew how to do — play a role. So I watched what other speakers did and mimicked them. I copied their wardrobe, stood behind the lectern like they did, and crafted a speech comprised of other peoples' wisdom. If *I* didn't show up — how could I be rejected?

None of this was conscious. As I said, it just happened. I had to fight hard to figure out who I was as a speaker and what I had to say. I had to find Doug's character. I had to discover Doug's voice.

Since then, I've worked hard to remove the mask. I've struggled to define myself as a person and as a speaker. I'm still working on it — I'm not finished.

I had to go very deep to discover what was holding me back. My personal revelation was the genesis for this work. I so wanted to be liked, I was petrified to say or do anything that might offend anyone. This was a direct crossover from my insecurity issues with women. Everything I did traced its roots back to "being chosen." That was a profound revelation for me. At its core, my problem was self-esteem. When I got up in front of a room full of people, my insecurity was blown all out of proportion.

I had to go deep to discover what was preventing me from standing in my power. When I wasn't speaking in public, I was a dynamo. When giving a speech, I was a wimp. In order to be an authentic speaker, I learned I had to accept and embrace myself first and foremost — to choose myself — before others would choose me. Now I teach what I've learned. I am no longer employing the insights of others. Because I went deep, I am now considered an expert in my field. Now I have something original — something of my own — to offer.

How about you? Are you wearing a mask to protect yourself? Are you afraid, like I was, to say something that may offend — to speak the truth that is in your heart? Are you playing it safe, hoping it will get you where you want to go? Remember, hiding behind a mask is a dangerous safety.

If you've been wearing a mask, it has probably served you well. If you want to impact your audience as fully as possible though, you'll need to take it off. The next few chapters will reveal how to do just that.

CHAPTER 24

Connect Your
Mind, Body, and Spirit

How do you prepare in the moments preceding a speech or presentation? If you're like most speakers, you look at your notes and think about your material. You focus on content — what you're going to say. That's fine, up to a point. But it's not enough.

The minute you step to the front of the room, your audience will size you up. They'll look for visual cues like how you walk, what you're wearing, and how comfortable you appear to be. They'll listen to the sound of your voice: is it confident or shaky? While they've doing that, they'll feel you out. On a gut instinct level — they'll take an internal reading that tells them whether they can trust you. All of this will take place in mere seconds.

If you were hoping to get by on your content, to be judged by the quality of the material you present and not on how well you present yourself, you're deluding yourself. Speakers beware! You must be ready to be your best the second you walk on the stage.

If you get so nervous before you speak that you shake, rattle and roll, listen up. You must develop a warm-up ritual that integrates your mental, physical and spiritual selves.

The Mind, Body and Spirit Connection

I approach speaking the same way I approached acting in the theater. I go through an elaborate warm-up ritual to prepare myself to be sized up by hundreds of people at a time. No matter how many speeches I give, and I've given more than one thousand, it's still a daunting task. My content is the least of my worries. My warm-up preparation is mostly about energy.

If you've ever experienced extreme anxiety before you speak, you know it's an overpowering experience. Fear creates energy. It pumps adrenalin into your veins and makes you want to run from the leopard. If you don't do something to deal with it, the fear wins and you lose. You can't breathe, think or swallow.

You are not just a brain. If you were, all your mental preparation alone would suffice. Your brain is sitting on top of this big clumsy thing called your body. It is either going to be your enemy or your ally. With a proper warm-up ritual, it will cooperate. It works just fine all day long — it will work fine during a speech as well. Besides, you're going to need it to illustrate your story.

Remember when I said that your audience is going to feel you out? What do you think they're feeling — your vibe, your spirit, your energy field? If you answered yes to all of the above, you'd be correct. Audiences can feel you. If you walk out and stand in your power with total confidence — they sense that and relax. If you wobble out shaking like a leaf in a hailstorm and sneak behind the lectern to hide, they feel your anxiety and get anxious.

From now on, synchronize your mind, body and spirit so they are in perfect harmony *before* you walk into the room.

Connect Your Mind, Body, and Spirit

The Rev-Up-and-Calm-Down Ritual

You can call your warm-up whatever you want. I call mine the Rev-Up-and-Calm-Down Ritual because first I rev my engines (my body parts) and get myself all energized, jazzed and warmed-up. Then I calm it all down with relaxation, breathing and spiritual practices that focus my energy.

The Ingredients of a Warm-up Ritual:

- Physical exercises to relax your muscles
- Brain Gym® exercises to integrate right-brain and left-brain
- Breathing exercises to oxygenate the blood and awaken the brain
- Vocal exercises to warm up your vocal cords
- Mental preparation to refresh the memory
- Attitude preparation to lift the spirit
- Spiritual preparation to put things in perspective

If you are going to take storytelling in business seriously because you want serious results, this last piece of the puzzle is essential. Over time you will discover what works for you. The following are some options for you to consider.

My physical preparation consists primarily of stretching exercises. I do Yoga. Ten minutes of Yoga stretches to loosen my spine and stretch my legs is all I need. Your physical warm-up should not be so strenuous that it saps your energy. Some people I know work out in the morning because that gives them energy. Just remember, your entire body is an instrument of communication — physical language. Don't let it send the wrong message by being stiff as a bored (pun intended!)

To prepare your body for storytelling, walk and talk the story out loud. Run through the staging and visualize yourself in front of the audience. Do some vocal exercises or run through some tongue twisters.

Get Ready to Go

Brain Gym® exercises are designed to create optimal whole brain functioning by balancing the left and right hemispheres of your brain. Your left-brain will keep you on track and focused while your right-brain helps you to think on your feet. You'll need them both functioning in balance for optimal performance.

Brain Gym consists of 26 easy and enjoyable targeted activities that bring about rapid and often dramatic improvements in concentration, memory, reading, writing, organizing, listening, physical coordination, and more. Dr. Paul E. Dennison and Gail E. Dennison developed these exercises. To learn more about how these exercises can help you on and off the platform, go to: www.braingym.org.

Deep breathing exercises are helpful for a couple of reasons. While deep-breathing sends needed oxygen to the brain, it calms the nerves and slows the rapid beating of the heart brought on by nervousness. If you begin to feel nervous, do some slow deep breathing for two minutes.

Many professional speakers make it a point to walk, run, or hit the treadmill the morning of a presentation. They make it a point to integrate physical movement into their preparation. If you're expecting to have energy on the platform, you better find some before you get there. You can't count on your audience for energy — they may not have any. They may be looking to you for a spark.

Perhaps you've been cooped up inside all day (or all week if it's

Connect Your Mind, Body, and Spirit

winter). Perhaps you've been in big, anonymous corporate build-
ings, waiting at airports, or stuffed into crowded airplanes. Your
spirit is dull, dark, or black. Don't take that energy to the stage or
it will undermine everything you've worked for. People come to
your presentation with one of three levels of energy.

1. **They're revved up.** Perhaps they've heard you before and they
    know you're great. Perhaps they have an interest in your topic
    or a desperate need for your information — and they paid
    their own way to attend the workshop. Perhaps your reputa-
    tion has preceded you and they're already on your side
    because previous attendees have told them to expect good
    things. Maybe they're eager learners who are committed to
    self-improvement and they're receptive to everything you say.
    This is a delightful situation because this type of group brings
    their own energy with them. They add their energy to yours
    to produce an animated, upbeat session from the get-go.

2. **They're neutral.** These people make up their minds whether
    this will be worthwhile based on your performance. They
    have a "wait-and-see" attitude. They're not against you or for
    you — they sit there evaluating the merit of your ideas and
    performance as your presentation unfolds. With this type of
    audience member, the first three minutes are pivotal. You
    either favorably impress them within that initial time period
    — or you fail to impress them within that time period. If you
    successfully grab them in the first three minutes, they're on
    board and will tend to give you the benefit of the doubt
    thereafter. If those first three minutes are flat, dull, or boring,
    they'll mentally check out and you'll have to do something
    spectacular to win them back.

3. **They're resistant:** These people don't want to be there for
    any number of reasons. Maybe their boss forced them to
    attend. Maybe they "hate" self-improvement seminars.

Maybe they have too much to do and they're thinking more about the work that's stacked on their desk than they are about the words coming out of your mouth. Maybe they have a personal challenge that is preoccupying them — they had a fight with their spouse; their teen-ager didn't come home until late last night; or they can't pay their bills and their credit card debt is getting worse every month. These people walk in with dark energy and their mental arms crossed. The good news is — you CAN win over even the most resistant audience members with universally relevant, well-told stories.

Why did I go into that? Because speaking is about energy. If everyone in your audience is enthusiastic, they actually send energy up to you on the stage. If most people are neutral, you will need to energize them. That means it's up to you to generate enough excitement about your topic to excite them too. If the group is predominantly resistant, you have to fill the room and the people in it with your conviction, passion, and commitment. The only way you'll be able to pull that off is if you are at your energetic best.

And there is no better way to be at your energetic best than taking some time the morning of your presentation, to get outside in nature and be physically active. Drink in the energy from the sunshine, the greenery, the mountains, or the water in a stream, lake, or ocean. Walk or jog with your arms swinging. You will walk into your presentation fully alive and almost vibrating with a positive spirit. Your personality will be lit up — and you will have a full reservoir of energy to infuse the crowd so everyone feels your excitement and then generates their own.

Review your notes a number of times on the day of your presentation. I suggest finding a private room away from any distractions. Practice some of what you plan to say out loud. Put your notes in

Connect Your Mind, Body, and Spirit

order. If you are using a PowerPoint presentation, look at the slides and memorize their order.

A simple attitude check is always in order before speaking. Monitor your self-talk. Replace any hint of negativity with positive affirmations. As an example, just before I step in front of my audience, I remind myself that my audience wants me to succeed. I remove any barriers to connection by affirming that I'm going to have a conversation rather than give a speech. I set my intention to tell the truth by being totally authentic and real. I remind myself that I'm enough just as I am — that simply being me is totally appropriate. Then I take the stage, get out of my own way and let my preparation and the magic of the moment mix.

Use Affirmations to Center Yourself

"You've got to find the force within you."
— JOSEPH CAMPBELL

The next part of my warm-up ritual is to calm down, using affirmations and spiritual practices. Try this set of affirmations before you speak:

> Today, I will embrace the gift that I am.
> Today, I will trust that what I have prepared is perfect.
> Today, I will tell the truth and be authentic and real.
> Today, I will stay connected with myself and let the audience come to me.
> Today, I will release the need to be perfect.
> Today, I will love myself and let them watch.
> Today, I will kick ass and take business cards.

The last part of any warm-up ritual is spiritual. Connecting with a higher power always seems to place things in perspective for me. It reminds me that there is a higher source of power and inspiration in the room and that I am the vehicle for a larger message. This connection to God through prayer gives me peace and helps me to get out of the way and let the miracle happen.

The time to do your warm-up ritual is at the very beginning of the day before you get caught up in the chaos surrounding a meeting. Make extra time for this essential practice. Then — 15 minutes before you are to speak, excuse yourself and find a private place to work on your energy. At that point you should know your material and have rehearsed your story. Don't stress about your content. Focus your energy.

Work yourself into a state of grace. Relax and have fun.

CHAPTER 25

Engage the Audience with Interaction Techniques

There are a variety of ways to keep your audience involved with your speech or presentation. In this chapter, we'll deal with audience interaction techniques both inside and outside of your stories.

Checking In

When I'm doing a keynote, I like to make it as interactive as possible, even though the room setup sometimes makes it awkward to do so. In a training room you can walk around and get close to people. You can have discussions where the trainer is not the focus of attention. In a keynote, that's not practical since the keynoter is usually the focus of attention and it's his or her job to do most of the talking.

I use a simple interaction technique called "checking in." It consists of short "Are you with me?" questions that make my presentation seem more like a conversation than a speech.

Checking In Questions:

> "Does that make sense to you?"
> "Do you know what I mean?"

"Has that ever happened to you?"

"Don't you hate it when that happens?"

"Do you see what I mean?"

"Am I the only one this stuff happens to?"

"Are you feeling my pain?"

"Doesn't it make you want to quit your job and raise llamas in Guatemala?"

"Do you ever get the feeling someone's out to get ya?"

"Do you ever just have one of those days?"

These are rhetorical questions that get people nodding in agreement, but don't require a verbal response. It allows them to feel connected to the experience and makes everyone feel like you're talking directly to them.

Occasionally, someone will respond by saying something out loud. If you're in a story, just nod and keep on going. If you're not in a story, take ten seconds to acknowledge the person who spoke. Say something like, "There you go. He knows what I mean. And I'll bet he's not the only one." Don't lose your momentum. Make a comment and move on.

Audience Surveys

I love to conduct audience surveys that get people thinking and raising their hands. I actually use one as a transition into my Streaking Story. In leading up to the story, I talk about the need to take risks and try new things. Then I ask people to share some of the wild and crazy things they've done to challenge themselves — to expand their comfort zones. They share things like jumping out of airplanes, hitchhiking across Australia, getting a divorce, taking a job in a different state and singing at a Karaoke bar.

I then ask those same people to tell me if their adventures made them feel more courageous and free. I ask them if doing those things expanded their comfort zones. They always say yes. Then I launch into my Streaking Story, which is about taking a risk.

Think about your subject. Can your audience help you prove your point by participating in a survey? If so, survey away.

Question and Answer Sessions

You may be expected to leave a few minutes at the end of your presentation for questions and answers. Although these techniques are not part of storytelling, I want to share a few of the techniques I've learned over the years.

How you handle questions when you're speaking to a group or running a meeting indicates your level of poise and professionalism. It illustrates calm under pressure, an admirable leadership trait.

How To Ask An Audience A Question

Audiences sometimes can't tell the difference between a rhetorical question and one you want them to respond to. That's because speakers often give confusing signals. Here's a helpful hint: before you ask a question, tell your audience what you want them to do. Preface your question with a comment like this: "I'm going to ask a question and I'd like five of you to respond." For rhetorical questions, try this: "Here is a question to ponder. You don't need to raise your hand, please just think about it."

How To Answer Audience Questions:

- If you are speaking in front of more than twenty people, always repeat the question. Don't paraphrase it; quote it as accurately as possible.

- Validate the person asking the question with a brief compliment such as, "That's a good question." This sends a message to everyone in the room that you really do welcome questions and will be nice to people who ask them.
- When responding to a question, qualify your answer with a simple disclaimer that lets your audience know you are open and receptive to other points of view. Begin your answer with: "In my opinion...," or "It's been my experience..."
- Is the person asking the question a rival? Does he have a hidden agenda? Can you tell from his tone he is aiming to discredit you? Try this: "I hear you and that's a valid question. Let me try to address it as best I can." Regardless of whether you agree with argumentative participants, to them, their question is valid. Deal with the questions logically rather than emotionally.
- If every answer you give to a challenging person leads to another question that is clearly designed provoke a conflict — take control by asking the person to meet with you after the program to continue the discussion. If s/he still won't take no for an answer, enlist other people in the room. Ask, "Does anyone else have an opinion on this issue he or she would like to share?"
- Assuming that you have done your homework and are prepared to answer questions on the subject you are presenting, there will still be questions you cannot answer. That is because you are human. Release yourself from the need to know everything about everything and admit it when you don't know the answer. Here are the best responses in such a situation: "That's a good question, Bob, and at this moment I don't have the answer. But I know where to find it, and I'll get back to you today with that information." A second option is to enlist other people in the room and let them be the hero. Try this: "Now that's a question I hadn't considered. Does anyone here have an answer?" The bottom line is that no one

has all the answers and it reveals weakness to pretend we do. Get real. When you know the answer, answer it. When you don't, tell the truth.

I believe one of the principle reasons people are afraid of speaking is they feel they have to be perfect and know everything about their subject. While it is rightfully assumed that you will be knowledgeable about your topic, there will always be different points of view. It is unrealistic to expect everyone will agree with all your opinions. It is also unhealthy to place an expectation on yourself that when you take the stage, you will miraculously become perfect. Get over it!

From now on, when someone asks a question, answer with humility and grace. Tell them what you know and admit to what you don't. They'll appreciate your honesty and will respect you for it.

Tap Into Your Audience's Stories

Nothing pleases an audience more than for you to show that you know them. A great way to do that is to include several audience members' stories in your presentation. They will probably each be a short vignette, usually less than two minutes.

Sometime before you speak, or the night before at the reception, begin your story safari. Start by approaching people and asking for their advice. I've discovered that almost everyone likes to be interviewed. It makes them feel special. Find out who the "stand-out personalities" in the group are, and put them on your list for an interview.

How to Find an Audience Member's Story:

- Pick one of your main points (i.e.: honesty is the best policy).

- Ask people to tell you a story about a time they learned that lesson.
- Ask if it's okay to take a few notes so you can get their remarks correctly.
- If it's a good story, ask their permission to use it in your presentation.
- When using their story, acknowledge the person by name to honor their contribution.
- Use their story to customize your message to make it timely and relevant to what they face on a daily basis.

Audiences appreciate it when speakers take the time and invest the effort to ask questions in advance. It is part of your responsibility as a speaker to include their terminology, address their trends, and incorporate some of their leaders' stories.

CHAPTER 26

Brand Your Message with Cards and Posters

The Phrase That Pays is designed to brand your message. It summarizes a story or philosophy into one memorable phrase. Perhaps you have three or four stories in your presentation and a Phrase That Pays for each of them. You must now pick the one "PTP" you want your audience to take home with them.

This is a strategic decision. If there is only one idea your audience takes away from your presentation, what would you want it to be?

The sad fact is, your audience will only remember one or two key points from your presentation. It's your job to make sure they remember the one you want them to remember. This is important because you want them to associate that particular PTP with you and your business. If you do a bang-up job with your message and brand it with a PTP, they'll always associate that phrase with you. They may forget your name, but if you put your PTP on your card, coffee mug, poster, or handout — at least they'll have your contact information and can get in touch with you.

Help Them Remember You and Your Message

A simple and cost-effective way to insure you live forever in their minds is to create and distribute a branding card or poster. I'm not talking about spending a lot of money on a four-color print job. What I have in mind is brightly colored card stock with bold black type. You can create it on your computer with common graphic design software like Microsoft Publisher. You can even do it in Word. See Figure 4 for an example of a branding card layout. See the Wall Signs at the back of the book for examples of 8½" x 11" posters.

The following directions are for Microsoft Publisher.

Creating a 5½" x 8½" Branding Card:

- Choose the Phrase That Pays that you want to put on the card.
- In the toolbar at the top of the page — go to File, Page Setup and click on landscape.
- In the toolbar — go to Arrange, Layout Guides.
- In Layout Guides reduce the right and left side margins to 0.3.
- Reduce the top and bottom margins to 0.5.
- Increase Columns to 4 and Rows to 2.
- In the Drawing toolbar, click on the Box icon. It's a square box.
- Create a box on the left side of the page approximately 4¾" x 7". This is your frame.
- Center it on the blue-grid lines on the top and sides.
- In the Drawing toolbar, click on the WordArt box and make a large box inside your frame.
- Choose a non-serif font like Ariel and type in your Phrase That Pays, one word per line.
- Click the WordArt box again and below the PTP create a horizontal box that contains your name, phone and email address.
- In the top toolbar go to Edit, Select All.
- Touch the Control button and then the letter C.
- Touch the Control button and then the letter V.

Brand Your Message with Cards and Posters

Stand In Your Power

Your name here — your phone — your e-mail address

Stand In Your Power

Your name here — your phone — your e-mail address

Figure 4

- You now have a duplicate of the card on the left.
- Drag it to the right, and center it.
- Print it, fold your page half and look to see if the two sides match when you hold the page up against the light. If not, go back and tweak it until both sides match.
- Take it to the printer. Choose a light card stock paper. Print half as many as you need.
- Have the printer cut the printed cards in half.
- That's it! You have a simple branding card.

Creating a Branding Poster:

Duplicate everything you just did for a card, but use the entire page for your Phrase That Pays. Where the page setup (second step above) for a branding card was created using "landscape," a full size poster will be created in "portrait." Use colored paper or card-stock to make it more interesting.

I'll leave it to you to fiddle with frames and fonts to make it look interesting. The main thing is that you now have a branding card with your main point or Phrase That Pays and contact information on it. People will take your cards back to their personal workspace and stick them up where they can look at them. You can hand them out before you speak or give them to people as they're leaving the room.

Congratulations — you're branded! (This is a good thing.)

CHAPTER 27

Heighten Your Impact with Audio/Visual/Technical Support

A fter all you've learned about crafting and presenting a story in the hopes of making a difference in someone's life, wouldn't it be a shame if you were sabotaged at the last minute by a lousy sound system? It can happen if you're not prepared.

Hotels and conference centers both have one thing in common — audio/visual nightmares. Believe it or not, meeting rooms are not designed to be speaker friendly. The lighting is insufficient, the heating systems are dysfunctional, and the speakers in the ceiling are inadequate. Be that as it may, it is your job to make it all work. In the end, the audience doesn't care whose fault it is if things go wrong. They just know things got messed up. More than once I have been the only person in the room who knew how to dim the lights or fix the volume level.

Prepare Yourself

Here are a few hints on how you can ensure the debut performance of your story doesn't turn into your own personal version of *Nightmare on Elm Street.*

- Arrive early and check out the room setup — move chairs if you must.
- Find all of the light controls and play with them until you're knowledgeable.
- Check the microphones and the mixer. Determine which volume knobs control each of the microphones, including everyone else's.
- Ask the A/V person if there are spare batteries available in the room. If not, get some.
- Figure out how to change the batteries in your microphone.
- Find the temperature control. It should be set at 69-degrees.
- If there is a stage, walk on it. Fix any wobbles or weak spots.
- If there is a lectern, check out the light and the microphone. Turn them both on and off.

Working with Notes and Outlines

It is perfectly permissible to use notes and outlines. I still use notes to this day because I customize my talks. I need the notes to remind me of the tailored stories and terms I've inserted for the client.

I avoid lecterns or as some people call them, podiums. If you are going to deliver your dramatic stories the way I have taught you, I hope you will get out from behind them too.

"What?" you say. "Use notes, but get rid of the lectern?" Yes! Lose the lectern. Ask for a small, skirted cocktail table and put it on the side of the stage where you can glance at your notes. Better yet, purchase a portable music stand. They collapse into a little cloth-carrying bag and are perfect for your notes.

Why is this so important? Remember earlier in the book where we talked about NOT hiding from the audience? When we stand

Heighten Your Impact with Audio/Visual/Technical Support

behind a four-foot tall lectern, we hide all but 25% of our bodies. This relegates us to being the dreaded "Talking Head." We have eliminated 75% of our dynamism, 75% of our gestures, 75% of our illustrative body language, and 95% of our movement. We have just eliminated the "acting-out" part of Story Theater.

Furthermore, we have placed a wall between the audience and ourselves. It will be hard to overcome this tangible barrier that is blocking us from connecting with the people in the room. Come out from behind that lectern. Open yourself to the audience. Do not conceal yourself. The audience wants to see who you are. Let them know that you are ready to be seen — and that you want to see them and connect with them too.

For the notes themselves, I use light cardstock. It's better than paper because paper is wimpy and tends to fall to the floor. Distill your speech down into bullet points. Print or hand-write your bullet points onto the cardstock in 24-point font letters. I use markers and hand-write them out. I like to use colors for my performance notes so I can differentiate them from my content. Use no more than two pages of notes.

Working with Microphones

As a proud disciple of The Story Theater Method, you will be requesting to use a wireless, lavaliere microphone. This type of microphone allows you to move freely and gesture with both hands. Remember to wear something with a lapel or collar to clip the microphone to. Your next best choice is a wireless, handheld microphone. It will give you more control over volume levels than a lapel microphone, however it will limit your gestures to one hand.

This is not a petty issue. If your voice is fuzzy or garbled, it will undermine everything you have worked so hard to achieve. It is worth requesting the wireless lapel or handheld microphone because it will allow you to deliver a Story Theater presentation in all its glory. If you plan to speak frequently, it may be worth investing in your own portable microphone equipment to guarantee that your presentation will be heard with the professional quality it deserves.

A Final Word

F or most of us who speak for a living — it is a calling. We *like* to stand in the front of the room and talk. Perhaps you, too, like to stand in the front of the room. You think you have something to say and you like it when people listen. You have stories to tell and believe in your heart of hearts that sharing them will benefit others. You're right. They will.

You and I share a common need. We need to feel we're making a difference in the world. We need to reach out to the hearts, minds and souls of those around us and tell them it's going to be okay. We're teachers and counselors and believe it or not — we're the philosophers of our age. I know that sounds grandiose, but it's true.

Do you sit around after something interesting happens and think, "This would make a great story?" It could be traumatic, but you're still trying to find the story and its meaning. Yep — you're a storyteller all right — a modern day Aristotle.

You're an idealist. While others look at their world and say, "Why me?" you look at the world and say, "Why not me?" You're the little train that could. You're Mother Teresa, Rocky Balboa, Yoda. The world needs more people like you.

There is a hitch however. Here it is:

You're going to spend countless hours working on your story and deciphering its deep meaning. Then you'll rehearse it to perfection and take it out into the world and perform it with everything you've got. People will sit inches away from you and take it all in. And then, when it's over and your speech is done — they'll applaud politely and get up and leave. If you're lucky and the stars are in alignment that day — you might even get a standing ovation. But even then, your audience will leave and go about their business.

At some point, later on that day, you will find yourself alone. You'll replay the moment in your mind for highpoints and low points. You'll be happy that they laughed at your Triple and disappointed with yourself for rushing through a Hold The Moment. And you'll give yourself a grade. Based on what you perceived to have happened in the room, you'll reduce the experience to an elementary school grading system. Be very careful. This is a dangerous habit. You have just made a difference in the world. Magic has just happened and you were the magician.

I have a theory. It's my own version of the one that says, "When a butterfly flutters its wings in Hong Kong, the air moves in New York." It's something like that anyway. Mine applies to those of us who stand at the front of the room and speak. It goes like this:

Doug's Spiritual Theory for Speaking Sanity

It takes 50 impressions for a person to change their behavior — 50 impressions for someone to finally get an epiphany and decide to change their life. An impression is any sign, clue or reminder that you are doing something that is non-productive, self destructive and/or hurtful to others.

If, as a speaker or trainer, it's your lucky day, you may get to be number 50. Your story and your message may have been the 50th impression for someone in your audience. If it is, they will come up to you. They will look into your eyes and squeeze your hand. They will find the words to tell you that you have made a difference in their life. Then again, they may just get up and leave — too stirred to speak. They will thank you for the rest of their life by changing — an act of supreme courage.

This is a Karmic principle. You are participating in a divine dance.

But, what about the others? What about the person for whom you were #3 or #17? They may have appeared to be bored or, worse yet, annoyed. Did you not play a part in their transformation? Certainly the person for whom you were #49 will speak to you. Certainly they will have something to say. Certainly they will seek you out and let you know that you helped shape their life.

When doctors heal someone, they can see the change. When teachers mentor a child, they can see the change. It's seldom like that for speakers. You seldom get to see the change in someone's life as a result of hearing your story. It happens in the days, weeks, months and years after you're gone. You can only know it in the stillness of your own heart.

You make a difference in the world. No one else has your story. It is your gift to the world. You must give it without expectation.

The magician practices for hours each day. Only he knows the secret to making the mechanical seem magical. So it is for you — the storyteller. Choose to practice your craft. Take responsibility for mining your dramatic turning points and sharing your lessons-learned. Dedicate yourself to mastering this process called Story Theater.

Then stand before the gathered crowd with a story or two up your sleeve. They are waiting for the show to begin. They need the magic power that only you can bring.

It's show time.

Love Yourself and Let Them Watch

Make Your Business Presentations Capture Attention, Inspire Action, and Produce Results

The Messenger is as Important as the Message

Stand In Your Power

Make Your Business Presentations Capture Attention, Inspire Action, and Produce Results

When They Laugh They Learn

Recommended Reading

About speaking and storytelling:

Did I Ever Tell You About the Time, Grady Jim Robinson, New York, McGraw-Hill, 2000.

The Power of Personal Storytelling, Jack Maguire, New York, Tarcher / Putnam, 1998.

Stories Trainers Tell, Mary B. Wacker and Lori L. Silverman, Pfieffer, San Francisco, 2003.

Leading Minds, Howard Gardner, New York, Basic Books, 1995.

Managing by Storying Around, David Armstrong, New York, Doubleday Currency, 1992.

An Actor Prepares, Constantin Stanislavski, New York, Routledge, 1936.

Present Yourself, Michael Gelb, Torrence, CA, Jalmar Press, 1988.

Taking Center Stage, Deb Gottesman and Buzz Mauro, New York, Berkley, 2001.

Don't Let The Funny Stuff Get Away, Jeanne Robertson, Houston, Rich Publishing, 1998.

Power Presentations, Marjorie Brody and Shawn Kent, New York, John Wiley & Sons, 1993.

About healing and personal growth:

Be Here Now, Baba Ram Dass, New York, Crown Publishing, 1978.

Do What You Love, The Money Will Follow, Dr. Marsha Sinetar, New York, Dell, 1987.

Elegant Choices, Healing Choices, Dr. Marsha Sinetar, Mahwah, N.J, Paulist Press, 1988.

Lost in the Shuffle, Robert Subby, Deerfield Beach, FL, Health Communications, 1987.

Healing the Shame That Binds You, John Bradshaw, Deerfield Beach, FL, Health Communications, 1988.

A Return to Love, Marianne Williamson, Harper Collins, New York, 1996.

Co-Dependant No More, Melody Beattie, Hazelden Information Education, Center City, MN, 1997.

Resource List of Professional Organizations, Websites, and Training

The National Speakers Association
1500 South Priest Drive
Tempe, Arizona 85281
480-968-2552
www.nsaspeaker.org

Toastmasters International
PO Box 9052
Mission Viejo, Ca 92690
800-937-7325
www.toastmasters.org

American Society of Training and Development
1640 Kings Street
Box 1443
Alexandria, VA 22313-2043
703-683-8100
www.astd.org

National Storytelling Association
International Storytelling Center
116 W. Main Street
Jonesborough, TN 37659
800-952-8392
www.storytellingcenter.com

Free Story Theater newsletter: www.storytheater.net
Speaking Industry Newsletter: www.speakernetnews.com
Storytelling for Knowledge Management: workingstories@lists.gjhost.com

Make Your Business Presentations Capture Attention, Inspire Action, and Produce Results

Contact Doug Stevenson

Feel free to call or email us. We'd love to hear from you with feedback on the book. Tell us how you are putting the techniques to use.

Doug Stevenson Unlimited   *a Division of Cornelia Corporation*
PO Box 9222
Colorado Springs, CO 80932-0222

To inquire about speaking engagements and personal appearances call:

  800-573-6196 or 719-573-6195
  Fax 719-574-2605 (Mountain Time Zone)

DOUG STEVENSON — *CEO and President*
  doug@dougstevenson.com

DEBORAH MERRIMAN — *VP of Everything*
  deborah@dougstevenson.com

Keynotes and Training Programs: www.dougstevenson.com

- NEVER BE BORING AGAIN: Capture Attention, Inspire Action and Produce Results
   Storytelling and Presentation Skills
- STORY THEATER: Making Content Come Alive
   Storytelling in Business
- STRATEGIC STORY*SELLING* FOR SALES SUCCESS — Sell It With a Story
   Sales
- THE POSITIVE POWER OF CHANGE — Elevate Your Attitude
   Change

Storytelling Retreats and Workshops: www.storytheater.net

- NEVER BE BORING AGAIN RETREAT   6–8 students
   Storytelling and Presentation Skills
- STORY THEATER RETREAT   6 students
   Corporate Storytelling
- STORY THEATER ONE-DAY WORKSHOP   Up to 100
   Story Crafting

Private Coaching: Call for details and customized arrangements

Audio Products: www.storytheater.net

- THE STORY THEATER SIX-PACK (coach in a box)
   Six cassettes or six audio CDs
- MAKE THE MOVE FROM TRAINING TO KEYNOTES
   Two cassettes
- TAKE YOUR STORY TO THE BANK (self promotion)
   Two cassettes
- ADVANCED DRAMA AND COMEDY PERFORMANCE SKILLS
   Two cassettes
- THE POSITIVE POWER OF CHANGE — Get Over It
   Two cassettes
- STORY THEATER LIVE
   (live performance includes the Streaking Story)
   Two cassettes

STORY THEATER RETREATS & SEMINARS

"The only person I know who can translate the art of storytelling in business into an understandable science is Doug Stevenson. You will be a better speaker after studying with this Master Storyteller. I know I am."

CHRIS CLARKE-EPSTEIN, CSP — Wisconsin
Past-President, National Speakers Association

"This is the best coaching I have had. Doug has designed a program that pushes the participant in both technique and authenticity. He creates an atmosphere to take risks. He models the behaviors. This is worth three times the cost. It is a must investment for any speaker."

MARJORIE BRODY, CSP — Philadelphia, Retreat Graduate
Author of 10 books including *Power Presentations*

"I left the class with a renewed confidence in my ability to deliver material and make it more entertaining than it's been in the past. I finally understand the block I've had with conveying my humor through storytelling to an audience. This retreat is an absolute must for anyone who wants to improve their ability to captivate an audience with a story. I will recommend it to anyone who will listen!"

DAN MADDUX — San Antonio, Retreat Graduate
Executive Director, American Payroll Association

"You are an insightful, helpful coach. What I liked best was that you helped us discover the best in ourselves. You made suggestions, not commands. To be honest, this is the best I've ever felt about my gifts and talents in this area. It was a true blessing."

DR. PAT GANGI — Phoenix, Retreat Graduate

"This retreat made me see the difference between amateur and professional speaking. It allowed me to compare my Toastmasters speaking against members of a professional speakers association. I learned that if I work hard I will be able to become a professional speaker. It was the best course for the money that I have been on in the last five years."

CIARAN BLAIR — Dublin, Retreat Graduate

"Thanks to you for helping me to tell my story more effectively. It was well received. I was shocked, however. I got emotional. So did they. In the middle of the day when I shared it, they gave me a standing ovation. Couldn't believe it."

LOIS CREAMER — St Louis, Retreat Graduate

"What worked about the retreat for me was lots of personal attention and the quality of your coaching. It was specific, supportive, on-point, and helped us improve our own story and style, rather than trying to make us clones of Doug. I knew I could make people laugh, but I learned that I can expand my range of ways in which I do that, and that there is a technique that can be applied that ups the percentage of times people will actually laugh."

RICK MAURER — Baltimore, Retreat Graduate

"I found the audio six-pack a great preparation but I needed the retreat to help me start doing it. The retreat is a great combination of well thought out methods that are easy to follow and a highly creative experience that helps everyone go outside their comfort zones. The magic ingredient was Doug. His coaching examples were practical and inspiring at the same time."

CARL FRENCH — London, Retreat Graduate

"Let me just say that Doug Stevenson's Story Theater Retreat was the best money I have ever spent on my speaking career … and I've spent a lot. I've been with several coaches and he's the best."

June Cline, CSP — Atlanta, Retreat Graduate

"Doug Stevenson has to be experienced. Words can't convey the uncanny ability he has to reach in and capture one's natural talent and masterfully stretch that talent to a new level. I was absolutely thrilled with the progress I was able to make and the tools I now have at my disposal.

Karyn Buxman, CSP, CPAE — St. Louis, Retreat Graduate

"Take this workshop now! This is the single best workshop on story-telling that I have ever attended. Doug is direct, to the point, positive and very helpful. I got so much more for my money here than at any other workshop. Just fabulous. Even better than I had hoped."

Mary Ellen Barnes — Los Angeles, Retreat Graduate

"I have just gotten a taste of the outrageous person I can be on the platform. I learned that I can be brilliant and hilarious. Doug helps you find your stories and yourself. I really appreciated Doug's loose style, very relaxed but also very attentive to each speaker. This is an unbelievable opportunity to practice, learn, develop and create your stories."

Diane Seig — Denver, Retreat Graduate

"The best money I've spent on my professional development all year."

Jan Carothers — Portland, Retreat Graduate

About the Author

DOUG STEVENSON gave his first speech at 13 years of age in Boy Scouts. He became a professional actor in his hometown of Chicago at 19 and at 22, hitchhiked to Hollywood where he acted on stage in everything from Snoopy to Shakespeare and in movies, TV and commercials. During his 16 years as a character actor he developed his unique style of physical comedy. His expertise eventually led him to direct plays and teach acting.

While in Hollywood, Doug owned a carpentry and remodeling business and a mobile disk jockey company. After 13 years of trying to become a rich and famous movie star, he did what many actors do when they fail to make it in Hollywood — he moved to Colorado Springs and became a real estate broker. Always the entrepreneur, he quickly opened his own brokerage firm, Sherlock's Homes.

While selling homes, Doug discovered the world of professional speaking. He began teaching presentation skills in 1990 and held his first Story Theater Retreat in 1996. He now presents keynotes and training seminars worldwide. He has performed in front of over 1000 audiences as an actor, rock singer, speaker, trainer and author.

Doug is the creator of *The Story Theater Method*™ for *Making Content Come Alive.* His articles and interviews have been published in many national publications including *Selling Power, Investors Business Daily* and *Professional Speaker Magazine.* He has contributed a monthly column entitled *Talk Your Walk* for the *Denver Business Journal*.

Doug is a member of the American Society of Training and Development and is Past-President of the Colorado Chapter of the National Speakers Association. He has produced five Story Theater audio albums, as well as the audio and video of his Positive Power of Change keynote.

Never Be Boring Again is Doug's first book.

His clients include: The National Association of Realtors, The American Medical Association, Southwestern Bell, Norwest Bank, Aetna, The National Education Association, GTE, Farmers Insurance, Compuware Corporation, UPS, Pharmacia, Commonwealth Edison, The Department of Defense, Maytag, John Deere and many more.

Doug lives in Colorado Springs, Colorado with his wife Deborah (VP of Everything), and their family pets: a neurotic but loveable black lab mix named Beta and an adorable old mutt named Maggie. His stepson Mike is a Hip Hop producer in Los Angeles. His stepson Bennett is a Cadet at the US Air Force Academy.

Index

Make Your Business Presentations Capture Attention, Inspire Action, and Produce Results

Cornelia Press
ORDER FORM

NEVER BE BORING AGAIN

MAKE YOUR BUSINESS PRESENTATIONS Capture Attention, Inspire Action, and Produce Results

To Order Individual Copies of the Book:
- Telephone Cornelia Press Consumer Sales at 800-573-6196, or
- Order Online at: www.storytheater.net, or
- Fax this form to 719-574-2605.

ORDER FORM FOR CONSUMERS ONLY
(1–5 COPIES) Payable in US funds only. Postage and handling: US/Canada $3.00 for one book, $1.00 for each additional book not to exceed $7.00; International $5.00 for one book, $1.00 for each additional. No cash / COD.

Number of copies @ $19.95 each . . . . _____

Total . . . . _____

CO sales tax 3% (Colorado residents only). . . . . _____

Postage and Handling . . . . _____

TOTAL AMOUNT DUE . . . . _____

Name _____

Address _____

City _____ State _____ Zip _____

Phone _____

Email _____

Charge my: ☐ Amex ☐ Visa ☐ Master Card

Credit Card # _____ Exp. _____

Signature _____

☐ Check or ☐ Money Order: Payable to Cornelia Corp.

Mail to: Cornelia Press
P.O. Box 9222
Colorado Springs, CO 80932-0222

Please allow 3–4 weeks for US delivery; 4–6 weeks outside US.